ATTACK
OF THE
DIFFICULT
POEMS

ATTACK

of the

DIFFICULT

POEMS

ESSAYS AND INVENTIONS

Charles Bernstein

The University of Chicago Press
Chicago and London

CHARLES BERNSTEIN is the Donald T. Regan Professor of English and
Comparative Literature at the University of Pennsylvania. Among his forty
publications are *All the Whiskey in Heaven: Selected Poems*, and *With Strings*
and *Girly Man*, the last two published by the University of Chicago Press.
He cofounded and edits PennSound (http://writing.upenn.edu
/pennsound) and the Electronic Poetry Center (http://epc.buffalo.edu).

Acknowledgments: Initial publication of these works (mostly in variant
versions) is noted alongside individual texts; thanks to the editors and
publishers. Conversations with Susan Bee, Felix Bernstein, and Emma Bee
Bernstein percolate through these works. Carol Saller's copyediting was
acute and always apt. To Alan Thomas and Randy Petilos of the University of
Chicago Press: continuing gratitude.

The University of Chicago Press, Chicago 60637
The University of Chicago Press, Ltd., London
© 2011 by Charles Bernstein
All rights reserved. Published 2011.
Printed in the United States of America.

20 19 18 17 16 15 14 13 12 11   1 2 3 4 5

ISBN-13: 978-0-226-04476-7 (cloth)
ISBN-13: 978-0-226-04477-4 (paper)
ISBN-10: 0-226-04476-9 (cloth)
ISBN-10: 0-226-04477-7 (paper)

Library of Congress Cataloging-in-Publication Data

Bernstein, Charles, 1950–
    Attack of the difficult poems : essays and inventions / Charles Bernstein.
        p. cm.
    ISBN-13: 978-0-226-04476-7
    ISBN-10: 0-226-04476-9
    ISBN-13: 978-0-226-04477-4 (alk. paper)
    ISBN-10: 0-226-04477-7 (alk. paper)
1. Poetry—Explication. 2. Poetry—Appreciation.   I. Title.
    PN1042.B475 2011
    808.1—dc22

                                                          2010044223

♾ The paper used in this publication meets the minimum requirements
of the American National Standard for Information Sciences—
Permanence of Paper for Printed Library Materials, ANSI Z39.48-1992.

In the Middle of the Way

In the middle of the way was a stone
was a stone in the middle of the way
was a stone
in the middle of the way was a stone.

Never, me I'll never forget that that happened
in the life of my oh so wearied retinas.
Never, me, I'll never forget that in the middle of the way
was a stone
was a stone in the middle of the way
in the middle of the way was a stone.

CARLOS DRUMMOND DE ANDRADE (TRANS. CH. B.)

CONTENTS

IV

"I'm not joking, and if I seem to talk in circles, it just seems that way. It all ties together—everything. Geiger and his cute little blackmail tricks, Brody and his pictures, Eddie Mars and his roulette tables, Canino and the girl Rusty Regan didn't run away with. It all ties together."

RAYMOND CHANDLER, *THE BIG SLEEP*

I

Professing Poetics

One of the Fathers, in great severity, called poesy *vinum daemonum*, because it filleth the imagination; and yet it is but with the shadow of a lie. But it is not the lie that passeth through the mind, but the lie that sinketh in and settleth in it, that doth the hurt.

FRANCIS BACON, "OF TRUTH"

It is a ridiculous demand which England and America make, that you shall speak so that they can understand you. Neither men nor toadstools grow so. As if that were important, and there were not enough to understand you without them. As if Nature could support but one order of understandings, could not sustain birds as well as quadrupeds, flying as well as creeping things, and *hush* and *whoa*, which Bright can understand, were the best English. As if there were safety in stupidity alone. I fear chiefly lest my expression may not be *extra-vagant* enough, may not wander far enough beyond the narrow limits of my daily experience, so as to be adequate to the truth of which I have been convinced.

HENRY DAVID THOREAU, *WALDEN*

Still, how to bear such loss I deemed
The insistent question for each animate mind,
And gazing, to my growing sight there seemed
A pale yet positive gleam low down behind

THOMAS HARDY, "GOD'S FUNERAL"

THE DIFFICULT POEM

All of us from time to time encounter a difficult poem. Sometimes it is the poem of a friend or family member and sometimes it is a poem we have written ourselves.

The difficult poem has created distress for both poets and readers for many years. Experts who study difficult poems often tie the modern prevalence of this problem with the early years of the last century, when a great deal of social dislocation precipitated the outbreak of 1912, one of the best-known epidemics of difficult poetry.

But while these experts have offered detailed historical discussions of difficult poems and while there is a great deal of philosophical speculation and psychological theory about difficult poetry, there are few practical guides for handling difficult poetry. What I want to do in this essay is explore some ways to make your experience with the difficult poem more rewarding by exploring some strategies for coping with these poems.

You may be asking yourself, how did I get interested in this topic? Let me be frank about my situation. I am the author of, and a frequent reader of, difficult poems. Because of this, I have the strong desire to help other readers and authors with hard-to-read poems. By sharing my experience of over thirty years of working with difficult poems, I think I can save you both time and heartache. I may even be able to convince you that some of the most difficult poems you encounter can provide very enriching aesthetic experiences—if you understand how to approach them.

But first we must address the question—Are you reading a difficult poem? How can you tell? Here is a handy checklist of five key questions that can help you to answer this question:

1 Do you find the poem hard to appreciate?
2 Do you find the poem's vocabulary and syntax hard to understand?

Harper's, June 2003.

3   Are you often struggling with the poem?
4   Does the poem make you feel inadequate or stupid as a reader?
5   Is your imagination being affected by the poem?

If you answered any of these questions in the affirmative, you are probably dealing with a difficult poem. But if you are still unsure, look for the presence of any of these symptoms: high syntactic, grammatical, or intellectual activity level; elevated linguistic intensity; textual irregularities; initial withdrawal (poem not immediately available); poor adaptability (poem unsuitable for use in love letters, memorial commemoration, etc.); sensory overload; or negative mood.

Many readers when they first encounter a difficult poem say to themselves, "Why me?" The first reaction they often have is to think that this is an unusual problem that other readers have not faced. So the first step in dealing with the difficult poem is to recognize that this is a common problem that many other readers confront on a daily basis. You are not alone!

The second reaction of many difficult-poem readers is self-blame. They ask themselves, "What am I doing to cause this poem to be so difficult?" So the second step in dealing with the difficult poem is to recognize that you are not responsible for the difficulty and that there are effective methods for responding to it without getting frustrated or angry.

The writers of difficult poems face the same troubling questions as readers, but for them the questions can be even more agitating. Often a poet will ask himself, if he is man, or herself, if a woman (transgendered individuals also find themselves asking these questions): "Why did my poem turn out like this? Why isn't it completely accessible like the poems of Billy Collins, which never pose any problems for understanding?" Like readers of difficult poems, these writers of difficult poems must first come to terms with the fact that theirs is a common problem, shared by many other authors. And they must come to terms with the fact that it is not their fault that their poems are harder to understand than Billy Collins's, but that some poems just turn out that way.

Difficult poems are normal. They are not incoherent, meaningless, or hostile. Well-meaning readers may have suggested that "something must be wrong" with the poem. So let's get a new perspective. "Difficult" is very different from abnormal. In today's climate, with an increasing number of poems being labeled "difficult," this is an important distinction to keep in mind.

Difficult poems are like this because of their innate makeup. And that makeup is their constructed *style*. They are not like this because of something you as readers have done to them. It's not your fault.

Difficult poems are hard to read. Of course, you already know this, but if you keep it in mind then you are able to regain your authority as a reader. Don't let the poem intimidate you! Often the difficult poem will provoke you, but this may be its way of getting your attention. Sometimes, if you give your full attention to the poem, the provocative behavior will stop.

Difficult poems are not popular. This is something that any reader or writer of difficult poems must face squarely. There are no three ways about it. But just because a poem is not popular doesn't mean it has no value! Unpopular poems can still have meaningful readings and, after all, may not always be unpopular. Even if the poem never becomes popular, it can still be special to you, the reader. Maybe the poem's unpopularity will even bring you and the difficult poem closer. After all, your own ability to have an intimate relation with the poem is not affected by the poem's popularity.

Once you have gotten beyond the blame game—blaming yourself as a reader for the difficulty or blaming the poem—you can start to focus on the relationship. The difficulty you are having with the poem may suggest that there is a problem not with you the reader nor with the poem but with the relation between you and the poem. Working through the issues that arise as part of this relation can be a valuable learning experience. *Smoothing over difficulties is not the solution!* Learning to cope with a difficult reading of a poem will often be more fulfilling than sweeping difficulties under the carpet, only to have the accumulated dust plume up in your face when you finally get around to cleaning the floor.

Readers of difficult poems also need to beware of the tendency to idealize the accessible poem. Keep in mind that a poem may be easy because it is not saying anything. And while this may make for undisturbed reading at first, it may mask problems that will turn up later. No poem is ever really difficulty-free. Sometimes working out your difficulties with the poem is the best thing for a long-term aesthetic experience and opens up the possibilities for many future encounters with the poem.

I hope that this approach to the difficult poem will alleviate the frustration so many readers feel when challenged by this type of aesthetic experience. Reading poems, like other life experiences, is not always as simple as it may seem to be from the outside, as when we see other readers flipping happily through collections of best-loved verse. Very often this picture of readerly bliss is not the whole story; even these now-smiling readers may have gone through difficult experiences with poems when they first encountered them. As my mother would often say, you can't make bacon and eggs without slaughtering a pig.

A BLOW IS LIKE AN INSTRUMENT:
THE POETIC IMAGINARY
AND CURRICULAR PRACTICES

I shall not see—and don't I know 'em?
A critic lovely as a poem.
DOROTHY PARKER

Recently, I went to a talk by Stanley Cavell at a bookstore in New York City. A crowd of perhaps fifty people gathered into the upstairs space of the store to hear the distinguished philosopher talk about Hollywood melodramas of a bygone era. The question period that followed Cavell's initial presentation was characterized by a mix of erudition and over-the-top enthrallment in these films, both by Cavell and the audience members. While I had seen some of the films being discussed, I had only the haziest recall of any of the details being pored over by the group as if they were a familiar part of a shared culture of those participating—a culture I also shared with them, but had fallen out of, at least to a degree. Toward the end, someone asked Cavell to talk about *Blond Venus*, and in the course of his remarks he noted that in the film Marlene Dietrich sings in both a gorilla costume and in a white tuxedo; he said one of the questions the film raised is whether the Dietrich figure can appear in these ways and still be taken for a responsible mother. I heard this question as reflecting on what Cavell himself was doing: Can you do philosophy in a gorilla suit or a white tuxedo and still be responsible to the profession and to the activity of philosophy (not the same thing)?

An early version of this essay was published in *Daedalus* 126.4 (Fall 1997), a special issue on the academic profession, based on presentations made at a seminar at the American Academy of Arts and Sciences. A later version was published in *Beyond English, Inc.*, edited by David Downing, Mark Hurlbert, Paula Mathieu (Portsmouth, NH: Boynton/Cook Heinemann, 2002). The essay was adapted for *The Poetry and Cultural Studies Reader*, edited by Maria Damon and Ira Livingston (Champaign-Urbana: University of Illinois Press, 2009).

Stanley Cavell is no guerrilla warrior in the trenches of the canon wars. And his suits, while appearing tailored, tend to be blue or gray. Nonetheless, what counts for him as an activity of philosophy, at least in this instance, is barely recognizable in terms of the ostensive subject matter of his talk. Because what is philosophical about his project is not the content but his mode of thinking, by which I don't mean a set of philosophical issues that he applies to a discussion of the subject, but rather an attitude of inquiry, a manner of listening, a mode of recognizing what is significant and proceeding from there to identifying networks of significance. So the answer to the question Can philosophy still be philosophy if it is performed in a guerrilla suit or a white tuxedo? is that philosophy can be philosophy only if it acknowledges the suits it is wearing and also that these suits are not (only) what are issued to us in central casting but (also) ones that we fashion and refashion ourselves.

There are no core subjects, no core texts in the humanities, and this is the grand democratic vista of our mutual endeavor in arts and letters, the source of our greatest anxiety and our greatest possibilities. In literary studies, it is not enough to show what has been done but also what it is possible to do. Artworks are not just monuments of the past but investments in the present, investments we squander with our penurious insistence on taking such works as cultural capital rather than capital expenditure. For the most part, our programs of Great Books amount to little more than lip service to an idea of Culture that is encapsulated into tokens and affixed to curricular charm bracelets to be taken out at parties for display—but never employed in the workings of our present culture. Ideas are dead except in use. And for use you don't need a preset list of ideas or Great Works: almost any will do if enactment not prescription is the aim.

I often teach works that raise, for many students, some of the most basic questions about poetry: What is poetry? How can this work be a poem? How and what does it mean? These are not questions that I always want to talk about nor ones that the works at hand continue to raise for me. Whatever questions I may have of this sort, I have either resolved or put aside as I listen for quite different, much more particular, things. My own familiarity with the poetry I teach puts me at some distance from most students, who are coming to this work for the first time. And yet, when I overcome my resistance and engage in the discussion, which I often find becomes contentious and emotional, I am reminded that when a text is dressed in the costume of poetry, that, in and of itself, is a provocation to consider these basic questions of language, meaning, and art. Inevitably, raising such questions is one of the uses of the poetry to which I am committed; that is, poetry marked by its aversion to conformity, to received ideas, to the expected or mandated or regulated form. These aversions and resistances have their history; they are never entirely novel nor free of traditions, including the traditions of the new; that history is nothing less than literary history. But the point of literary history is not just that a selected sequence of works was created nor that they are enduring or great (or deplorable and hideous) nor that they form a part of a cultural fabric of that time or a tradition that extends to the present. All that is well and good, but aesthetically secondary. The point, that is, is not (*not just*) the transcendental or cultural or historical or ideological or psychoanalytic deduction of a work of art but how that works plays itself out: its performance not (just) its interpretation. But as history is written by the victors, so art (as a matter of professional imperatives) is taught by the explainers.

It needn't be so, for we are professors, not deducers: our work is as much to promote as to dispel, to generate as much as document. I am not—I know it sounds like I am—professing the virtue of art over the deadness of criticism but rather professing the aversion of virtue that is a first principle of the arts and an inherent, if generally discredited, possibility for the humanities.

I suspect part of the problem may be in the way a certain idea of philosophy as critique, rather than art as practice, has been the model for the best defense of the university. Critique, not as opposed to aesthetics but *without* aesthetics—that is, the sort of institutionalized critique that dominates the American university—is empty, a shell game of Great Books and Big Methods full of solutions and cultural capital, signifying nothing. That is, Professionalized Critique dogs every school of criticism when as a matter of routine (and perhaps against its most radical impulses), it turns art into artifact, asking not what it does but what it means; much as its own methods are, and quicker than a wink, turned from tools to artifacts. Like I told the man at the agency, if you want the guy to talk maybe you need to remove your hand from his throat, even if it looks to you like that's the only thing keeping him upright.

Poetry and the arts are living entities in our culture. It is not enough to know the work of a particular moment in history, removed from the context of our contemporary—our public—culture; such knowledge risks being transmitted stillborn. Just as we now insist that literary works need to be read in their sociohistorical context, so we must also insist that they be read into the present aesthetic context. So while I lament the lack of cultural and historical information on the part of students, I also lament the often proud illiteracy of contemporary culture on the part of the faculty.

I do not suggest that the (contemporary) practice of poetry should eclipse literary history (as, for a time, the contemporary practice of analytic philosophy eclipsed the history of philosophy). I do believe, however, that literary history or theory uninformed by the newly emerging forms of poetic practice is as problematic as literary criticism or literary history uninformed by contemporary theoretical or methodological practices. I realize that my insistence on the aesthetic function of poetry and the significance for literary studies of contemporary literature has an odd echo with some of the tenets of the New Critics. But I point this out mainly to debunk the dogma that works that "create linguistic difficulty and density and therefore make meaning problematic" have remained, or were ever, the center of attention of literary studies from the New Critics until the present, as Catherine Gallagher suggests.[1] As far as English literary studies of this century is concerned, *The Waste Land* and *Ulysses* have had to bear most of the weight of this claim. But these cease to be difficult texts insofar as they are fetishized as Arnoldian tokens of "bestness," a process that replaces their linguistic, aesthetic, and sociohistorical complexity with the very unambiguous status of cultural treasure; in any case, they have not been contemporary texts for well over half a century. Despite the homage, "difficult" or "ambiguous" literature has not, as a rule, meant teaching disorienting or unfamiliar works of literature to college students, and especially not works that challenged the professor's critical or ideological paradigms or were written in unfamiliar or disruptive dictions, dialects, or lexicons. Rather it has meant turning a narrow range of designated difficulties into puzzles resolvable by checking off the boxes on the "Understanding Poetry" worksheet, while rejecting ways of reading poetry that do not produce "understanding" but rather response, questions, disorientation, interaction, more poems. In fact, if you look at the anthologies of English and American literature that have been used in humanities classes over the past fifty years, you will see that if "difficulty" is a criterion at all, it is as likely to be one for the exclusion of a work as for its inclusion; a tendency that has only accelerated in recent years as "accessibility" and moral uplift have taken on both a political and pedagogic

---

1. "The History of Literary Criticism," in *Daedalus* 126.1 (Winter 1997), 133–53.

imperative. In the end, despite their defense of difficulty, the New Critics were primarily responsible for defanging radical modernism and enthroning its milquetoast other, High Antimodernism (a reference to their own work certainly, but also bringing to mind the work they abjured). Moreover, as Gallagher accurately points out, and it is also a point made with synoptic brilliance by Jed Rasula in *The American Poetry Wax Museum*,[2] the New Critics and their heirs actively discounted much of the demotic, folk, vulgar, idiosyncratic, ethnic, erotic, black, "women's," and genre poetry for which their reading methods were inadequate. This is not, I would insist, because this work was not ambiguous or difficult enough, but because it posed the wrong kind of difficulties and ambiguities.

The academic profession is not a unified body but a composite of many dissimilar individuals and groups pursuing projects ranging from the valiantly idiosyncratic to the proscriptively conventional. Most of the popular generalizations about what professors do or don't do are unsupported by facts; for example, it turns out that, as a whole, professors work very long hours, generally beyond anything required of them. Moreover, there is a disturbing trend to equate classroom hours with work hours, leading to a fundamental misrepresentation of the nature of academic labor. It's as if you measured the work of a lawyer only by the hours spent in her client's presence, or the work of a cook by how long it takes to eat his soufflé, or the work of a legislator by the number of pages of legislation he or she has written. Yet comparable misrepresentations of the academic profession are having dire consequences, most specifically in abetting the increase in non-tenured part-time employment that is eroding not only the working conditions of the university but also the quality of education that universities can provide.

Misinformation feeds on misinformation, so it is particularly unfortunate that political expediency has encouraged many of those who speak in the name of the university to abandon any vision of the radically democratic role the university can, but too often does not, play in this culture. That is to say, tenure and academic freedom are not primarily valuable because they provide job security to individual faculty members but because they serve the public good. There is no conflict between the public interest and full-time tenured employment: short-term cost savings cannot justify the

2. *The American Poetry Wax Museum: Reality Effects 1940–1990* (Urbana, IL: NCTE, 1996).

long-term economic folly of compromising one of the most substantial intellectual and cultural resources this society has created. The question is not whether our society can afford to maintain the intellectual and cultural space of the university at present levels but whether it can afford not to.

The greatest benefit of the university is not that it trains students for anything in particular, nor that it imbues in them a particular set of ideas, but that it is a place for open-ended research that can just as well lead nowhere as somewhere, that is wasteful and inefficient by short-term socioeconomic standards but practically a steal as a long-term research-and-development investment in democracy, freedom, and creativity—without which we won't have much of an economic future or the one we have won't be worth the flesh it's imprinted on. At its most effective, the university is not oriented toward marketplace discipline and employment training, but rather toward maximizing the capacity for reflection and creativity. When it is most fully achieving its potential, university classes are not goal-oriented or preprofessional but self-defining and exploratory. Attempts to regulate the university according to market values only pervert what is best and least accountable about these cultural spaces. We cannot make education more efficient without making it more deficient.

My plea then is for enriched content, especially aesthetic and conceptual content, over a streamlined vocational goal orientation. There is a educational payoff, but it has to do with degrees of intellectual resonance and creativity not measurable (always) in immediate job readiness (for which, as Silicon Valley has shown, college may be unnecessary). Almost everyone agrees there is a practical value in students' being able to write in conventional business English, but minimum standards are notoriously hard to achieve, as even those who emphasize basic skills realize. To create good writers you need to create good readers. There is no shortcut. A correction-oriented expository writing drill might produce barely competent writers (it often doesn't), but such competence may come at the cost of alienating students from their own language practices (talking and writing and reading). Taking an image from Rousseau's *Émile*, if we swaddle the young scholar in the strictures of grammatical correctness, we may induce immobility while fostering uprightness. And mobility is a practical skill for a "people in transition," to use a phrase from Langston Hughes that speaks to our American social space at the beginning of the twenty-first century. In correcting a perceived deficit, we must keep in mind that teachers, just as doctors, need to be sure to do no harm.

Arthur Levine, then president of Teachers College, suggested, at the meeting where I first presented this essay, that we imagine our relation to our constituents on the model of a bank's relation to its depositors.[3] With a bank, you deposit something you have already acquired. With education, you are seeking to acquire something you don't already have. For at its best, education delivers nothing—it enables, animates. That is, the information imparted is embedded in an interaction. Information stripped of this interaction is largely inert: it is as if you are given the database but not software to use it, or, perhaps more accurately, you are given the data and the software but not tools to question the collection method, reframe the categories, or collect new data. Let the buyer beware: the new "consumer-oriented" education may be cheap, but it also may not be worth very much.

The university I envision is more imaginary than actual, for everywhere the tried and sometimes true pushes out the untried but possible.

Within the academic profession, fights are often intramural as new disciplinary and methodological projects threaten older ones, the new and old both claiming to be the victims of unprecedented dogmatism, bad faith, and lack of intellectual or cultural values. In literary studies, these conflicts tend to be among three different conceptions of the field. One group defines literary studies in terms of its traditional subject matter, that is, the literary works that have traditionally served as the principal object of study in the field. This group maintains relative consensus among its constituents. A second group accepts the idea of the field as defined by its subject matter, but proposes a new range of subject matters—from works underrepresented in traditional literary study to works that challenge the very idea of the literary. There is consensus among the constituents of this second group on broadening the subject matter of the field but necessarily no consensus on exactly what the new subjects should be. A third group consists of those who define the field primarily in terms of a particular method of analysis, critique, or interpretation. There is little consensus among the constituents of this third group, since the approaches adopted are often seen to be mutually exclusive. No doubt many in the profession are sympathetic, to varying degrees, with all three of these conceptions of the field. The danger for the academic profession is not that one side or another will "win"—that the new barbarians will become the old boys or the traditionalists will block innovation. Rather, the problem is the idea that consensus should prevail. The

3. "How the Academic Profession Is Changing," in *Daedalus* 126.4 (Fall 1997): 6–7.

manufacturing of consent always involves the devaluing or exclusion of that which doesn't fit the frame. What I value is not temperance but tolerance, for an insistence on temperance can mark an intolerance not only of the intemperate but also of unconventional—or unassimilated—forms of expression. We don't need to agree—or even converse—so long as we tolerate the possibility of radically different approaches, even to our most cherished ideas of decorum, methodology, rationality, subject matter. The university that I value leaves all of these matters open, undecided—and not just open for debate, but open for multiple practices. The point is not to replace one approach with another but to reorient ourselves toward a kind of inquiry in which there are no final solutions, no universally mandated protocols—an orientation that is fundamental to the essays collected in this book. The point is not to administer culture but to participate in it.

In discussions about the state of the university, complaints about "tenured radicals" abound. I am more worried about tenured smugness and tenured burnout. While I respect the authority of scholarship, I reject the authoritativeness of any prescribed set of books, methods, experts, standards. The problem is not that there has been too much reform but that there has hardly been any at all: the content has shifted, but this reflects demographic changes more than ideological ones; the structure of authority remains the same. Given the passionate engagement with their research shown by most of the graduate students I know, the often deanimating mandates of perceived professional success are the surest symptom of the problem. From the time they enter graduate school, the passions, commitments, and creativity of young scholars are routinely reoriented toward a cynical professional wiliness that emphasizes whom it is opportune to quote or what best fits market prospects rather than what the young scholars are most capable of doing or what best suits their passions or aesthetic proclivities. The profession, both panicked by the market and temperamentally conservative (even in its apparently nonconservative guises) seems bent on shaping young scholars in its own image rather than encouraging the production of new and unexpected images. In these circumstances, professors—sometimes unintentionally, sometimes with the best intentions—often seem less inclined to offer themselves as aids to the young scholar's research than to act as living roadblocks.

While specialization is appropriate for a scholar's own work—and there is nothing more sublime about the university than those obsessive scholars who seems to know everything about a specific subject, writer, or period—

specialization is too often projected on students at large, as the same few books get taught over and again, while the vast wealth of new books and old books remain "outside my field" (why not take a walk on the adjacent fields from time to time?). The problem may well be that many professors do not feel they have the authority to teach or supervise work in which they do not have expertise. I suppose imagining I have no expertise at all may be my greatest advantage: I can consider teaching or discussing almost anything if a student makes a compelling proposal for its necessity. My subject is contemporary poetry, but I find it stretches from there to almost anywhere—by which I mean to say that whatever time students have in the university, in college or graduate school, should be a time of indiscriminate, prodigal, voracious reading and searching: *one text must lead directly to the next.* Against the mandated hypotactic, rationalized logic of conventional syllabi, I suggest we go avagabonding: let our curriculums spin out into paratactic sagas. I propose we focus less on adducing the meaning of a homogenous sequence of works and more on addressing the relation of heterogeneous series of works (Li Po next to Oulipo, "Jabberwocky" with Newton's *Optics*). Nor is this another appeal to interdisciplinarity, which assumes the constituent disciplines that are already established and carefully preserves their distinctness through the process. Indeed, I've come to realize that poetry is one of the most infra- or transdisciplinary fields in the humanities, but this is because—since well before Lucretius—poetry already potentially encompasses all the disciplines of the humanities.

I realize my approach will not be to everyone's taste, nor do I wish to impose my sensibilities on the academic profession at large. What I ask for is greater tolerance for such approaches in a university that allows for the multiple and even incommensurable not just in its theories but in its practices.

It's not that I overstate my case; I am making a case for overstatement.

This wild adventure in learning is surely what inspired many of us to make the arts or humanities our calling, yet we lose the passion as we go from this adventure in texts to administering culture by teaspoon. And this is very like what we do when we imagine our graduate programs primarily in terms of vocational training in narrowly predefined fields, rather than opportunities for open-ended research, centers for the study of the arts, lavish emporiums of further thinking. Does anyone doubt that we deaden the potential of future research and future teaching with our cramped, vocational/preprofessional disciplinary fantasies? And what a travesty, in particular, this training for jobs that do not even exist—though we must all do all we can to reverse the pernicious trend toward poorly paid adjunct work in place of full-time, tenured employment. Yet I must disagree with those who, with great probity, advise that we reduce graduate programs to make them conform more precisely to the job market so as to avoid overproduction of PhDs. Rather we should welcome into our graduate programs those whose goal is not to have the same job as their teachers, but who, for a number of reasons, want to take one, two, or five years, modestly funded in exchange for some teaching, to pursue their studies, in ways they must be primarily responsible to define.

And what of academic standards? Aren't these the dikes that protect us from the flood of unregulated thought? Or are they like the narrow Chinese shoe that deforms our thinking to fit its image of rigor? When I examine the formats and implied standards for peer-reviewed journals and academic conferences, they suggest to me a preference for a lifeless prose, bloated with the compulsory repetitive explanation of what every other "important" piece on this subject has said. Of course, many professors will insist that they do not subscribe to this, but the point is not what any one of us does, but the institutional culture we accept. It seems to me that the academic culture of the humanities places more emphasis on learning its ropes, on professional conformity, than it does on any actual research, writing, thinking, or teaching of the people who make up the profession. Indeed, it doesn't really matter what constitutes this conformity: the distinction being made is in an important sense antipathetic to substance. This is the chief function of anonymous peer review: ensuring not quality or objectivity but compliance.

Anonymous peer reviewing enforces prevalent disciplinary standards, especially standards about the tone or manner of an argument, even while permitting the publication of a wide range of ideas—*as long as the ideas are expressed in the dominant style.* While it might seem that anonymous review would encourage greater textual freedom, in practice the submission of an anonymous article to multiple anonymous readers ends up favoring work that comes closest to conforming to accepted norms of argument and writing style—indeed such a procedure is one of the best ways to determine what these norms are. Of course, it's not a big surprise that institutions perpetuate their institutional styles. But perhaps what may make what I am saying sound—to some in the profession—exaggerated is that I find it deplorable that the academic profession is, well, too *academic.* Maybe this is because I am more accustomed to a form of cultural exchange and production among poets and through independently produced "small press" books and magazines that seems more vital, and more committed to the values often ascribed to the academic profession—that is, more committed to fomenting imagination than controlling imagination—than is the academic profession itself. The academic profession has a lot to learn from such communities of independent artists and scholars. I also feel that the academic profession has an obligation to provide a sanctuary for the arts, especially in a period of devastating defunding of government support for the arts.

What I object to is disciplinarity for the sake of disciplinarity and not in the service of inquiry. Too often, the procedures developed by the academic profession to ensure fairness and rigor end up creating a game that rewards routinized learning over risk. Blind peer reviewing, like its cousins standardized testing and evaluation, is certainly an advantage when it comes to discouraging preferential treatment for individuals, but the price it often pays for this is bolstering preferential treatment for the most acceptable types of discourse and fostering the bureaucratization of knowledge production. Anonymous peer review, like standardized testing and uniform assessment, encourages blandness and conformity in the style of presentation and response, leading those whose futures are dependent on such reviews and evaluations to shy away from taking risks with their writing styles or modes of argument or ideas. The policy is to reward the best test-takers but not necessarily the most engaging or culturally significant achievements. The result is that academic prose, like the career patterns it reflects, tends to avoid animation in favor of caution and to defer exuberance in favor of interminable self-justification and self-glossing that are unrelated to the needs of documentation or communication, research or teaching. I am not saying there is no place for anonymous peer reviewing, nor that it should be abolished, but that there is far too much deference given to a system that in trying to eliminate one kind of bias actually institutes another kind. In contrast, not enough recognition is given to those activities of the members of the academic profession who question the rules of the game, who champion rather than adjudicate, who see universities as places for wild questions and not just the prescribed answers.

Emphasis on conventional testing is antipathetic to an aesthetically charged encounter with art. Testing students on their ability to memorize names or dates or on their skill at identifying passages taken out of context encourages them to focus on mastering information rather than on reading literary works: the two goals are in opposition.

The best way I can describe how I teach is by calling it a reading workshop, for I am less concerned with analysis or explanation of individual poems than with finding ways to intensify the experience of poetry, of the poetic, through a consideration of how the different styles and structures and forms of contemporary poetry can affect the way we see and understand the world. No previous experience with poetry is necessary. More important is a willingness to consider the implausible, to try out alternative ways of thinking, to listen to the way language sounds before trying to figure out what it means, to lose yourself in a flurry of syllables and regain your bearings in dimensions otherwise imagined as out of reach, to hear how poems work to delight, inform, redress, lament, extol, oppose, renew, rhapsodize, imagine, foment . . .

The stigmatization of the poetic and the aesthetic in writing is a foundational component of the judgment of academic prose, to the detriment of students and teachers alike. As something of a prank, call it empirical research, I submitted my essay "What's Art Got to Do with It: The Subject of the Humanities in the Age of Cultural Studies," which was written as the keynote speech for the annual convention of the Northeast Modern Language Association (and subsequently collected in *My Way: Speeches and Poems*),[4] to *PMLA*, since I was aware that the flagship publication of the profession welcomes talk about poetic function as long as it doesn't involve actively engaging in poetic acts. That is, I was aware that the publication committees of *PMLA* might support some of what I say "in theory" but never in practice, never as a writing practice. I mention this not because *PMLA* is an important place of publication for a poet or essayist, but because its attitudes set a tone of conformism and hypocrisy that governs the profession and sharply delimits the possibilities for the writing styles of graduate students and untenured faculty—that is, the groups most likely to do innovative work. And the reason for this is that the accrediting and legitimating function of the literary academy rests not on a particular subject matter or political view or methodology but rather on the control of the means of expression. In short, legitimation lies in the control over the means of representation.

4. "What's Art Got to Do with It" was published in *American Literary History* and anthologized in *The American Literary History Reader*, edited by Gordon Hutner (New York: Oxford University Press, 1995) and in *Beauty and the Critic: Aesthetics in an Age of Cultural Studies*, edited by James Soderholm (Birmingham: University of Alabama Press, 1997). I collected the essay in *My Way: Speeches and Poems* (Chicago: University of Chicago Press, 1999).

Consider, for a start, *PMLA*'s statement on the form for readers' reports that submissions are to be evaluated for "importance of the subject, originality of thought, accuracy of the facts, clarity and readability of style . . ." Readability of style? *PMLA*? Compared to what? Importance of subject? That phrase is expected to be understood only in the narrowest professional sense; that is, in terms of the concerns of specialization and scholarly detail that in most other contexts would argue against the "importance of the subject" of most *PMLA* articles but should not, I would argue, undermine their legitimate place in this publication. For the *PMLA* of the 1990s to hold onto "originality" as a criterion, given the decisive eroding of that concept in articles it has sponsored, suggests the problem to which my irritable charge of "hypocrisy" gives vent. I suppose I am naïve enough to believe that bad faith does not have to be mandated. So the "clarity" of which the editorial policy statement speaks becomes, in this context, an entirely disciplinary affair, an empty marker of legitimation that confers value on outmoded and indefensible principles of writing.

Both *PMLA* readers rejected my essay—and I suspect that few of you who have gotten this far in this essay will wonder why. One rejection, anonymous, says that the essay "is provocative" but "not appropriate for *PMLA*. I would suggest the author rewrite it—tightening it up, clarifying the argument—for submission elsewhere." The essay should be rejected because it (1) "lacks focus," (2) has an "inconsistency of tone," (3) "is disjointed, loose, in need of revision to make it more 'punchy.' The reader wonders at times what the point is." And (4) "Many readers will consider self-indulgent the author's reference to writing his essay 'lying down on the couch, the pad propped up by my knee.'" (As I write this coda I am standing upside down floating over Manhattan in a helium balloon.) The referee goes on: "The author makes intriguing assertions, with sweeping generalizations, which he or she does not support with any evidence. In order to convince the reader that he or she is not simply expressing eccentric opinions on literary matters, the author ought to explain in greater depth the reason for which he or she has come to a particular conclusion."—But I *am* expressing eccentric opinions on literary matters, without *PMLA*'s brand of "clarity" and "evidence": eccentric, indulgent, disjointed, loose, inconsistent—and proud. But evidently not punch-drunk: though I do wonder what articles in recent *PMLA*s the professor finds stylistically "punchy"? While it is easy to poke fun at this sort of *Elements of Style* fundamentalism, such a constrained approach to reading has dire effects in the classroom, where it alienates students from writing and reading. That is something our culture cannot afford.

The other rejection, signed by Richard Ohmann, a prominent progressive whose critical work on the English profession I admire, makes a witty reply suggesting that it's not so much that the essay is "not recommended for *PMLA*" but that "*PMLA* not recommended for this essay." (I quote Professor Ohmann with his permission.) Still, Ohmann thinks I am being unfair to cultural studies, which may be true, but fails to register that the essay subsumes cultural studies in a much broader polemic in which many individual practitioners of cultural studies come out ahead. Indeed, I imagine my poetry and essays are themselves forms of cultural studies. Ultimately, the reviewer, famous for his own sharp and useful critiques of the academy in decades past, feels that my essay falls outside "the academic humanities" since it doesn't "refer specifically to texts, generalize about them, construct an historical framework of analysis, all that academic stuff." He concludes, "I don't think the author wants to write this kind of article. I'd go for the aphorism and provocations and some other venue." I feel like a dance-hall performer in *Gunsmoke* being thrown out of town by Marshal Dillon. "That may be awright for Paree or SoHo, but we don't cotton to that around here."—"But, Marshal, I have as much right to be in this territory as you and so maybe I just won't mosey along!"

In contrast to the sciences, in the humanities we shrink from teaching difficult or hard-to-grasp material in a desperate, self-defeating effort to make literature and art accessible. From an educational point of view, it might be better to insist that what is inaccessible or impossible to grasp is exactly what needs to be taught in our schools. This is why I feel that, with all the attention to radical changes in the humanities, we have not changed nearly enough. The focus on teaching representative and expressive works, where representation and expression are understood in an almost entirely unrelated sense, marks a continuity from 1890s to the 1990s. If the earlier phase of humanism marked literature as expressive of mankind, the new humanism of identity politics condemns the universalization but adopts the underlying structure: literary works are expressive or representative not of mankind but particular subsets of human beings (by means of which their basic humanity shines forth). The almost total absence of poetry from primary and secondary school curriculums certainly suggests the problem. Light fiction seems to be the best vehicle for the new humanism, and if poetry comes into the picture at all it is almost surely going to be sincere, sentimental, instructive, and uplifting. This entails reading poetry not for its aesthetic values, which is to say as aesthetic construction, but as moral sentiment; or else recognizing that as moral discourse poetry will often seem inaccessible, immoral, without values, decadent.

Moreover, I can't help but feel that the unwillingness to teach difficult or challenging or unconventional work is based less on good intentions than on condescension: the false belief that students are not smart enough to understand anything other than the most artless art. (Just between you and me, it turns out that lots of students get enthusiastic about much of the poetry that most high school and college English teachers have long since redlined, but are bored to tears by the poetry of uplift foisted on them.)

SHORTY PETTERSTEIN INTERVIEW (Henry Jacobs and Woodrow Leafer)

How would you compare the kind of music you play with a, how would you compare that with art, you know, what kind of art, artistic . . . ?

Man like I think Art blows the most, I mean, uh, he came with the band about three years ago, man, dig, and, uh, like, he was a real uh you know small town cat—and I mean he was swinging, man, but he was a small time cat. And I mean he started to blow with us and he was a real nut, you know, cool. . . .

What would you advise the young artist, the young musician, to do? Would you advise him to get an academic education or strive immediately for self-expression?

Well, man, I mean, I'm a musician, dig. And I mean to me the most important thing is that you should blow, you know. . . . If a cat wants to blow and he wants to blow, and uh then he's got to have a scene where he can blow.

That would apply to the artists playing horns and wind instruments—they would have to blow. What about those, for example, who are playing string instruments? Or would you say, how's the picture there?

Well, I mean, you know, it's, uh, pretty much all the same, man. A blow is like an instrument, you know.[5]

5. My transcription from *Howls, Raps & Roars: Recordings from the San Francisco Poetry Renaissance* (Berkeley: Fantasy Records 4FCD-4410–2, 1993), disc 1; produced by Bill Belmont, compiled by Ann Charters. Originally released as Henry Jacobs & Woody Leafer, "Two Interviews" (Fantasy EP 4051, 1955) and later on *Interviews of Our Times* (Fantasy F-7001, 1958).

The arts and sciences of this century have shown that deductive methods of argument—narrow rationalizing—hardly exhaust the full capacity of reason. Induction and discontinuity are slighted only at the cost of slighting reason itself. There is no evidence that the conventional expository prose that is the ubiquitous output of the academic profession produces more insights or better research than nonexpository modes. There is no evidence that a tone of austere probity rather than tones that are ironic or raucous furthers the value of teaching or inquiry. It may be true that standard academic prose permits dissident ideas, but ideas mean little if not embodied in material practices, and, for those in the academic profession, writing is one of the most fundamental of such practices. Writing is never neutral, never an objective mechanism for the delivery of facts. Therefore the repression of writing practices is a form of suppressing dissidence—even if it is dissidence, I would add, for the sake of dissidence.

So while my attitude to the academic profession is highly critical, I want to insist that one of the primary values such a profession can have results from its constituents challenging authority, questioning conventional rhetorical forms, and remaining restless and quarrelsome and unsatisfied, especially with the bureaucratizing of knowledge that is the inertial force that pulls us together as a profession. Which is to say: *The profession is best when it professionalizes least.* As negative as I am about the rhetorical rigidity of the academic profession, comparison with journalism, corporate communications, or technical writing will show that these other professions police writing styles far more completely than the academic profession. That is why it is vital to raise these issues about rhetorical and pedagogic practices: because universities remain among the few cultural spaces in the United States in which there is at least a potential for critical discourse, for violation of norms and standards and protocols, in which a horizon of poetics remains possible.

At the SUNY-Buffalo, I am the director of the Poetics Program, cofounded in 1991 by Robert Creeley (our first director), Susan Howe, Raymond Federman, Dennis Tedlock, and myself.[6] The program has its roots in the forma-

---

6. I came to Buffalo as Butler Chair visiting professor in the fall of 1989; Susan Howe had been Butler Chair the year before. I had scant teaching experience. I first taught in the winter quarter of 1987 at the University of California–San Diego's writing program. In the summer of 1988, I taught my first literature class at Queens College. I also had taught a class in Princeton's Creative Writing Program for two semesters (spring 1989 and spring 1990). I was

tion of the English Department at Buffalo in the early 1960s by Albert Cook. Cook had the idea that you could hire literary artists to teach not creative writing but literature classes, and in particular literature classes in a PhD program. It was with this in mind that he hired Creeley, Charles Olson, and others; it marked a decisively other path from far more prevalent graduate (usually MA and MFA) "creative writing" programs that emerged at the same time.

By formalizing this concept in the early nineties, shortly after Howe and I came to UB, we were suggesting an alternative model for poets teaching in graduate, but also undergraduate, programs. The Poetics faculty teaches in the English Department's doctoral program, supervising orals and directing scholarly/critical dissertations, even if our license to this is more poetic than formal. A frequent question I get from students applying to the program is whether they can write a creative dissertation. I always do a double take: "I hope it will be creative, but it can't be a collection of poems or a novel." For the fact is that Poetics students have the same requirements as all other graduate students and are admitted by the same departmental committee. And while we encourage active questioning of the conventions of critical and scholarly writing, we remain committed to the practice of poetics as something distinct from, even though intersecting with, the practice of poetry. The implications of this perspective are perhaps more pragmatic, not to say programmatic, than theoretical: while the "creative writing" approach at universities often debunks the significance of critical reflection, sometimes pitting creativity against conceptual thinking, the Poetics Program insists that scholarship, historical research, and critical writing are at the core of graduate education.

This is not to say that a PhD program is appropriate for most poets. I tend to discourage people who ask my advice from pursuing this degree at any institution, partly to ensure that they have considered the limitations of the academic environment in terms of artistic freedom, compensation, and

---

appointed David Gray Professor of Poetry and Letters in the fall of 1990 (Creeley had been the first Gray Chair, but had been promoted to the Capen Chair a couple of years earlier). We hired Susan Howe and she came back to Buffalo in the fall of 1991. In Buffalo that first year, Bob and I cooked up the idea for the Poetics Program, though Bob had wanted to secede from the English Department and move to the Center for the Arts then under construction. I argued that we should use the administrative support of the English degree and have our students receive the more generic English PhD. In 2003, I was appointed Donald T. Regan Professor of English at the University of Pennsylvania.

future employment. But if this is the choice they make, it is likely because they want to be teachers, editors, and writers and because their writing is as likely to be criticism or poetics as poetry.

The Poetics Program is fully integrated into the English Department, presenting seminars and sponsoring events within that context, even while marking such offerings as our own. We also provide modest funding to students to publish magazines and books (print and electronic) as well as to organize their own poetry readings, talks series, and conferences: over the past decade, this has resulted in dozens of magazines, scores of books, and numerous visitors, not to mention our website, the Electronic Poetry Center, created by Loss Pequeño Glazier (http://epc.buffalo.edu).

While many doctoral programs in English expect students to choose between being poets and scholars, we suggest that the one activity may enhance the other, for those so inclined. The poets, as I've suggested, do their poetry and their editing on their own: it informs their graduate work but is never the explicit content of it. And, equally significant, the Poetics graduate students form a vital community among themselves, where their shared interest in criticism and scholarship, editing and publishing, poetry writing, and teaching makes for an active bond. As it turns out, this mix seems to produce PhDs who are eager and well qualified to teach literature as well as writing.

The status of dialect, or nonstandard English, is another politically charged issue for the academic profession. Indeed, the issues raised by the controversies that rage around standardized language go to the heart of the ideology of education and the kinds of language practices sanctioned by the academic profession. At the same time, the controversy illustrates the either/or thinking that, as I have suggested, also plagues discussions of issues such as the core curriculum, academic standards, and objectivity.

In the most visible form of the conflict, black English is reviled by the conservative mainstream as deformed English and celebrated by Afrocentrics as the mother tongue. What's sanctified as ordinary for one group is derided as spurious by the other. The very ordinariness of black English is what makes it seem of self-evident value to its speakers, and rightly so, but this ordinariness is a red herring to conservatives because it is not ordinary to them. The problem is that there is no one ordinary language, but many ordinary languages. All language are social constructions—black English as much as standard English. In this case, there is paradoxical conflict between the ordinary and the conventional, between the dialect and the standard, between the normal and the spoken, between the intelligible and the vernacular. It's the ordinary versus the really ordinary. Conventional, standard English derives its authority from being perceived as the normal, the intelligible, and also the transparent. "It must be ordinary 'cause it's what I understand." Dialect, however, casts the conventional or standard as artificial or other or learned or imposed—"it's not my ordinary"—while sometimes claiming to be authentic or natural or spoken.

In this situation, the academic profession finds itself caught in a double bind that turns it against itself, for authenticity and normalcy both misconceive the dynamic and essentially rhetorical or trop(e)ical social fact of language. Black English is just as rich a language as standard English, just as valid (all languages are equally valid). The point is not to go from fetishizing (or naturalizing) the standard to fetishizing (or naturalizing) the authentic, but to acknowledge the multiple possibilities, and different social valances, of language. And to recognize that the ordinary lies not in any one type of language but in the between.

The most salient values of the university are reflected by the fact that it is the largest and most vibrant noncommercial quasi-public space in the United States. As others in this collection note, this is changing as universities are increasingly governed on output-driven consumer-oriented business principles. Yet at its best, education delivers nothing—it enables, animates. That is, the value imparted is embedded in an interaction not measurable by output alone. The bright ideas of managers and politicians to adopt commercial decision making on campus are almost always an erosion of the immutable value of the institution, destructive beyond measure. To put it more bluntly, we must move beyond what the editors of *Beyond English* provocatively call "English, Inc."

Yet, it is no longer taken for granted that immersion in the literature, art, and philosophy of the past and present has any practical benefit for society, and this too often has had the perverse effect of making those who would believe otherwise respond with a narrow, and often shrill, insistence on the necessity of one list or other of treasured or representative works that must be taught (since we can't ensure that they will be read or understood). The boat is sinking and we spend our time debating which pieces of furniture ought to go into the main dining room—instead of fixing the leaks. But, the value of the noncommercial space of the university is independent of any particular work or method, no matter how much any one of us loves the works or methods we have chosen to profess. For the values taught are reading values: critical thinking, reflection, social and bibliographic contexts of meaning, the relation of forms, styles, dictions, and genres in determining what any work has to say. While distance learning and large lecture classes are efficient on cost-per-student terms, for most students, who come out of media-intense but breathtakingly narrow cultural confines, they are ineffective. Teaching in our culture at this time is more than ever a labor-intensive activity. It requires prolonged engagement with individual students: gauging their reactions and responding to each one, individually. The answer is never in the technology—audiovisuals, web connections, books included—but how we learn to use these technologies.

My commitment is to public education: the education of the public at large and an education about the public, how it is constituted. Yet we are writing off our large public institutions of learning with the cynical assumption that graduates of such colleges have no practical need for the sort of open-ended education in the arts and sciences that most of us in the humanities support. "I never learned anything in college so why should they." Indeed, from a corporate point of view, having too many people in the workforce who think too much may be detrimental if they find themselves in dead-end jobs that require little thought. Such ideas are fundamentally antidemocratic of course; they are a breeding ground for a passive and malinformed citizenry that is unable to make sense of the complex issues that confront the nation. What price do we have to pay for an informed citizenry, one that can understand the complex multiplicity of American culture, can read into events, not simply register them as a series of fated accomplishments? What sort of investment are we willing to make in the intellectual and cultural development of our citizens so that we can remain, as a country, innovative, vibrant, socially responsible? How can we prepare ourselves for the unexpected, the difficult, the troubling events that are sure to lie ahead for all of us? Will we spend billions for defense while begrudging any money spent on what we are defending? The great experiment in mass education is not even a hundred years old: it has had virtually no downside. That we teeter on abandoning this commitment now is a testament to a smallness, to a lack of generosity, and to a contempt for noncommercial values that can only make us poorer—not only cultural, but economically.

AGAINST NATIONAL POETRY
MONTH AS SUCH

And they say
If I would just sing lighter songs
Better for me would it be,
But not is this truthful;
For sense remote
Adduces worth and gives it
Even if ignorant reading impairs it;
But it's my creed
That these songs yield
No value at the commencing
Only later, when one earns it.
GIRAUT DE BORNELH (12TH CENTURY, TRANS. CH. B.)

April is the cruelest month for poetry.

As part of the spring ritual of National Poetry Month, poets are symbolically dragged into the public square in order to be humiliated with the claim that their product has not achieved sufficient market penetration and needs to be revived by the Artificial Resuscitation Foundation (ARF) lest the art form collapse from its own incompetence and irrelevance, and as a result of the general disinterest among the broad masses of the American People.

The motto of ARF's National Poetry Month is: "Poetry's not so bad, really."

National Poetry Month is sponsored by the Academy of American Poets, an organization that uses its mainstream status to exclude from its promotional activities much of the formally innovative and "otherstream" poetries that form the inchoate heart of the art of poetry. The Academy's activities on

University of Chicago Press website, April 1999.

behalf of National Poetry Month tend to focus on the most conventional of contemporary poetry; perhaps a more accurate name for the project might be National Mainstream Poetry Month. Then perhaps we could designate August as National Unpopular Poetry Month.

Through its "safe poetry" free verse distribution program, the Academy of American Poets' major initiative for National Poetry Month is to give away millions of generic "poetry books" to random folks throughout the country. This program is intended to promote safe reading experiences and is based on ARF's founding principle that safe poetry is the best prophylactic against aesthetic experience.

Free poetry is never free, nor is free verse without patterns.

Oscar Wilde once wrote, "Only an auctioneer admires all schools of art." National Poetry Month professes to an undifferentiated promotion for "all" poetry, as if supporting all poetry, any more than supporting all politics, you could support any.

National Poetry Month is about making poetry safe for readers by promoting examples of the art form at its most bland and its most morally "positive." The message is: *Poetry is good for you.* But, unfortunately, promoting poetry as if it were an "easy listening" station just reinforces the idea that poetry is culturally irrelevant and has done a disservice not only to poetry deemed too controversial or difficult to promote but also to the poetry it puts forward in this way. "Accessibility" has become a kind of Moral Imperative based on the condescending notion that readers are intellectually challenged, and mustn't be presented with anything but Safe Poetry. As if poetry will turn people off to poetry.

Poetry: Readers Wanted. The kind of poetry I want is not a happy art with uplifting messages and easy-to-understand emotions. I want a poetry that's bad for you. Certainly not the kind of poetry that Volkswagen would be comfortable about putting in every new car it sells, which, believe it or not, is a 1999 feature of the Academy's National Poetry Month program.

The most desirable aim of the Academy's National Poetry Month is to increase the sales of poetry books. But when I scan some of the principal corporate sponsors of the program of the past several years, I can't help noting (actually I can but I prefer not to) that some are among the major institutions that work actively against the wider distribution of poetry. The large chain bookstores are no friends to the small presses and independent bookstores that are the principal supporters of all types of American poetry: the chains have driven many independents out of business and made it more difficult for most small presses (the site of the vast majority of poetry publishing) to get their books into retail outlets. I also note this year that the *New York Times* is a major sponsor of National Poetry Month; but if the *Times* would take seriously the task of reviewing poetry books and readings, it would be doing a far greater service to poetry than advertising its support for National Poetry Month. The whole thing strikes me as analogous to cigarette makers sponsoring a free emphysema clinic. Indeed, part of the purpose of the Academy's National Poetry Month appears to be to advertise National Poetry Month and its sponsors—thus, the Academy has taken out a series of newspaper ads that mention no poets and no poems but rather announce the existence of National Poetry Month with a prominent listing of its backers, who appear, in the end, to be sponsoring themselves.

The path taken by the Academy's National Poetry Month, and by such foundations as Lannan and the Lila Wallace–*Reader's Digest*, has been misguided because these organizations have decided to promote not poetry but the idea of poetry, and the idea of poetry too often has meant almost no poetry at all. Time and time again we hear the official spokespersons tell us they want to support projects that give speedy and efficient access to poetry and that the biggest obstacle to this access is, indeed, poetry, which may not provide the kind of easy reading required by such mandates.

The solution: find poetry that most closely resembles the fast and easy reading experiences of most Americans under the slogans Away with Difficulty! Make Poetry Palatable for the People! I think particularly of the five-year plan launched under the waving banners of Disguise the Acid Taste of the Aesthetic with NutraSweet Coating, which emphasized producing poetry in short sound bites, with MTV-type images to accompany them, so the People will not even know they are getting poetry.

This is the genius of the new Literary Access programs: the more you dilute art, the more you appear to increase the access. But access to what? Not to anything that would give a reader or listener any strong sense that poetry matters, but rather access to a watered-down version that lacks the cultural edge and the aesthetic sharpness of the best popular and mass culture. The only reason that poetry matters is that it has something different to offer, something slower on the uptake, maybe, but more intense for all that, and also something necessarily smaller in scale in terms of audience. Not better than mass culture, but a crucial alternative to it.

The reinvention, the making of a poetry for our time, is the only thing that makes poetry matter. And that means, literally, making poetry *matter*, that is making poetry that intensifies the matter or materiality of language—acoustic, visual, syntactic, semantic. Poetry is very much alive when it finds ways of doing things in a media-saturated environment that only poetry can do, but very much dead when it just retreads the same old same old.

As an alternative to National Poetry Month, I propose that we have an International Anti-Poetry Month. As part of the activities, all verse in public places will be covered over—from the Statue of Liberty to the friezes on many of our government buildings. Poetry readings will be removed from radio and TV (just as they are during the other eleven months of the year). Parents will be asked not to read Mother Goose and other rimes to their children but only . . . *fiction*. Religious institutions will have to forego reading verse passages from the liturgy and only prose translations of the Bible will be recited, with hymns strictly banned. Ministers in the black churches will be kindly requested to stop preaching. *Cats* will be closed for the month by order of the Anti-Poetry Commission. Poetry readings will be replaced by self-help lectures. Love letters will have to be written only in expository paragraphs. Baseball will have to start its spring training in May. No vocal music will be played on the radio or TV or sung in the concert halls. Children will have to stop playing all slapping and counting and singing games and stick to board games and football.

As part of the campaign, the major daily newspapers will run full-page ads with this text:

> Go ahead, don't read any poetry.
> You won't be able to understand it anyway: the best stuff is all over your
> head.

And there aren't even any commercials to liven up the action.
Anyway, you'll end up with a headache trying to figure out what the poems
    are saying because they are saying NOTHING.
Who needs that.
Better go to the movies.

INVENTION FOLLIES

I think Pound was a sort of prototypical American writer. Another would be Edward Dahlberg, another in obvious ways Williams, another Emily Dickinson, or Marianne Moore, or H.D., all of these. What's interesting about them, variously and as a company, is that they all have the necessity of inventing not only themselves but the literature they purport to be a fact of. They have to invent everything. That's why I love Williams' *In the American Grain,* which is absolutely vivid instance of creating anew thoughts for oneself to be fact of.
ROBERT CREELEY

1. *Noise That Stays News*

Make it noisy.
NATHANIEL MACKEY

Radical formal innovation in modernist and contemporary art has, at times, been seen as undermining the aesthetic, but it is more accurate to say that such work reinvents the aesthetic for new readers and new contexts. While modernist art remains a crucial site for any consideration of the aesthetics of poetic invention, I want to ground the discussion in the vicinities of the immediate present, where innovation, the new, ingenuity, and originality, perhaps even more than the aesthetic, are vexed terms, jinxed, perhaps ironically, by their own historical weight.

American Official Verse Culture operates on the premise that innovation and originality are not criteria of aesthetic value, and while not an absolute barrier to quality, are something to be held against a work, as if there were something unpleasantly immodest about any poetry that trades in the untried, something that smacks of elitism or arrogance or vulgarity. This

Ward Phillips Lecture, Notre Dame, November 27, 2006, subsequently published in *The Consequence of Innovation: 21st Century Poetics*, edited by Craig Dworkin (New York: Roof Books, 2008).

attitude, while relatively easy to ridicule, has deeper roots than might be apparent on first blush (the blush that comes over the cheek after the first few slaps).

Innovation is not so much an aesthetic value as an aesthetic necessity. Nevertheless, I understand full well the great suspicion with which claims to innovation and originality are now held. Indeed, there is, at present, an enormous circumspection about the necessity of the new, even among many whose work is fresh and adventurous. Some of this suspicion is a justified response to progressivist ideas in modernism (and modernization) that value the new over any other aesthetic quality, with the concomitant beliefs that the new replaces the old or that the new is better than the old. Too often claims for innovation seem to mime the marketing (and generational) imperative for "new and improved" (cultural) products. But such claims fail to recognize that poetic innovation is not necessarily related to improvement; at its most engaged, it is a means of keeping up with the present, grappling with the contemporary. We have to constantly reinvent our forms and vocabularies so that we don't lose touch with ourselves and the world we live in. The need for change in art is prompted by changes in the social and economic environment. The responses of the past are not always able to engage the present.

But such arguments for aesthetic innovation too often fall on deafened ears. For example, it is now fashionable to attack innovative poetry as frivolous, as the product of privileged individuals who do not have to face the harshest realities of poverty, war, or social injustice. This attitude, while often morally motivated, is aesthetically and ethically treacherous. For one thing, it risks denying the extraordinary innovations made by poets in the grip of just these harsh realities, without which the poetries of the Americas, for example, could not have developed as dynamically as they have. More accurate would be to say that innovation comes as a response to the human crisis: innovation is the mark of rethinking, trying to break out of the obsessive repetition-compulsion that we see all around us, whether in an individual or a family, or politically (in the conflict between states or groups). The idea that innovation is a luxury for the privileged or those who remove themselves from struggle creates, at best, a Romantic, at worst, a demagogic nostalgia for the greater authenticity of the experience of the imagined less well-off "other," as if only severe forms of oppression can create "relevant" poetry, as if we are so well off ourselves, with so many things to keep us company.

You might say that severe forms of oppression rob a people of its right to poetry—and the crisis for poetry, for the aesthetic, is to create a space for poetry again and again.

For that, anything less than invention falters. Sometimes that faltering can be exquisitely beautiful and sometimes the fall away from faltering can seem crass or crude. But the human need to create anew is no less strong than our need for lamentation. And even lamentation is not safe from the erosion of our consuming culture; even lamentation must be reinvented lest the dead be mocked and the living become ghost walkers, zombies of the tried and no longer true.

For well over a hundred years, we have been living through a period of aesthetic disruption, which is to say, shifting and readjusting to, reeling and spinning from, the social and technological changes of the long twentieth century. Of course, the risk for invention is that your invention fails; it usually fails, since most art produces failure, no matter its successes. The risk of not inventing is to succeed—at little or nothing. So these are poles: it can admirable to succeed at nothing (I have made a point of it) just as it can be illuminating to fail at innovation.

According to Henry Petroski, in *The Evolution of Useful Things*, his great study of inventions, from paper clips to zippers, *form follows not function but failure*.[1] According to Petroski, it is the frustration with existing things that produces innovation. I am interested in thinking through how this applies to poetic invention and originality, where the motivation may be less to produce the new than a frustration with aspects of existing work, not just in terms of form or content, but also means of reproduction and distribution. Petroski states his central idea succinctly:

> The form of made things is always subject to change in response to their real or perceived shortcomings, their failures to function properly. This principle governs all invention, innovation, and ingenuity; it is what drives all inventors, innovators, and engineers. And there follows a corollary: Since nothing is perfect, and indeed, since even our ideas of perfection are not static,

1. *The Evolution of Useful Things: How Everyday Artifacts—From Forks and Pins to Paper Clips and Zippers—Came to Be as They Are* (New York: Vintage Books, 1994). Chapter 2 is entitled "Form Follows Failure." I am grateful to James Shivers for underscoring the relevance of Petroski's work in *Charles Bernstein: American Innovator* (Doctoral dissertation, Université de Lausanne, Switzerland, 2002).

everything is subject to change over time. There can be no such thing as a "perfected" artifact; the future perfect can only be a tense, not a thing. (22)

Petroski's engineering perspective is remarkably free of the self-conscious unease that is the occupational hazard of the American poet working against accepted practices. Not surprising, Edgar Poe, in "The Philosophy of Composition" (1846) anticipates this peculiarly American struggle both for and against invention and originality along with Petroski's negation of the famous Bauhaus slogan, *form follows function*:

> My first object (as usual) was originality. The extent to which this has been neglected, in versification, is one of the most unaccountable things in the world. Admitting that there is possibility of variety in mere *rhythm*, it is still clear that the possible varieties of metre and stanza are absolutely in-finite—and yet, *for centuries, no man, in verse, has ever done, or ever seemed to think of doing, an original thing.* The fact is, originality (unless in minds of very unusual force) is by no means a matter, as some suppose, of impulse or intuition. In general, to be found, it must be elaborately sought, and although a positive merit of the highest class, demands in its attainment less of inven-tion than negation.[2]

What's needed is a transvaluation of the concept of innovation, so that we can think of innovation in a modest and local way, as responses to histor-ical and contemporary particulars—as situational, not universal. More like the weather—and one's everyday adaptation to it—than like the forward march of scientific knowledge. Very often innovation comes in reaction to a sense of the perceived failure of the artwork that precedes it (no matter how innovative it may appear to be). That sense of perceived failure creates a space for the new in the sense of the now. And it may often look like a swerve away from the innovations of the past, which, quicker than a wink, seem historical, fossilized. Innovation is a constant process of invention in the face of the given. From the outside, some of the innovations may seem very minor or technical, but in poetry the minor is the major and the major is often a bit tedious, like the windbag that keeps bellowing even after the air conditioning has been installed. Sometimes, the best thing you can do is stall, bunt, pass, loop, dodge, or just sit down and take a load off your feet.

2. Edgar Allan Poe, "The Philosophy of Composition," in *Poetry, Tales, & Selected Essays* (New York: Library of America College Edition, 1996), 180–81.

I am particularly interested in the ways that inventive poetries can be disruptive not only to forms of poems but also to reading habits, audiences, and distribution systems. And how a poetics of invention can be seen in contrast to a poetics of refinement—not one better than the other, but one with radically different aesthetic and social concerns in a given point in time.

I am interested, that is, in what business theorist Clayton Christensen calls "the innovator's dilemma."[3] In literary terms (my own highly contentious translation of Christensen's theory), the dilemma has to do with the desire of some practitioners to produce refined and improved works based on the perceived expectation of the "best" readers, what Christensen calls the "sustaining" approach. The alternative model is to abandon the needs of these "best" readers and produce works that are disruptive of perceived ideas of quality, understood in terms of refinement (one might also speak of skillfulness, craft, fluency). That alternative may require finding new readers, as Whitman insists, or having no readers, as Dickinson found. In any case, if the art form changes, then that which was out of it, impossible to read, may end up somewhere quite else, though where this elsewhere is I have a hard time saying.

Poetic innovations are often noisy, messy, disruptive, disorienting. They do not form a neat line with the innovations of the past, but often seem to swerve from a progressivist course. This may be because they are not only reconceiving the nature of the poem but reconstituting the audience for the poem, reevaluating the contexts that give the poem not only its meaning but its social force. On this model, you can contrast disruptive innovation with refinement. Very often the refined work that comes after disruptive innovation is "better" than the originals but may lack some of the initial energy. On a vertical (or diachronic) axis, Louis Zukofsky's "Poem Beginning 'The'" and "*A*" are refinements of, respectively, Eliot's "The Waste Land" and Pound's *Cantos*; at the same time, on a horizontal axis, vis-à-vis Official Verse Culture of the period, Zukofsky's poems are surely examples of disruptive innovation. For this reason, the terms need to be contextualized rather than treated as true or absolute values. While movements toward refinement are especially useful to consider across generations, you can also see such shifts in a single poet's work, say the difference between early and late Eliot, or early and late Ginsberg for that matter.

---

3. *The Innovator's Dilemma: When New Technologies Cause the Great Firms to Fail* (Boston: Harvard Business School Press, 1997).

Still, it's important not to accept the refinement of initially disruptive innovation as innovation while losing sight of actually existing innovation because it doesn't look like you think it "should."

After all, my own motto is still "should never say should."

Should you?

I realize I may appear to be valuing innovation over refinement, or at least registering my sense of how important inventiveness and indeed ingenuity have been for American poetry in the past century. But I want to suggest that the innovations of American poetry have not necessarily been toward improvement, but, in contrast, have worked to disrupt the ascent of an American poetry of refinement and assimilation. At the same time, I want to flag the danger of morally coding either end of this spectrum of disruption or refinement. Great works certainly exist in both modalities, and bad ones too, nor can the modalities always be differentiated. I am talking relative direction, not absolute qualities.

Inventive poetries, each in its own way, often very explicitly, abandon models for refining and improving poetry, avert meeting the expectations of existing poetry audiences with more beautifully articulated poems that consolidate the innovations of the prior generations. They resist assimilation. Such poetries may be willing to discard the existing poetry audience by creating works—and imagining alternative poetic lineages—that call into being new kinds of language reproduction technologies, new constellations of readers, new methods of reading, and new methods of distribution: by reconstituting the field. As in the business model of innovation, inventive poetry is disruptive of existing values and indeed may appear to be—may actually be—messier, noisier, and cruder than other available poetic works.

Christensen's business model provides an uncomfortably accurate description, especially since discourse about the arts often goes to great lengths to distance itself from market models. Yet categories such as "mainstream" and "fringe" are familiar to both discourses, as is the underlying notion of received historical value. And aren't the poetry products of Official Verse Culture served up to customers expecting a certain kind of product performance that innovative poetries fail to provide, often because the work either doesn't register as poetry or because it lacks (or rejects) expected literary values? In any case, Christensen is a relief from tiresome clichés derived from Peter Bürger's and Renato Poggioli's theories of the avant-garde as well as Harold Bloom's theory of influence:

What all sustaining technologies have in common is that they improve performance of established products, along the dimensions of performance that mainstream customers in major markets have historically valued. . . . Occasionally, however, *disruptive technologies* emerge: technologies that result in *worse* product performance, at least in the near-term. Ironically, in each of the instances studied in this book, it was disruptive technology that precipitated the leading firm's failure. Disruptive technologies bring to a market a very different value proposition than had been available previously. Generally, disruptive technologies underperform established products in mainstream markets, but they have other features that a few fringe (and generally new) customers value. (*Innovator's Dilemma*, xv)

A good recent example of a disruptive and messy new technology is the digitalization of poetry, which is not just reproducing but producing new possibilities for both the art of poetry and the archive of poetry. There has been much fuss made in the press about copyright issues concerning the exchange over the web of digital sound files, but I am far more interested in the implications of MP3 files for poetry, since we are now witnessing a transvaluation in poetry from the printed book to the sound file of an individual poem.

Poetry doesn't improve nor do new modes of poetry replace existing modes; indeed, the new may bring back into play previous and even apparently outmoded styles, forms, contents, and dictions. In insisting on a poetics of invention, invention more than innovation, I am imagining a poetry that is not progressivist or developmental or even evolutionary, not about replacement, not us/them; a poetics that is based more on dissatisfaction with previous inventions than any distinction between new/old, conventional/experimental, mainstream/outsider.

"What's new" can be an oppressive market constraint that stifles poetic work, but it can also be a form of human exchange as when we say to one another "What's new?" meaning "What's up?" or "What's happening?" What allows for a sense of opening, of a blank page that is not already completely inscribed? The problem here may be the rote evocation of Emerson, more than Michael Fried or Clement Greenberg or Ron Silliman; but the discourse of the avant-garde is too thick to cut through even with the new electric ideology weeder I bought last week at X-Mart.

The invention of which I speak is not a matter of choice, not one among many possibilities, but a necessary probe of perception for grappling not only with things as they are but also things as they might be. For that task, words such as innovation and invention may be inadequate; perhaps better to invoke the aesthetic force of NO: a resistance to the given state of things as not working or not working right or not working anymore. That doubt, that refusal, refusal especially of innovation, may be the mark of any such endeavor so conceived and so dedicated.

As blank may be its space.

2. We Cannot Retrace Our Steps

A phenomenology of invention would suggest a poetry's particularizing responses to shifting conditions. This would be a poetics of the temporal or processural, of contemporaneity, as Stein has it in her key work of poetics, "Composition as Explanation," where she insists that poets are neither "ahead" of their time nor "behind" their time but *in* or *out of* their time. Readers are mostly "out of it": their problem is not the difficulty of comprehending the advanced, but the inability to grapple with the present.[4] This, then, is not newness or the new, but *news*: "news that STAYS news" is Pound's formulation in *ABC of Reading*.[5] William Carlos Williams puts it best in "Asphodel, that Greeny Flower"—

It is difficult
    to get the news from poems
        yet men die miserably every day
            for lack
    of what is found there.[6]

As Stein writes in *The Mother of Us All* (in the voice of Susan B. Anthony)—"We cannot retrace our steps, going forward may be the same as going backwards."[7] And she adds: "Life is strife. I was a martyr all my life not to what was won but to what was done." It's this distinction between done and won that I am counting on here.

---

4. "Composition as Explanation," in *Selected Writings of Gertrude Stein*, edited by Carl Van Vechten (New York: Vintage Books, 1972).

5. *ABC of Reading* (New York: New Directions, 1934), 29.

6. *Collected Poems*, vol. 2, 1939–1962, edited by Christopher MacGowan (Princeton: Princeton University Press, 2001), 337.

7. *The Mother of Us All*, in *Last Operas and Plays*, edited by Carl Van Vechten (New York: Vintage Books. 1975), 87. The quotation is the next sentence is from page 88.

And also the idea that moving forward may always be moving backward. The more involved I become in twenty-first-century digital production and reproduction, the more I feel compelled to consider earlier histories of material textualization, from the invention of the Greek alphabet through the Gutenberg revolution and onto the era of photo/electronic language reproduction, in which we now find ourselves.

CREATIVE WREADING & AESTHETIC JUDGMENT

I am professor of poetry. I take that term quite literally. I profess poetry in a society, and often a classroom, where poetry is at best a half-forgotten thing, something confined to the peripheries of cultural imagination, a once grand enterprise perhaps, but today eclipsed by more compelling media. Many readers—current students and long ago graduates alike, those who have never been to school and those who teach school—have no experience at all with poetry and certainly little contact with poetry as an active contemporary art form. Indeed, college is a crucial site for the introduction, the continuing reintroduction, to poetry in both its historical and contemporary particulars.

A poem is a work of art using words (or related verbal materials). New poems often challenge prior definitions or understandings of poetry. Another way of saying this is that a poem is any verbal construction that is designated as a poem. The designation of a verbal text as poetry cues a way of reading but does not address the work's quality. Disagreement over the nature of what poetry is, or what constitutes a poem, is as much a part of the history of poetry as disputes about what makes a good poem. The most contentious of these disputes are fundamental to poetry's continuing social and aesthetic significance.

Confronted with a poem, many seem to go silent, or what they say tends to treat the poem as if it were not a poem at all but a statement of opinion, experience, or sentiment—or a cultural artifact of a time more benighted than our own that can perhaps give us a glimmer of the dim consciousness that guided those in days gone by. It's as if these readers were trying to access a Windows program with DOS tools, not realizing that you can click on the icons, not just scroll up and down and type in commands at a prompt

Adapted from an essay in *Poetry and Pedagogy: The Challenge of the Contemporary*, edited by Joan Retallack and Juliana Spahr (New York: Palgrave, 2006).

line. Or it is as if the poems, with sound and in color, were being viewed with a silent monochrome screen.

My response to this chronic poetic aporia (CPA) is to provide intensive poetry immersion courses, something like teaching poetry as a second language. That means I try to immerse the class in a wide yet distinct variety of poetic forms, sounds, dictions, and logics.

I am committed to bringing into play the performance of poetry—both the reader's performance of the printed poem and the poet's performance at a reading, in this way also bringing into the discussion the histories of performed poetry. At PennSound (http://writing.upenn.edu/pennsound) and other websites, sound files of poetry readings are available to use in conjunction with printed texts. Still, there is nothing like having live readings and discussions with poets as part of the class. (I find it helpful to assign a book by the visiting poet before the visit and have that form the basis for an active conversation either before or after the reading.) There is no more powerful way to bring home the materialities of voice or the specificities of the contemporary than through a reading. Readings offer a concrete countermeasure to the relentless abstraction and reification of the poem as something existing disembodied in an anthology. The lessons of the live poetry reading are significant for historical and contemporary poetry, since they provide a model for imagining poems not just as meaning formations but as social productions and material texts, and can provide a very concrete introduction to the study of literary works through both their bibliographic and performance contexts.

As for the art of reading, I try to create possibilities for reading as creative performance and as a ground for subsequent critical interpretation, based on the aesthetic principle that *you can't interpret what you don't experience*. Many new, but also many highly experienced, readers of poetry have a difficult time accessing the poetic strata of a work, that is, those elements that make a piece of writing a poem as opposed to . . . well let's just say prose. To counter this anaesthesia, I have a threefold plan.

First, I ask students to do interactive and creative responses to assigned readings, including imitations, memorizations, rearrangements, word or phrase substitutions, homolinguistic (English to English) translations/ transpositions, and other "wreading" experiments that involve reordering or rearranging a poem's words, lines, or stanzas, as well as locating or isolating certain key linguistic, figurative, and rhetorical features of the poem. (A list of wreading experiments is available at http://writing.upenn.edu/ bernstein/wreadiing-experiments.html.) The point here is both to investigate the recombinant structure of a poem—to what extent it retains its identity through modification of its constituent elements—and also to allow for a more intuitive, even visceral, contact with the materials of the poem, call it "sounding" the poems, as Thoreau speaks of sounding Walden Pond.

The Poem Profiler (http://writing.upenn.edu/library/Bernstein-Charles_ Poem-Profiler.html) is the second fold of Creative Wreading. The Poem Profiler is a delirious extension of New Criticism, one of whose significant virtues was a focus on the formal and linguistic features of a poem. I developed the profiler in response to the paucity of terms many students, not to say readers, have for discussing poems. In reading a poem, I ask students to assess the levels of a wide range of rhetorical features. "The Poem Profiler" has ten overall categories and over 125 individual features: "Stylistic Textures and Poetic Diction" includes such items as ambiguity, humor, eloquence, plainness, sincerity, smoothness (versus roughness, bumpiness, striation), and subtlety (versus bluntness). "Content" assesses the main types of subject matter in the poem. "Developmental/Temporal/Compositional Structures" assesses what holds the poem together—is it fragmentary or expository, stream of consciousness or dream-like/surreal, fast paced or jerky, procedural or employing traditional forms? The profiler also inventories "Devices," from irony to hyperbole, simile to metonymy. The "Mood/Tone" features are given as contrasting pairs, as in scary/reassuring, dark/light, impersonal/emotional, turbulent/calm. "Counting" is a way to note various features of a poem that are organized by number, while "Visual Shape/ Form" asks for an account of the physical arrangement of the poem on the page. In "Sound," the acoustic elements of the poem are assessed, while "Point of View" assesses whether there is a narrator, persona, first-person, and the like. Finally, in the most explicitly un–New Critical gesture, I have a list of sociohistorical contexts to consider.

The Poem Profiler is a guide for the perplexed and hopefully not a perplexing guide. The profiler is not meant to be applied to every poem or else it could become a tool for rote, laborious, microanalysis of a given poem. For that reason, I suggest doing comprehensive profiling on only a couple of poems. After that, the profiler should be used as a resource to add specificity to more open-ended responses to poems, through journal responses and interactive experiments and performances. For the Poem Profiler is not just a delirious form of close reading, it is also an approach to literary criticism as a form of thick description, in several senses of the term: dense (you don't get it do you, huh?), richly detailed, and opaque. Criticism should be at least as opaque as the poem and twice as opaque as the reader.

In the first class, I ask the students to run the profiler on themselves, to gauge their current preferences. In going over the results, hours can be spent defining, expanding, and détourning the terms. I go through the whole profiler, asking students not only to give their rating for each term but also to make up an example to illustrate what the term means. I am fascinated by the occasional student who marks everything "5," since it's close to unimaginable that anyone would like all the possible qualities of a poem equally, irreverence as much as piety. Such a response suggests a lack of engagement with, or confidence in, one's own aesthetic judgment. The value of the exercise is that it makes explicit the set of aesthetic values each reader brings to a poem and helps to explore how these affect the evaluation of, and more important, the response to, a poem. For this reason, the profiler may enable some students to appreciate that a poem achieves, to a significant degree, something that he or she rated very low on the profiler.

The profiler also can provoke a discussion of why some poets choose poetic values that are not necessarily highly rated on an individual student's initial self-assessment. Indeed, the different ratings students give to the same poetic feature make palpable that there is no consensus in the class on what factors are valued in a poem. In the Wreading Workshop, disagreement is encouraged as a way of generating exchange rather than as an obstacle that needs to be overcome. Disagreement is not a means to a consensus (or the imposed consensus of the professor's judgment): dissensus is the goal of the Wreading Workshop. I always try to give extended attention to the negative reactions that students have to a poem or set of poems. By emphasizing the range of disagreements in the initial self-assessment via the profiler, it becomes apparent at the start that disagreement is as much a product of initial orientation as of the qualities of any given poem studied. Since I often ask students to rank the poems they read for a given week in order of their preference, the profiler provides a means to pursue the basis of these initial judgments. Asking about preferences is just a beginning, however; the more useful question is asking students to articulate (if necessary with the help of the profiler) the criteria for their preference. The next step is to explore the relation between initial preferences and quality assessment by asking whether a student's initial preferences for one set of poetic textures is a sufficient basis for determining the aesthetic value of a poem. After a while, most students will acknowledge the value of a poem whose profile is aversive to their own initial preferences. Some students may even, as the class progresses, choose to reset the factory preset aesthetic preferences in the options menu of their Imaginary.

(Beyond the second fold, which is not a school activity, is to reconfigure that options menu so that it works as a dynamic, nonlinear system. Basic reprogramming skills are required.)

As with all wreading exercises, the value of the Poem Profiler diminishes when the work it generates ceases to be engaging and exploratory. The point is not that all poetic study needs to be fun, but that thematic or formal analysis needs to be connected with the experiential dimension of the poem. In many cases, it would be better to have a student read a poem out loud, type it out, or repeatedly play a recording of it than to write a paper trying to figure out its meaning. I don't see much use, in poetry teaching, of exams, test identifications, or traditional theme-based papers. By *experience* I mean a movement away from a summary of what the poem is about or a catalog of its devices or images or conceits and toward the sound and tone and mood of the poem perceived intuitively, as one hears a song without necessarily concentrating on it or being able to say what it is about. Concentration may be an obstacle to the sort of ambient reading that is a fundamental prerequisite to accessing the experiential dimension of a poem. Without access to this dimension, analysis is worthless: it may say something about the "idea" of a poem but cannot engage a poem's inner life. Scholarship and interpretation are of tremendous value, but they need to be informed by tone and rhythm as much as theme.

Favorite poems I have read and taught many times remain opaque to me or I forget whatever conclusions I may have come to upon earlier readings. It's often the case that I have no idea what a line means or why exactly it appeals to me. In the Wreading Workshop, such nonunderstanding flourishes. Reading ambiently and associatively rather than rationally and systematically, a poem may come to life even as it remains out of our grasp. Paradoxically, the harder we try to grasp a poem's meaning, the more elusive it may become. Given that most students are drilled to think in a linear and logical manner and to express themselves in directly expressive or expository prose, the Wreading Workshop becomes one of the very few sites at a university that encourages and explores intuitive thinking and writing; its not that such poetic work is better than rationalistic or directly expressive work, but it provides a necessary counter to the dominance of one type of knowledge over others.

The final, or third, fold of Creative Wreading is weekly intensive journal entries in which the students respond to each week's assigned readings, and to the supplemental material posted on the online syllabus. As with the wreading experiments and the Poem Profiler studies, I ask that all student work be posted directly to a common class e-mail list or web log. In this way, everything that I see as the teacher is also seen by all students. Nothing is private. The most radical result of the public postings is that students direct their comments to each other, rather than to the professor/authority figure. The class discussion extends and intensifies online; it might even be more accurate to say that class discussion is an extension of the online discussion.

I emphasize to students that the week's responses are meant to be spontaneous, informal, and unedited. These notebooks entries are not drafts for papers, nor are they necessarily expository. Fragments, lists, incomplete thoughts are fine—in the service of noting reactions and thoughts. The purpose of the writing is to encourage interaction with the poems and also serve as a record of individual reading.

Creative Wreading actively counters the fear that "difficult" or "negative" poetry is harder for students to engage than simple or affirmative poetry. In a Creative Wreading environment, difficulty means more layers with which to grapple and therefore more opportunities for a multilevel engagement with a poem. When reading poetry is not directed to the goal of deciphering a fixed, graspable meaning but rather encourages performing and responding to overlapping meanings, then difficulty ceases to be an obstacle and is transformed into an opening.

WREADING, WRITING, WRESPONDING

1. Writing

Laptops are open and everyone's online and chattering away at the same time. I pass around a yellow pad and it circulates from one person to the next, in zigzag order, for the length of the seminar. The participants are writing an ongoing serial collaboration and will continue to work on this, during the class, for the full fourteen weeks we meet. Each week one student takes the pages home and posts a verbatim transcription and an edited version. From my laptop I project, on the large LCD display screen, the index of the class e-mail list, to which everyone has posted their work for the week.

Each week students write works based on the experiments list (http://writing.upenn.edu/bernstein/experiments.html), a set of constraints and procedures, which has served as a foundation for much my undergraduate teaching over the past twenty years. You could call this class "creative writing," but I resist the label, since it comes with all the weight of the prototypical poetry workshop, which is often focused on content-based exercises rather than experiments in form. *Write a poem about the first time you saw your Dad shaving*: "the blood dripped down his face / and I trembled in the corner, / unseen, whimpering." Not being particularly interested in sincerity, description, or traditional craft, I've long made a point of teaching modernist and contemporary poetry classes rather than writing classes, but the twist is that these literature classes—what I call "creative (w)reading" workshops—are run as if they were creative writing classes (students write creatively in response to the readings, but the focus is entirely on poems assigned).

Teaching Modernist Poetry, edited by Peter Middleton and Nicky Marsh (London and New York: Palgrave/Macmillan, 2010).

Over time, you see, I've become more interested in small seminars devoted just to the students' experiments, and so, through a kind of trap backdoor I've fallen through, tripping up my apparent prejudices, I've ended up in a very common space of creative writing (poetry), which I simply call "Writing Experiments Seminar"—or English 111, after the number of the room in which we meet.

My phobia to creative writing poetry workshops, like all phobias, is exaggerated and no doubt unfair to the eccentric range offered under the rubric; but I cling to it as to an untrustworthy friend. But then again I know what I don't like. I am so stubborn that I am sure if someone advised me on how to improve a poem I'd probably do the opposite, just out of sheer contrariness. From the get-go I tell 111 participants that writing good poems, or learning to write better poems, or learning the craft of poetry, or improving your work, is not the focus or goal of the seminar (but it may happen as a by-product). I think of 111 as a nonexpository writing class, or a course in anti- or para- or pluricomposition, something that, if I had *my way* (and not just a book by that name), I would require as an antidote to Freshman Comp. The class has its value not for budding poets, only, or primarily, or exclusively, but also for all writers. It's less a workshop than a lab, with experiments in mutant forms conducted on the textual body of the living language. (I play the role of a kinder, gentler Frankenstein.) Still, as an elective course, the students who enroll in it think of the class as a poetry class, since that is the only academic slot associated with what one of the students likes to call abnormal writing, but I prefer to think of as r & d (research and development). I figure the more you know how to take words apart and put them together, the more aspects of language you've turned up, down, left, right, inside out, and outside in, the better you will be able to respond to the many contingencies, screwballs and curve balls and monkey wrenches that language will inevitably throw your way. Like my main man says, "Whose in control, me or the words?" (*Whose* is, that's who.) And then—I am slowly getting around to the subject of teaching modernist poetry—an approach like this makes for proactive readers by potentiating proactive approaches to writing. So, yeah, busted again: this is just another kind of lit'r'ture class, a reading workshop not so much in disguise as in drag.

Let me circle back to the question of craft and improvement. The scene: my grossly caricatured creative writing workshop, led by a teacher who (unlike me) knows good from bad and (also unlike me) prefers the good. A teacher who's not afraid to tell a student what she's doing wrong and how to fix it. I have my tastes too, but am wary of legislating them, since I know they are minority tastes, particular and eccentric tastes, and I don't expect students to share them, much less adopt them. I try as much as possible to steer discussions away from good or bad and don't, as a rule, give my opinions about quality or improvement. I do the best I can to direct attention to what is happening in the work, alternative means of construction, and the possibilities of the form.

And I encourage distractions and digressions. Something reminds someone of a cartoon on the web so they turn their laptops around and play that. That reminds me of my boyhood in ancient Greece, so I carry on about etymologies. And I do tend to wax aesthetic and philosophical about any or all of the forms employed; and have a trigger finger ready to fire off examples from modernist and contemporary poetry, many of which I have linked to the web syllabus. Someone laughs, after reading something funny on the yellow-pad collaboration being passed around, or maybe in a text message sent from one class member to another, or maybe just at one of my innumerable, problematic jokes. Laughter is the necessary yeast of good class conversation and opens the possibility for listening, not just hearing.

The best advice I can give to the student in a conventional creative writing workshop is that if your peers or teacher tell you not to do something, because that something doesn't make sense to them, appears as a blur, then probably the thing you need to do is *not cut it out* but pursue it: develop. (But then some teachers in a more conventional workshop will tell you that, and others in a more experimental one won't.) Something germinal in a young writer isn't necessarily, or even usually, going to make sense even to the most open-minded teacher or generous classmate. Often the most problematic things about a germinal work have the greatest potential for development. That is why the typical workshop environment, with cross-comments toward creating a "better" piece of writing, that is, one that a group will agree is "better" (more fluid, less awkward, clearer, more logical or expressive, more direct) runs counter to poetic invention and aesthetic process, which will more likely (but not necessarily) produce work that is not legible by such workshop criteria. But you can rely on something: the quizzical, puzzled, and overtly negative responses are signs you are on to something.

How many creative writing workshop members does it take to change a well-crafted light bulb?: Three—One to screw it in (the student), one to hold the ladder (the peer), and one to block the light (the teacher).

I block the light too. But I try to use that as a point of rhythmic oscillation, as I move in and out of the rays.

The Writing Experiments seminar focuses on transformation, metamorphosis, substitution, and deformation. It has a typical order (you can see a recent example of the syllabus at http://writing.upenn.edu/bernstein/syllabi/111.html), starting with a reading of Raymond Queneau's brilliant variations of the "same" story in *Exercises in Style*:

1   Substitution
2   Homolinguistic translation
3   Recombination
4   Homophonic & dialect translation
5   Ekphrasis
6   Chance operation & the aleatoric
7   Without rules, (k)not!, or is free writing free?
8   Short lines / short poems (attention)
9   Memory
10 Novel forms
11 The art of constraint
12 Flarf & conceptual poetry: web-generated poems, found poems, appropriation
13 Digital & visual poetry
14 Performance
15 Class anthology / chapbooks /web site

The syllabus itself is subject to deformative performance; as a final assignment, Kimberly Eisler (a Penn freshman at the time) did a set of substitutions for the experiments, making something of a bestiary of possible modernist forms. Here's my edited version:

§   Homolinguistic transduction: Take a pretense (someone else's or your own) and traverse/rewrite/rate it by substituting warp for word, phase for phrase, load for line, or "free" troupe as repose to each phantom or sentence. Or: traditionalize the poem into another, or severely other, illegitimate style.

§   Recombination (1): Write a piece and crack it somewhere in the middle, then recharge with the "best" part following the enjoyable part.

§   Reposition (2)—Doubling: Starting with ominous sentence, write a series of penitentiaries each doubling the number of sexes in the punitive paragraph and including all the words used previously.

§ Homophonic translation: Take a poem to a foreign country that you can pronounce but not necessarily understand and never make it back. Take the sound of their lips before the clouds.

§ Use the wet dream engine.

§ Acrostic charades: Pick a book at random and use the title to feather your pinkie nails and scratch off your wings. For each letter, create a pore and cover every faucet in your multiverse.

§ Poem is made according to the order in which it swells like icicles. Solo: pick a series of ferns or vines from your closet to put in the vat.

§ Dream work: Use the moon to sweep every fur coat under the couch for 30 days. Double the length of each diamond. Borrow a friend and apply these techniques to him or her.

§ Write a poem just when you are on the verge of being forced into the back of a police car.

§ Read the Bible with a stranger's chapped lips.

§ Bring your brain storm into a bomb shelter.

§ Fertilize your pipe dreams.

§ Write a poem in which all the events never happen.

§ Write a poem made up entirely of hydrogen.

§ Let the morning come and tell each of your addled minds a lie.

§ Do something five times, then pray.

§ Create a blueprint of the way thoughts speak like tiger lilies at the center of gravity.

§ Bite your tongue until it bleeds.

§ Write a poem in the form of the future.

& the moral of that is: the syllabus is an imaginary map to a constantly transmogrifying place: the process begins with the readings and assignments but ultimately engulfs every aspect of the class and perhaps the psychic spaces beyond. The syllabus (like the pronouncement of the teacher) is subject to its own mandates to question and reorder. & the moral of that is: students in an "experiments" class are as likely to play follow the teacher as students in a traditional forms class. & the moral of that is: leave no turn unstoned.

2. Reading

Modernist poetry projects futures, even if that means concatenating the present as if it were a future. The modernist poem is always in the future because that's where you catch it, just beyond the poem, in Wallace Stevens's "what's after" ("Thirteen Ways of Looking at a Blackbird"). And once you catch it, it dissolves into air; the butterfly net is empty. In other words, the more I try to pin the poem down, the more it eludes me and elates me. I come to the poems I know best as an enigma comes to a weigh station. I'm the enigma, the poem's my grounding.

In the 1970s, many of us, batty as hornets in a bee's nest, spoke of reader's response, the reader not the poem makes the meaning. This was true in a deliciously magical sense of "makes," as in my favorite Lenny Bruce joke, where the kid comes into the candy store, where the genie is behind the counter while the owner's out: "Make me a malted." "YOU'RE A MALTED!" But as readers, and teachers, we all know that not all readings are equally good; that for all the range of readings some can be entirely off-base, while others, off-beat, offer new horizons for interacting with the poem. In the end, the poem makes malteds of us all.

But even so, there is no one meaning to a poem, and the poems I know best, like Stevens's "The Plain Sense of Things," have no plain sense. It's less the heresy of paraphrase than the paraphrase of heresy.

I remain mystified by the culture of testing in modernist and contemporary poetry classes. I couldn't pass a multiple-choice test of one of my own poems. A friend once sent me a passages-identification quiz and I couldn't quite remember if the passage in question, which the written record will show that I wrote, was by David Antin, Moses Maimonides, Madonna, or me. Confusion can be more productive than adjudication. If we ask the mind to wonder in reading the poems, let's accept some collateral drift too.

"The student is always right." No that's not quite an adoption of the corporate ethos for the classroom, where we don't teach but offer client services. I mean if a student says something, within the context of the classroom, she can't be wrong about her perception, though it may not correlate with the poem at hand. So the question is: what about this poem evoked this apparently unsupported response? And how does *that* relate to what is going on in the poem? A misperception can be just as generative for engaging a poem as a supposedly correct perception, especially one grounded in schooling, in rational analysis. The first thing to learn (you can't quite teach it) about modernist and contemporary poetry is that you have to get the hang of it, trust your intuitions before your analytic faculties come into (and try to keep in) play.

At the University of Pennsylvania, I teach two basic undergraduate twentieth-century poetry classes: one focused on U.S. poetry (http://writing

.upenn.edu/bernstein/syllabi/88.html) and one focused on poetry outside the United States (http://writing.upenn.edu/bernstein/syllabi/62.html). I've become increasingly agitated about the Anglomania of our literature classes. I see no problem with actively reading poetry in other languages, working through our own translations in class, or reading multiple translations, together with the originals, where possible. Listening to the sounds and rhythms of the poem, even in the absence of knowing the language, can be exhilarating.

The web syllabus is a key part of the course, as I have moved away from photocopied course packs and anthologies and toward greater reliance on web materials, many of which I have compiled for this purpose. I do use print anthologies, but I see these more as background information and further readings than at the center of the class. Wherever possible, I make available sound files of the poets reading their work (together with texts of the poems), something that has been a central focus for Al Filreis and me in starting PennSound (http://writing.upenn.edu/pennsound/), our huge sound recording archive. (And we are working on developing select recordings of non-English language poetry.) The Electronic Poetry Center (http://epc.buffalo.edu), which I edit with Loss Pequeño Glazier and Jack Krick, provides additional digital resources for many of the poets in the syllabi. And fundamental to the project is to make as much of this material as possible available not just to the students registered in the class, but to anyone who accesses our web pages (all free both of charge and advertising).

I developed the Poem Profiler (discussed above in "Creative Wreading & Aesthetic Judgment") to expand the range of possible responses to the poems, so I use that to generate the first-order response.

Second, I ask that each week students do "creative wreading" experiments on the poem—a set of deformations, transformations, and imitations that involve doing things with the poems rather than analyzing them (http://writing.upenn.edu/bernstein/wreading-experiments.html). These exercises are designed to provide interactive engagement with the assigned reading. I also ask that for each experiment, the student provide a short commentary on the process, the results, the relation to the original, and an assessment of the value of the experiment. The point of these wreadings is not to create "original" poems of value, though that may well happen. Rather, these exercises are designed to create a greater engagement with the assigned reading and a greater understanding of the structures of, and possibilities for, poetic composition. Indeed, before you can discourse about a poem you need to think *with* it, get it inside your ears; for that, typing it, or hand-writing it, or reciting it over and again, or putting the poet's reading on our iPod playlist, might be a better first encounter with a poem than a thematically unified composition explaining it. The poem cries out: *I don't want to be understood—just listened to!* For a last class, there is nothing better than having students recite memorized poems from the syllabus. Imitation and memorization are as old-fashioned, and future-directed, as poetry itself.

Third, I ask students to keep an intensive journal of their responses to the readings. I emphasize that these journals are to be, as far as possible, integrated with the flow of everyday life. Often students include the comments of their roommates or the responses of their friends. At Penn, reading a poem out loud or playing a sound file of a poem is bound to seem odd and provoke quizzical responses; these too become part of the journal. I ask the students to consider a specific set of questions and instructions:

> What do you think of the poem? Give as much detail as you can as to why you feel the way you do. What does the poem sound like, what does it remind you of? Quote specific lines or phrases that seem relevant. Being specific is the hardest part of this assignment and I almost always request descriptions of the form and style of the different poems: which can be as simple as a description of the visual shape of the poem, its length, the type of lines (long, short, metrical, enjambed), the sort of style or rhetoric or vocabulary (unusual, common, pastoral, urban, urbane, fast-paced, slow-moving, pictorial, bombastic, introspective, descriptive, narrative, fragmentary, etc.).
>
> The point is not for you to analyze or explain the poem but rather to try to react to it. Cataloging the features of the poem won't explain it but it may enable you to enter into the poem more fully.
>
> Of the poems read for this week, which is your favorite? Why? Which is the best. Why? Are favorite and best the same? Rank the poems in your order of preference.
>
> Of the poems read for this week, which did you like least? Why?
>
> Of the poems read for this week, which is the worst. Why? What are your criteria for deciding the quality of poem. Can poems that you don't like or understand still be good poems?
>
> If you have heard the audio performance, describe the performance and how it extends or contradicts the written version of the poem.

Issues of quality are foregrounded while remaining provisional. The point is not to compare my judgment, or literary history's, with those of students who are perennially new not only to the difficulties of poetry but also to the pleasures attendant to these difficulties.

The responses to the poems might be mixed with a list of things to do (as in Ted Berrigan's "Things to Do in New York"), with dream entries, with comments on other classes, or with more typical diary entries.

So what then of the class meetings? Student discussion is central, but with the online forum I pick up themes, concerns, interpretations and take off from there. I try less to lecture and more to be a respondent to the stated (and unstated) responses of the students, as expressed in their journals, wreading experiments, and poem profiles. My motto as a teacher comes from Dominique Fourcade's "tout arrive," which he, in turn, found on Manet's stationery. The class time is a blank page on which a composition takes place: *everything happens.* Like an upside-down Boy Scout, Fourcade coins my pedagogic method in a phrase: "Be ready but not prepared."[1] This stands for nothing less than the multitrack improvisation of possibility. "Let, and not force to happen" (Fourcade again) is not the idea but a method played out in each class. "The light is in the dark."

A few weeks into the class, after a spirited discussion of Mallarmé's *Un coup de dés,* one of the students half asked, half interjected—"So you're saying this is art?!"

Or, better (as Carolee Schneemann put it in an e-mail): "a perfection of the unexpected."

1. *Everything Happens,* translated by Stacy Doris (Sausalito, CA: Post Apollo Press, 2000).

ANYTHING GOES

Al Filreis's *Counter-Revolution of the Word: The Conservative Attack on Modern Poetry 1945–1960* is less a work of literary interpretation than a penetrating historical and sociological study.[1] As such, it is comparable to such now-classic studies as Jed Rasula's *The American Poetry Wax Museum: Reality Effects*, Alan Golding's *From Outlaw to Classic: Canons in American Poetry*, Robert Von Hallberg's *American Poetry and Culture, 1945–1960*, and Cary Nelson's *Repression and Recovery: Modern American Poetry and the Politics of Cultural Memory*, 1910–1945. I mention these works as context because of their archival and historical focus. For Filreis's book is chock full of fascinating, yet disconcerting and often puzzling, quotations and accounts. Filreis shows the very real devils in the details.

Against the grain of received history, Filreis reveals the deep engagement of many of the left poets of the 1930s with modernist poetic innovation (the converse is also true: in an earlier book Filreis reads the putatively conservative Wallace Stevens within the sociocultural context of the 1930s). He also tracks a number of thirties poets, showing the dire effect of McCarthyite red-baiting on their careers. However, his principal focus is on the conflation of anticommunism with antimodernism in the immediate postwar period. Such a conflation might seem counterintuitive, since the left is often associated with populist styles that reject modernist difficulty, while radical modernism is often associated with an aesthetic at odds with explicit left political content. But the toxic mix of what Filreis calls "anticommunist antimodernism" is not only pervasive in the 1950s but also provides an ideological foundation for the Official Verse Culture of the 1970s onward.

Filreis's book is filled with telling examples of how the aesthetic and political right denounced nonconventional poetry as if it were a part of the communist menace. Such poetry was smeared as unnatural and corrupting,

Boston Review 33.4 (July–August 2008).
1. *Counter-Revolution of the Word* (Chapel Hill: University of North Carolina Press, 2007).

as an affront to moral values as expressed in proper grammar, and, moreover, as foreign and therefore un-American. "The vocabulary of thirties-bashing was cast in the idiom of incurability; tropes of cancer and mass death abounded. Leftist writing of the 1930s was dismissed 'in a phrase: it was an alien growth' . . . 'a poison'" (36, 37), while, by extension, modernist poetry was denounced as "barbarous dissonance" (170) fomenting "death and decay" (169). Writing in the *New York Times* in 1949, Howard Devree was already warning of the conflation of communism and modernism, both "possessed of the devil . . . and dangerous to American culture and realism" (169):

> Another curious, disconcerting and, in fact, frightening part of the new attack has been the tendency of the attackers to refer to modern art in practically the same terms used by Hitler and the Communist hierarchy. It is called "degenerate art," and there are thinly veiled accompanying demands for its suppression and censorship.[2]

Filreis is not alone in relating these images of the alien and nonhuman to the imagery of Don Siegel's 1956 movie, *The Invasion of the Body Snatchers*. In the charged environment, the lyric became a symbol for antimodernist resistance, clearly "identified with the postideological moment," a bulwark against what Col. Cullen Jones, in a 1951 article, "Abnormal Poets and Abnormal Poetry," derided as modernist effeminacy and its "sexual abnormalities."[3]

One thing the anticommunist antimodernists had right was that the poetic form of radical modernist work was political; Filreis calls this the "cold war politics of poetic form" (288). A perfect example is a 1953 article by Donald Davidson in which he targets parataxis in poetry for its "treacherous political irresponsibility in the act of eschewing relations of cause and effect while letting the related elements stand in unordered, unsubordinated lists" (Filreis, 292). Just a few years earlier, Robert Hillyer, in the widely cir-

---

2. Howard Devree, "Modernism under Fire," *New York Times*, September 11, 1949, sec. 10, p. 6.
3. "Abnormal Poets and Abnormal Poetry," in Stanton Coblentz, *The Music Makers: An Anthology of Recent American Poetry* (New York: Bernard Ackerman, 1945), quoted by Filreis (245–46). Based on the evidence from a headnote in Coblentz's anthology, Jones would certainly qualify as part of the Official Verse Culture of his time, given that he published thirty-five poems in 1944 in such widely circulated publications as the *New York Times* and the *Atlantic* (Coblentz, 122).

culated *Saturday Review of Literature* had assailed modernism in poetry as an "illusion of independent thought" and a "propaganda" machine of "the powers of darkness" ("Poetry's New Priesthood," June 18, 1949). Writing in the *Bulletin of the Poetry Society of America*, Hillyer accused modernists of "a cold conformity of intellectualism" that eliminated "diversity" and insisted on "a critical censorship, in its effects like that of the Kremlin" (Filreis, 165).

Filreis documents the smearing of modernist poets as perpetuators of the "Big Lie" (that it's really poetry), who, if they capture the free world, would enforce their worldview by means of "secret police, concentration camps, and execution squads," in the words of Stanton Coblentz in 1950 (Filreis, 166). Coblentz, a central figure in the study, had been featured in the *New York Times Magazine* in 1946 with his article "What Are They?—Poems or Puzzles?" In a later essay, Coblentz casts modernism in the role of a "mosquito that sucks your blood"; in other words, a "parasite that must be contained" (Filreis, 207). Images of purity versus degeneration abound. Consider Ben Lucien Burman's "The Cult of Unintelligibility," published in the November 1, 1952, issue of the *Saturday Review*. The influences of Gertrude Stein, Burman says, "still to be found in many strategic strongholds, like the lurking genius of yellow fever, . . . must be constantly fought and sprayed with violent chemicals lest the microbes develop again and start a new infection" (Filreis, 205–6).

As Filreis shows, it gets worse:

> The editors of *Pinnacle*, the magazine of the League for Sanity in Poetry, described modernism as genocide: poets were being exterminated ("The actual mandate, to be precise, prescribes not that all poets be exterminated, but only those who respect the literary traditions of three thousand years"). To this murderous "revolution," wrote another antimodernist, "there must be a counterrevolution. . . . The world has no . . . use for any kind of bigotry and regimentation." It was "futile . . . to seek the cause of the rise of our poetic dictators in any agency or factor outside their own little, warped minds and hearts," a conservative editor wrote, and so, she continued, "the only way to eliminate the trouble is to eliminate them." By imposing a "tabu against beauty, modern poets . . . have unwittingly signed their own death sentence." (166)

If the connection of radical formal innovation to genocide strikes contemporary sensibilities as bizarre, it's important to note that these ideas were mainstreamed in the immediate postwar period and that they underwrite the allegorical unconscious of the antimodernist factions of Official Verse Culture in our time.

While the postwar polemic takes a sometimes apocalyptic turn, there is nothing new about such viscerally negative responses to radical modernism. Russian futurist poets allied themselves to the 1917 revolution while Italian futurists allied themselves with the right; either way, those who rejected radical change expressed shock and dismay at the new art and the social disruption to which it was symbolically, and actually, attached. The confusion as to whether radical formal innovation is leftist or rightist, ethical or nihilistic, persists. In the United States, during the first decades of the twentieth century, the modernist "revolution of the word," and even the simple practice of free verse, were more often debunked than celebrated. Nowadays, we take Whitman and Dickinson as canonical, but the contemporary responses to their work were chilling and pre-emptive. In "The Philosophy of Composition," Poe located the problem as quintessentially American, as a phobia of the aesthetic; a fear that sensation undermines morality. The battle erupts on many fronts, historical and contemporary. Eugene O'Neill epitomizes the modernist-as-degenerate credo in Tyrone's famous blast at his too-poetic son in *Long Day's Journey into Night* (1942):

> That damned library of yours! . . . Voltaire, Rousseau, Schopenhauer, Nietzsche, Ibsen! Atheists, fools, and madmen! And your poets! This Dowson, and this Baudelaire, and Swinburne and Oscar Wilde and Whitman and Poe! Whoremongers and degenerates![4]

Brian Reed, in his recent study *Hart Crane: After His Lights*, is able to chart how both the body of this poet and the body of his work remain a site of acute aesthetic and political struggle, which plays out, in what must seem an odd passion play to the uninformed, in contemporary responses from the 1920s and 1930s and also in reviews of his work in our time.

What is significant about Filreis's study is that he traces how these antimodernist dynamics, fully alive in the first half of the century, morphed into effective, and even necessary, tools for Cold War hegemony. In this context it becomes harder to shrug off such now peripheral figures like Peter Viereck, who writing in *Political Science Quarterly* in 1952, "argued that the modern 'anything goes' aesthetic led to communist (and fascist) mass murder" (Fil-

---

4. *Long Day's Journey into Night* (New Haven: Yale University Press,) 135.

reis, 250). Filreis associates this noxious doctrine with the emergence of neoliberalism as articulated by Daniel Bell. "Bell's social narrative telling of the convergence of communism and modernism led him to propose a 'vital center'—in Arthur Schlesinger Jr.'s celebrated term—where limits could be placed on the urge toward 'anything goes,' an attitude symptomatic of both communists and modernists" (250).

While the anticommunist antimodernists claimed that modernist obscurity and unintelligibility constituted an elitist betrayal of the general reader, they failed to recognize that this general reader was the pure product of an elitist Cold War ideology. But the greater irony is that much of what the anticommunist antimodernists rejected in radical modernist poetry was also reviled by the totalitarian governments that they opposed. In the defense of human freedom as articulated by the individual poet in the lyric poem, these cold warriors hollowed the lyric of its enunciative and sonic richness and undermined the articulation of human freedom through unfettered expression.

The demonization of the aesthetic left in poetry does not end in the fifties or expire with the end of the Cold War; it persists, often in defensive, if not farcical, form, in the teaching and writings of those who, ironically, may sense they are on the wrong side of history. As with anticommunist antimodernism, dogmatic protest against the dogmatism of others is the standard operating procedure. The intellectual heir of anticommunist antimodernism is a post- or neoliberalism that underwrites its defense of dominant aesthetic values as common sense. Critiques are dismissed as unjustifiable agonism (the ideology of the avant-garde), part of a struggle that is deemed outmoded. The postpartisan creed is that the avant-garde, like the left, has won its battles and now it's time to return to kinder, gentler forms; poetry with a human face. It's the end of ideology all over again. On these Cold War terms, the only way not to be divisive is to accept the dominant poetic values as inevitable and natural, as craft rather than ideology, sincerity rather than artifice.

The kookiness of much "anticommunist antimodernism" can make it seem blithely dismissible, as if Filreis is flogging a possibly never living horse. And I have to confess to a ghoulish delight, mixed with the smugness of ridicule, to cruising Filreis's extreme detail. And yet, I can't help feeling that the underlying literary values articulated by anticommunist antimodernism remain central to a still contemporary dogma of conformism, masked as compulsory humanism, that constrains the reception of new poetry while repressing the dialectics of literary history that Filreis charts. Looking back, what's perhaps most striking is that American poetic invention flourished despite—indeed was fueled by—its detractors. For the perverse result of such attacks in postwar American culture is that they encouraged the development of an alternative poetry infrastructure that persists to this day.

Filreis provides a vivid lineage for a literary culture that promotes anti-intellectualism in the pursuit of monovalent "core values" (traditional form, the authentic subjective voice, legibility, the common reader) that are still claimed as fundamental literary virtues. The ideology of the fifties anticommunist antimodernists is now embedded in the mainstream; it has come to shape common assumptions of popular taste about poetry.

While it may be tempting to mock the antimodernist claims documented in *Counter-Revolution of the Word*, Filreis's sober approach acknowledges the social cost for many poets. Ludicrous attacks on formal innovation become ominous when they cost someone a job or erase significant poets from cultural memory. But beyond the individual price paid by poets, there is also a high social cost for demonizing aesthetic invention and poetic difference. We pay that price with the diminished intellectual fare served up daily by the mediocracy and with the stunted conception of literature promoted in too many school classrooms.

Those who do not want to repeat poetic history in the form of farce are condemned to study it. *Counter-Revolution of the Word* does just that.

OUR AMERICAS: NEW WORLDS STILL IN PROGRESS

The conceited villager believes the entire world to be his village.
JOSÉ MARTÍ, "OUR AMERICA"

Sou um tupí tangendo um alaúde!
(I am a Tupí strumming a lute!)
MÁRIO DE ANDRADE, "O TROVADOR" (THE TROUBADOUR)

Tupy, or not tupy that is the question.
OSWALD DE ANDRADE, "ANTHROPOPHAGITE MANIFESTO"

1.

One day I want to write an essay called *The Americas Still in Process*. In this essay, I would explore the still-imaginary cultural space of a "poetics of the Americas" in terms of José Martí's "Our America" and Emerson's "moral perfectionism." My discussion of moral perfectionism, indebted to Stanley Cavell, would no doubt lead to a declaration of interdependence: that the poetics of the Americas cannot be complete, for if we ever arrive at its end, we will have destroyed its promise to be ongoing, regenerating, and self-cannibalizing.

In this essay, I would proclaim, like a Dada Edgar Poe dreaming of Nicolàs Guillén doing Google searches, that the poem of the Americas does not exist. For the Americas is an imaginary cultural space whose mutant and multiform manifestations are as evanescent as the last breaths of a dying tongue.

& then I'd say that this is why the imperative for the poets of the Americas—contra conventional wisdom—has been to tell rather than show. For telling is the task, as Langston Hughes calls us, of a people "in transition."

First published in a Spanish translation by Ernesto Livon-Grosman in *S/N: New World Poetics* 1 (2010).

2.

In his 1972 anthology *Shaking the Pumpkin: Traditional Poetry of the Indian North Americans*, Jerome Rothenberg makes a modest proposal: let's study the indigenous epics of the Americas rather than those of Europe—the *Popol Vuh* in place of *The Odyssey*.[1] Rothenberg here echoes the sentiments of José Martí in "Our America," eighty years earlier:

> The history of America, from the Incas to the present, must be taught in its smallest detail, even if the Greek Archons go untaught. Our own Greece is preferable to the Greece that is not ours; we need it more.[2]

Rothenberg's two early anthologies, *Technicians of the Sacred* (1967) and *Shaking the Pumpkin* (1972) insisted on the immediate (rather than simply historical or anthropological) relevance of the "tribal" poetries of Native Americans (on both American continents), Africans, and peoples of Oceania. As such, they should be read as crucial poetic documents of the 1960s and '70s, works that accelerated a reconceptualization of American poetry as a poetics of the Americas. Rothenberg presented a concerted assault on the primacy of Western high culture and an active attempt to find, in other, non-Western/non-Oriental cultures, what seemed missing from our own.

3.

The singular, unitary idea of American literature is based on a set of often violent Anglonormative erasures: of pre-Conquest cultures, of the Middle Passage, of the languages of immigration, and of newly emerging tongues.

4.

In 1951, Charles Olson's visit to the Yucatan inspired a significant and influential move toward a Poetics of the Americas, the most important, among U.S. poets, in the years immediately following the Second World War. Olson's expansive rejection of the trap of what Robin Blaser, in an es-

1. *Pre-Faces & Other Writings* (New York: New Directions, 1981), 175.
2. "Our America," in *Selected Writings of José Martí*, translated by Esther Allen (New York: Penguin, 2002), 291.

say on Olson,[3] calls "The Western Box," both echoes Martí and anticipates Rothenberg:

> It is not the Greeks I blame. What it comes to is ourselves, that we do not find ways to hew to experience as it is, in our definition and expression of it, in other words, find ways to stay in the human universe, and not be led to partition reality at any point, in any way. For this is just what we do, this is the real issue of what has been, and the process, as it now asserts itself, can be exposed. It is the function, *comparison*, or its bigger name, *symbology*. These are the false faces, too much seen, which hide and keep from use the active intellectual states, metaphor and performance.[4]

Olson went on to articulate a poetics of place that rejects the metaphysical in favor of the historical and particular. Coming into direct contact with our Americas, he realized that the way in is not by analogy but through a process of active juxtaposition that produces a third term.

Our Americas is a performance.

5.

I want to insist on the word *Americas*, not just to encompass North and South America, but also as a way to register the multiplicity of our senses of America, as a way of registering this multiplicity, not comparison, as foundational for the poetics of our Americas.

In *Ül: Four Mapuche Poets*, Cecilia Vicuña quotes Jorge Teillier: "My weapon against the world is another vision of the world."[5] What poetry lacks in efficacy it makes up for in conceptual power—Blake's "Mental Fight," or, as Martí puts it in "Our America," "weapons of the mind, which conquer all others. Barricades of ideas are worth more than barricades of stones."

No issue has dogged poetry so much in the past two decades as identity—national, social, ethnic, racial, and local. Like the Americas, identity

3. "The Violets: Charles Olson and Alfred North Whitehead," in *The Fire: Collected Essays of Robin Blaser*, edited by Miriam Nichols (Berkeley: University of California Press, 2006); a digital version is available at PEPC Library, http://writing.upenn.edu/library/Blaser-Robin_The-Violets.html, accessed May 15, 2010.

4. "Human Universe," in *Collected Prose of Charles Olson*, edited by Benjamin Friedlander (Berkeley: University of California Press, 1997), 157.

5. *Ül: Four Mapuche Poets*, edited by Cecilia Vicuña, translated by John Bierhorst (Pittsburgh: Poetry in Indigenous Languages Series, Latin American Literary Review Press, 1998), 21.

is always plural. And like the Americas, identity is necessarily, *a priori*, syncretic and braided, indeed, self-cannibalizing, as surely as the DNA that flows in our psyches and concatenates our mental projections.

In developing our thinking of a poetics of the Americas and also, far more importantly, in our activities in creating a poetics of Americas, we would do well to keep in mind Teillier's remark that we are creating another vision of the world, one that in its globalism does not follow the dictates of the World Trade Organization and World Bank and in its localism does not become the site of the creation of strange fruits for export, but rather commits itself to a cannibalizing process of self-creation, as first defense against the "Western Box." A possibility never better set out than in Oswald de Andrade's 1928 Anthropophagite—cannibalism—Manifesto:

> Only anthropophagy unites us . . .
>
> Against all importers of canned consciousness. The palpable existence of life. And the study of prelogical mentality left to Mr. Levy-Bruhl . . .
>
> Against the truth of the missionary nations, defined by the wisdom of an anthropophagous, the Viscount of Cairu:—It is a lie repeated over and over . . .
>
> But there came no crusaders. There came fugitives from a civilization we are eating up, because we are as strong and as vengeful as the Tortoise.[6]

6.

Martí again: "The trees must form ranks to block the seven-league giant!" (289).

An ever intriguing model for our global/local/loco poetics is the Scots poet Hugh MacDiarmid, not the name he was born with but the name he aspired to, who was thrown out of the Scots nationalist party, despite his poetic work in synthetic Scots dialect, for being too international; and thrown out of the Communist Party for being too localist.

In the collection of Mapuche poets, Elicura Chihuailaf writes that "poetry does not merely safeguard the cultural identity of a people, it generates it." In this way, Chihuailaf emphasizes the productive forces of poetry in contrast to the reproductive reflexes of cultural theory. A poetics of the

---

6. "Anthropophagic Manifesto," translated by Maria do Carmo Zanini, in *Sibila*, http://sibila .com.br/index.php/sibila-english/395-anthropophagic-manifesto, accessed May 17, 2010.

Americas would be less concerned with analyzing the themes and cultural narratives produced in Spanish and English fiction than in listening for— and composing—a collage of distinct language practices across the Americas. In replacing theme and system—"comparison" and "symbology" in Olson's terms—with overlays, palimpsests, and collage, I am suggesting that we conceptualize our Americas as a hypertextual or syncretic constellation, with alphabetic, glyphic, and a/oral layers. A constellation is an alternative model for understanding what is often characterized as fragmentation, parataxis, isolation, insularity, atomization, and separate development. Hypertextuality maps a syncretic space that articulates points of contact and that potentiates both spatial connections among discrepant parts and temporal overlays that merge or melt into one another.

The Mapuche volume's palimpsestic approach emerges directly from the material conditions of the poetics of the Americas: not multiculturalism, but what Chihuailaf usefully calls (in John Bierhorst's English translation of the original Spanish text of this Mapudungun-speaking poet): *interculturalism*. Indeed, this book is in three languages: English, Spanish, and Mapudungun (the language of the Mapuche). Mapudungun is the most recent of the three language to be alphabetized, that is, to be transliterated into writing. At first I was confused as to why no translator was listed for the Spanish, but then I realized it was taken for granted that the poets represented in Mapudungun had made their own translations, or more likely worked bilingually, perhaps moving back from the Spanish into Mapudungun as much as going from a fully original Mapudungun and translating into Spanish, as if it were a foreign language. Perhaps what makes this *indigenous* for our Americas is not the single strand of the Mapudungun but the braided layers of the aboriginal, the colonial, the immigrant: specifically the joining of any two against a third, which is perceived to be the greater threat.

Martí speaks of us as laboring with "English trousers, Parisian waistcoat, a North America overcoat, and Spanish bullfighter's cap [as the] Indian circles about us, mute," and goes on to emphasize the necessity of rejecting racism by acknowledging not only those here before the Europeans but also those who were violently wrenched from Africa for a rough landing in a New World, those who sojourn alone and unrecognized among the rivers and wild animals (293). Martí is at pains not to erase the personhood of those brought to the Americas as slaves. But he also registers that the new worlds of our Americas require an *ecopoetics*, as Jonathan Skinner proposes in his magazine of that name.

In the imaginary space of our Americas, none has sovereignty, either of suffering or land, for sovereignty is reserved for the ghosts and the wind, which are forever lost both to and in time.

7.

The poetics of the Americas has for hundreds of years been creating syncretic indigenous languages distinct from the received dictions of the languages of conquest or emigration: indigenous in the sense of born in a region, originating in a place. The place of here, the time of now: necessarily a crossroads.

That's why I would stress, in looking for the threads that interconnect the poetries of the Americas, innovation and over refinement, as a way to register how important ingenuity has been for our Americas. That is, the points of contact that we may find in our mutual inhabitations of the Americas may not be in how we have extended and refined a poetic language we have inherited, for example from Europe, from London's English or Madrid's Spanish, or Lisbon's Portuguese, but rather how these poetries have worked to disrupt the ascent of a literature of refinement and assimilation.

I hope this may suggest a response to a criticism, often heard, to proposals for expanding the study of American literature to the literature of the Americas. If American, in the sense of U.S., literature is understood as an extension or development of earlier, primarily British literature, then we need, necessarily, to look first to the earlier literature of England to understand our own. This is a primary rationale behind the structure of the English department, where the teaching of U.S. literature was itself a hard-won battle in the earlier part of the last century. I say U.S., not North American, literature because U.S. English departments have paid scant attention to either Canadian or Mexican literature, which are seen, at best, as collateral to, rather than foundational for, the development of U.S. literature.

In a recent essay, Frank Davey points out how few points of contact there have been between U.S. and Canadian poets and that these have come almost entirely after 1950. When they have occurred, these confluences have allowed poets on both sides of the border to put forward a set of shared aesthetic and political engagements against more conservative, if not nativist, poetic positions in their own countries. At the same time, the official narratives of the national poetries of each country have largely been traced as separate and disconnected:

Always latent in Canadian culture are the facts that Canada's roots began in dissent from the U.S., and that Canada has been repeatedly re-affirmed by U.S. citizens themselves as the alternate North American nation. . . . Canada's first wave of English-speaking immigrants were United Empire Loyalist refugees from the American Revolutionary War. Canada's formation as a nation in 1867 was in part a response to the large U.S. armies created by the Civil War. Just as Canadian governments have been restricted by this complex cultural history in the extent to which they have been able to affiliate themselves with U.S. policies, Canadian poets have necessarily been both unconsciously and consciously selective in their associations with U.S. poetries and poetics. In general, Canadian poets have avoided association with hegemonic U.S. poetries or poetries that have celebrated the U.S. nation.[7]

As Roland Greene argues, the need to reform the disciplinary boundaries of literary study and move toward what he calls "New World Studies" is urgent. See especially his essay "New World Studies and the Limits of National Literatures" (from which I have taken the epigraph from Andrade's "O trovador"). Greene writes:

For new world studies the contact zone is not only the literal places of cultural encounter, but the concatenated spaces where worlds—that is, intellectual or spiritual systems represented by versions through which they can be understood or evaluated—move into critical relation with each other; the coming into play of the term and the concept of "world" is vital to the enterprise.[8]

8.

A syncretic poetics of ingenuity and invention, of collage and palimpsest, is averse to the accumulative and developmental model of literature still reigning in the U.S. literary academy (and elsewhere in the Americas). If we think of literature as developing through cross-fertilization and cannibalization, toward the invention of a synthetic indigenous, of new worlds, then

7. Frank Davey, "Canadian Poetry and Its Relationship to U.S. Poetry," in *The Greenwood Encyclopaedia of American Poets and Poetry*, edited by Jeffrey Gray (Westport, CT: Greenwood Press, 2006), 229.

8. Roland Greene, "New World Studies and the Limits of National Literatures," in *Stanford Humanities Review* 6:1 (1998), http://www.stanford.edu/group/SHR/6-1/html/greene.html, accessed May 17, 2010.

we may find it necessary to consider parallel poetries rather than causal poetries: coincidence will become more significant to us than lineage, points of contact more resonant than common origin. *Or anyway: as significant.* This is why Ernesto Livon-Grosman's notation of the synchronicity of New York's $L=A=N=G=U=A=G=E$ (1978–1981) and Buenos Aires's *Xul* (1980–1997) is so appealing: it makes no claim to influence, to cause and effect; these are simultaneous developments, yet structurally and poetically related, even twined.[9]

The poetics of the Americas that I am imagining is not about comparisons: it is about encounter, and change through the encounter; for if you are the same after such a meeting, then there was no encounter.

9.

The project of America—of the Americas—is a process not yet complete, a process that shall never be finished.

For when it's finished, it's over.

Our Americas is still in progress: as a talk, an experiment, an essay. Then again perhaps our Americas is a formal procedure, a hypothesis or conditional, requiring aesthetic intervention, seat-of-the-pants ingenuity, and otherworldly reinvention. And this is why, it could just be, that we see the possibilities of our Americas most acutely in poetry: our poetics viewed under the sign of our exchange.

9. See Livon-Grosman's "The Questioning of the Americas," in *99 Poets/1999: An International Poetics Symposium*, which I edited for *boundary 2* in 1999, and which is the starting point for my reflections here.

THE PRACTICE OF POETICS

1.

While poetics brings to mind a long history of laws of composition, poetics can also stress poiesis—the actual making or doing: poetry as process. Every doing carries the potential of something new, emergent, something not already predicated by poetics. Practice overtakes theory, practice changes theory. And not just writing practice but also performance.

2.

To practice poetics is to acknowledge the inevitability of metaphor, the linguisticality of perception, the boundedness of thought, the passion of ideas, the beauty of error, the chains of logic, the possibilities of intuition, and the uncanny delight of chance. In contrast to the syllogistic rationality of expository writing, poetics is situational, shifts with the winds, courts contradiction, feeds on inconsistency.

3.

The profession is best that professionalizes least.

The sociologist C. Wright Mills got this just right when he wrote, "The aim of the college, for the individual student, is to eliminate the need in his life for the college; the task is to help him become a self-educating man. For only that will set him free."[1]

Introduction to Scholarship in Modern Languages and Literature, edited by David Nicholls (New York: Modern Language Association, 2007).
1. "Mass Society and Liberal Education," in *Power, Politics and People* (New York: Oxford University Press, 1963), 367–68. Thanks to Joel Kuszai for bringing this quotation to my attention. See also William Carlos Williams's *The Embodiment of Knowledge* (New York: New Directions, 1974).

4.

In a culture that too often derides learning, complexity, and nuance, and where the demand for intelligibility is consistently used as a weapon to suppress unwelcome or difficult ideas: there is no higher aspiration than scholarship. But students caught up in the "major," just as faculty caught up in the "profession," often act as if scholarship requires adherence to a set of norms, either in subject matter or style, that define the field. Consistency of tone, standardization of documentation formats, and shopworn modes of analysis are more likely to anesthetize a required paper than allow entry for the aesthetic. Rewriting may be admirable, but not if it means stating a rote idea more clearly: rewriting should add reflection to a paragraph, not strip it of its unresolved thoughts. Felt inconsistency is preferable to mandated rationalization.

To state the obvious: an unorganized (or "differently" organized) essay that suggests active thinking is often more useful in response to a literary work than a paper of impeccable logic that has little to say. I realize that I am setting up a false dichotomy: It is not a question of choosing logic versus thinking but rather of understanding the value, and implications, of each. And yet, for the young scholar, the demands of expository normalcy may compete with the demands of poetics.[2] Shall we demand all students be extravagant? No doubt, this would be rash. But shall we continue to demand that all students curb their writing, as if composition were a dog and not a god?

I prize the adventure of learning: scholarship not as a predetermined ride to selected port of calls but as an exploration by association, one perception leading to the next, a network of stoppages, detours, reconnaissance. Not double majors with extra requirements and ever more protocols, but multicentered *minors*, connected by peripheral routes, less-traveled passages, hunches.

Art students used to be told that the fundamental requirement for drawing or painting was to accurately render figures. But this confused one modality of representation with the entire process of visual aesthesis. It might have been better to say *you can't draw if you can't see*, but it would be even better to say *you can't draw if you can't perceive*. Correlatively, we might say, you can't write if you can't think. Scholarship requires poetics.

2. Emerson's essays, and in particular "The American Scholar," his address to the Phi Beta Kappa Society, at Cambridge, on August 31, 1837; and "The Poet," remain foundational for American poetics. See especially Stanley Cavell's extensive writing on Emerson. And behind Emerson, think, for the purposes of this brief for poetics, of Montaigne and Pascal.

Paratactic writing, thinking by association, is no less cogent or persuasive than hypotactic exposition, with its demands that one thought be subordinated to the next. Poetics reminds us that the alternate logics of poetry are not suited just for emotion or irrational expression; poetics lies at the foundation of all writing.

Poetry is a name we use to discount what we fear to acknowledge.

The accurate documentation of information used in a work is a vital principle of scholarship. Similarly, scholarship requires writers to consider challenges to their views: but this too often is assumed to mean considering challenges to the content of what is being said while ignoring challenges to the style and form. The importance of poetics for scholarship is not to decree that anything goes, but rather to insist that exposition is an insufficient guarantor of reason. Poetics makes scholarly writing harder, not easier: it complicates scholarship with an insistence that the way we write is never neutral, never self-evident.

Clarity in writing is a rhetorical effect, not a natural fact. One man's eloquence can be another's poison; one woman's stuttering may be the closest approximation of truth that we will ever know.

5.

As a literary genre, *poetics* refers to works on the philosophy of composition, from Aristotle's *Poetics* to many contemporary works on the poetics of one thing or another, from scholarship to architecture. Poetics also is the term used for works about poetry written by poets. There is a long and storied history of both kinds of poetics, but this is to be an account not of the history of a literary form but rather of the significance of poetics for literary scholarship. With that in mind, it is important to note a distinction among literary theory, philosophy, and poetics. Literary theory can be described as the application of philosophical, political, or psychoanalytical principles or methods to the study of literary or cultural works. Theory suggests a predilection for consistency and explanation and, like philosophy, may take the form of stand-alone arguments. Poetics, in contrast, is provisional, context-dependent, and often contentious. Theory will commonly take a scientific tone; poetics will sometimes go out of its way to seem implausible, to exaggerate, or even to be self-deprecating.[3] (Since this is a work of poetics, I

3. There are, of course, many theories about theory. Two of the best overviews of this topic, both of which suggest useful parallels between theory and the argument for poetics made

won't note that poetics can also take a form directly opposite to what I am proposing; like *politics*, *poetics* is plural.)

In some ways, literary theory, in its many forms, has displaced poetics as a model for scholarship. Anthologies of literary theory, while often including statements by poets from earlier centuries, largely turn their attention to literary theorists and related philosophers when they come to the twentieth century.[4] Perhaps this seems a more sensible choice as a model for both scholarship and literary criticism. Poetics, in this system, becomes another form of poetry—something to be subjected to criticism and analysis but not the model for the practice of criticism, scholarship, or interpretation that it, nonetheless, continues to be.

6.

One of the two most important lessons of poetics is that the contemporary practice of poetry informs all readings of poetry. Poetry begins in the present moment and moves backward and forward from there. With no orientation in contemporary poetry and poetics, young scholars will remain ungrounded, without a direct connection to how works of literature are engendered in their own time. Without this knowledge, it will be all the harder to understand the relation of older works to their own times or to ours, or, for that matter, future works to the times yet to come. The absence of this visceral connection to poetic practice may be disguised by the demeanor of disinterested or clinical professionalism, but it will be betrayed in the body of the text of any scholarship produced.

The second fundamental lesson of poetics is that literary works do not exist only, or even primarily, on the page. Alphabetic writing in books remains the dominant medium for poetry in our time, as it has been over the past many hundreds of years; but there was poetry and poetics before the invention of the alphabet, just as new poetries and new poetics will emerge from our postalphabetic environment of digital and electronic language

---

here, are Jean-Michel Rabaté, *The Future of Theory* (Oxford: Blackwell, 2002); and Herman Rappaport's *The Theory Mess* (New York: Columbia University Press, 2001).

4. For example, *Critical Theory Since Plato*, edited by Hazard Adams, rev. ed. (Fort Worth: Harcourt Brace Jovanovich, 1992). Works of poetics (by poets) dominate the book up until the twentieth century, when the contribution by poets almost entirely disappears; nonetheless, this anthology remains a useful collection of poetics and indeed of the twentieth century "critical theory" that has been closely connected with the work of the most socially engaged and innovative poetics of the same period.

reproduction. Indeed, the *now*, as well as the archive of poetry, is as likely to be found on the web as in books. Modern reproduction technologies have also made available recordings of poets reading their work. These recordings, together with live performances, are a crucial part of any critical or scholarly approach to poetry over the past hundred years.[5]

New poetry is being created and performed every day. All scholarship in poetry occurs against this backdrop. Poetry readings and poetry on the web are directly relevant to literary scholarship of any type and of all periods. In this sense, poetry and poetics, as I am imagining them here, are a core value of the literary academy. It is exhilarating to see new poetics emerging in literary magazines and small press books, in local reading series and electronic discussion lists and websites and blogs. The ongoing creation of new poetics offers us a glimpse into how literature is made in response to ever-changing conditions. And it offers us a chance not just to observe the unfolding story but to change it.

7.

Read globally, write locally.

Narrowing down a "field" to one period, genre, or method inhibits one of the most important possibilities for scholarship: making connections across these divides. Lots of knowledge about a specific area of interest is admirable and sometimes invaluable; knowledge about lots of different areas is invaluable and sometimes admirable. It is not a question of being eclectic, but of developing your senses of association.

8.

What is the aim of literary scholarship? What is the purpose of a literature class? For some, it may be the accumulation of verifiable information that can be extracted from the literary work—social, political, historical, linguistic, or psychoanalytic. I have no wish to undermine such approaches to scholarship and teaching. Rather, I want to suggest an equally significant, but distinct, motivation for literary scholarship and teaching, a motivation for which thematic approaches to interpretation may prove detrimental. This "other"

---

5. *Close Listening: Poetry and the Performed Word* (New York: Oxford University Press, 1998), which I edited, provides a set of essays on the significance of the poetry reading for poetry and poetics.

approach to reading centers on the aesthetic experience of the literary work; thus, it presents an epistemological dilemma for thematic criticism. For if a literary work is not experienced aesthetically, the reader will not experience what makes it a work of art; this, in turn, will compromise any thematic reading. Poetics is a prerequisite for literary study.

9.

Everybody talks about the crisis in the humanities but nobody takes responsibility for it.

It is often lamented that humanists make a poor case for their values in the face of the powerful claims by those who advocate, on the one hand, invariant, often religiously derived, principles and those who advocate, on the other, technorationality—the idea that knowledge must be observer-independent and reproducible. I want to propose poetics as the foundation for a realm of values that is neither scientistic nor moralistic.

Poetics is an ethical engagement with the shifting conditions of everyday life. If it is poetic license to contrast ethics, as a dialogic practice of response in civil society, with morality, as a fixed code of conduct and belief, then poetic license I will happily claim.

Ethics is ironic, morality sincere. Ethics secular, morality religious. Poetics is the ethical refusal of morality in the name of aesthetics.

Poetics is an activity, an informed response to emerging circumstances. As such, it cannot claim the high ground of morality or systematic theory. Poetics is tactical, not strategic. Indeed, it is the lack of strategy, the aversion to the high ground, that often causes poetics to appear weak or confused or inconsistent or relativistic.

Yet, in the struggle between ethics and morality, ethics has the advantage even when it appears to be wandering in the wilderness. This advantage is too rarely taken advantage of. What is needed is a *poetics of poetics*; that is, a defense of the ethical grounding of poetics. A poetics of poetics would allow for a greater self-awareness of the history and value of poetics. In that sense, my approach is closely related to what George Lakoff argues in *Moral Politics*: that we must be as strong in our advocacy of our values, what he calls the values of nurturing parents, as the moralists are for their values, what he calls the values of the strict father.[6]

6. *Moral Politics: How Liberals and Conservatives Think* (Chicago: University of Chicago Press, 2002).

A poetics of poetics refutes the charge of relativism, just as a philosophy of aesthetic judgment refutes the idea that tastes are merely personal.[7] Indeed, a poetics of poetics makes the case that value judgments are better when they take into account multiple, and often competing, factors and refuse the simple solution of pre-existing rule.

10.

I want a visceral poetics that articulates the value of the particular over and against the rule of the universal; that refuses to sacrifice the local in the name of the national or corporate; that is dialectical rather than monologic, situational rather than objective; and that prizes knowing and truthfulness more than knowledge and truth.

I want a social poetics that is embodied rather than neutral, that actively acknowledges context dependence as a counter to the appearance of objectivity. Social poetics, like what Kenneth Burke calls "sociological criticism," begins with a conception of the poem as an action to be read in relation to its social motivation, not its intention.[8] The motive or design is the underlying reason for a work to come into being in the world, its orientation or trajectory; in contrast, intention is the calculated effect of style and technique. Social poetics acknowledges the agency of a work of art, not simply its historicity, where agency is recognized in the work's response to particular conditions.

11.

How can such aesthetic or poetic readings be accomplished? So much literary training directs us toward the themes and content of a work as if they were the meaning, that we have almost come to believe, against ourselves, that all the rest is window dressing. Perhaps we've lost the hang of listening; perhaps we just don't hang in long enough. Perhaps we've lost the hankering.

7. See Ludwig Wittgenstein, *Lectures & Conversations on Aesthetics, Psychology, and Religious Belief* (Berkeley: University of California Press, 1972). For a full account of the relation of Wittgenstein to poetics, see Marjorie Perloff's *Wittgenstein's Ladder: Poetic Language and the Strangeness of the Ordinary* (Chicago: University of Chicago Press, 1999).

8. See Kenneth Burke's "Literature as Equipment for Living," in *The Philosophy of Literary Form* (Berkeley: University of California Press, 1973). See also Burke's *A Rhetoric of Motives* (New York: Prentice-Hall, 1950).

But maybe it is just a matter of practice.

The aim of a course in poetics is not the memorization of facts but the engagement with works—and not so much with the themes of work as with their material emanations as sound and form. Tests in such an environment are counterproductive. And the emphasis on undergraduate essays that mimic the style of professional academic conference papers is replaced by interactive "wreadings" that echo, distort, translate, reform, and imitate the poems that are under active consideration. What is called for is not so much analysis as responsiveness, for it is only after the work has gotten under the skin that there is a basis for an analysis.

The Art of Immemorability

But knowing not love nor change nor wrath nor wrong,
No more we knew of song.
ALGERNON CHARLES SWINBURNE, "ON THE CLIFFS"

. . . to communicate you must speak clear . . . first of all . . .
though I soon learned that immediacy and force take priority . . .
LARRY EIGNER

EVERY WHICH WAY BUT LOOSE

I am writing this sentence in Word for Windows 95: the 12-point Times New Roman letters are white dropout against a blue background, and when I first typed "blackground" a wavy red line automatically appeared under it until I corrected it with a word found in the Microsoft vocabulary list that comes with the program.

In the book, the one I imagine you to be holding in your hands, the text is printed in black ink on white-like sheets, and the light needed to read the letters is coming from above or to the side of the book and is reflected off the opaque surface of the paper.

But is it even the "same" text?

If I chose to put this piece up on the web (but not without the editors' permission in writing, for which a signed fax would be OK but e-mail would not), the light would come from the back of the document, toward you as you read the text on (or is it off?) the screen. For an HTML version, I would need to make a number of additional decisions. First I would need to choose a background color or image, something few writers have had much choice about in the past five hundred years. If I pick an image—say a blowup of the holograph text of Blake's *Jerusalem*—I risk making my text illegible, or, to put it a different way, risk making my text into an image as I efface the contrast between figure (that is, the text) and ground (that is, the underlying image). As much as I want to tease at the idea of the text melting into an image, I also want each of my words to be identifiable, so I take the image into Photoshop and tone it down, ensuring that the letters I superimpose on it will be readable. Although I am interested in the merging of text and

Reimagining Textuality: Textual Studies in the Late Age of Print, edited by Elizabeth Bergmann Loizeaux and Neil Fraisat (Madison: University of Wisconsin Press, 2002). This essay was adapted from my response to several essays in the collection. I used the final section of the original essay on Arakawa and Madeline Gins (not included here) for a preface to *With Strings* (Chicago: University of Chicago Press, 2001).

image in HTML, the mark-up language itself allows for clear differentiation between the two, treating the text as a layer separable from the background. Even if a text is illegible in the browser view, I can copy it and paste it into another field with a neutral background and read it, now without interference (or was it enhancement?). If I want to fuse the text and image I need to make a single graphic file of the layers, "flatten" them is the term of art, but then the text loses many of its unique user-friendly digital features: the reader/viewer can't change the font or size or color, can't copy it and paste it into another document—can't, that is, treat the text as we have come to expect texts to be treatable in an electronic environment. Ironically, converting (or is it translating?) a text into an image file re-creates just the immutability (materiality?) of text that we assumed before the advent of electronic textuality.

The new computer technology—both desktop publishing and electronic publishing—has radically altered the material, specifically visual, presentation of text. It begins to seem as natural to think of composing screen by screen or link by link as page by page. Many text-based works now exist primarily for the screen rather than as transcriptions from another medium. The printed versions of such works might be considered the reproduction and not the other way around, though reciprocity is a better way than hierarchy to understand the relation among textual media.

For the generation now learning to read and write on computers, the medium of writing has radically and inalterably changed in ways that can be called hyperalphabetic if not postalphabetic. The association of picture, font, color, sound, link, and design creates a writing space that is closer to William Blake's or Arakawa and Madeline Gins's or Johanna Drucker's practice than it is to the school notebooks I grew up with. Their primary pictorial feature was the tiny holes I created in the paper from rubbing the eraser too hard in one spot (or maybe from just making the same correction over and over and never getting it right). The ineradicable stubbornness of writing is one of the most powerful qualities of nonelectronic writing media, and it is therefore understandable that with the partial eclipse of these media we have come to appreciate this feature of writing more and more.

In her essay in *Reimagining Textuality*, Drucker explores the implications of the premise that electronic textuality may be a technical realization of what had previously been an idealization of the literary work (for example, in G. Thomas Tanselle's textual theory, as discussed in *Reimagining Textuality* by Morris Eaves) or geometry (for example, in Husserl's philosophy, as discussed by Drucker), because digitalized text appears to exist in a form that is separate from and prior to any given embodiment. Insofar as binary coding produces virtual texts, alphabetic sequences exist in an immaterial form for which any visible manifestation displayed on screen or printed "out" on paper is a second-order phenomenon. After thinking through these textual conditions, Drucker rejects the dematerialization of electronic textuality, pointing to the materiality not only of format and configuration but also of the emplacement of the digital code. The coding is not the antecedent original but an anoriginal source from which multiple versions emerge (to pursue a concept I develop in *Close Listening: Poetry and the Performed Word*).[1]

Drucker's speculations make for some suggestive parallels between analphabetic and postalphabetic language environments. Like oral performance, virtual textuality creates an original material work in each presentation. The computer screen provides a stage for the transformation of texts into works. Writers become language environment designers—textual architects—who need to foresee how the texts they write will be brought to life in particularized enactments. This entails anticipating the inevitable variances made by the different systems on which the work will be displayed. It also allows for creating variants in the configuration of the work; for example, randomizing the sequence of a hypertext so that each time it is viewed it is read in a different order. Moreover, readers can participate in the constitution of the work (and not only in its interpretation) by taking advantage of options for determining the graphic and acoustic environment in which they experience a work and for altering the text of works whose configuration allows for, or indeed mandates, variance.

Electronic textuality is expanding the pool of linguistic signs while at the same time "flattening" the alphabetic into an intensely and undeniably visual medium. In the West, alphabets replaced more icon-heavy writing systems because of their technical efficiency: Alphabets utilizing twenty-six or a few more characters replaced writing systems that required memorizing dozens of characters. With electronic textuality, however, icons can once again proliferate because there is almost no limit on the capacity of the computer to unzip (decode, translate) these icons to meet the needs of particular readers (one example of this is the context-sensitive help provided by a mouse-over on an unfamiliar pictogram on your screen). James Sherry recently pointed out to me that in the world of financial computing words

1. Charles Bernstein, ed., *Close Listening: Poetry and the Performed Word* (New York: Oxford University Press, 1998).

are beginning to be characterized as too slow, at least in comparison with the amount of information that can be transmitted with semiotically packed icons. Twenty-five hundred years ago, the verdict was in: the alphabet is swifter than the hieroglyph. In 1999, the reverse appears possibly to be the case. In *Briggflats*, Basil Bunting laments, "Pens are too light. / Take a chisel to write."[2] Is this something we are now in a position to understand? Or is it just another modernist shibboleth, as in—pens are not light enough? In any case, the more disembodied our language environment becomes, the more we may learn to value the materiality of writing. The aura of the prior stages of linguistic production and reproduction increases as each is displaced.

Art media emerge from culture and from the activities of the produc-ers of culture; they are not intrinsic projections of materials or technolo-gies. Pigment and canvas (or cave walls) do not necessitate the invention of painting as an art medium, any more than the alphabet prescribes the emergence of writing as a medium of art.

As a poet interested in the material and social dimension (you might also say social material) of writing, I find many of the most exciting ideas suggested by the new explorers of hypertext well worked out in the radically paratactic explorations of both modernist and contemporary work that have been aversive to the "humanist" ideology dominant within the university and also in the mass media. To be reductive about it: On the level of mass culture, humanist values emphasize mimesis of human presence and con-ventional modes of "realistic" representation as a means of maximizing the audience for cultural products by maximizing consumer passivity. On the level of high culture, humanist ideology works to maintain control of those free-floating value sectors not determined by market dominance. In this sense, the radical art of the modernist and contemporary periods is both anti-mass-consumer art—trying instead to create works that require the active participation and critical reflection of viewers and readers—and anti-high art, critiquing the ideological assumptions and cultural biases behind the valuation of the Great Books, the Core Curriculums, Cultural Literacy, and the like. For this reason, it is fascinating that John Unsworth, in his essay "Electronic Scholarship; or, Scholarly Publishing and the Public," de-votes so much of his space to a critique of Sven Birkerts as representative of the criticism of scholarly work in the electronic medium.[3] Unsworth under-

2. *Briggflats* (London: Fulcrum Press, 1966), 14.
3. "Electronic Scholarship; or, Scholarly Publishing and the Public," http://village.virginia .edu/~jmu2m/mla-94.html, accessed May 1, 2010; but by late August, the link did not work for

scores Birkerts's fear of the new computer technology as engendering "de-personalization, of inauthenticity, of substitution to the mechanical, and ... substitution of quantity for quality"—exactly the charges that Birkerts and others typically make against the sort of poetry and art to which I am alluding. Indeed, a version of Birkerts's critique that Unsworth cites was featured in the newsletter of the Associated Writing Programs, home of self-styled "anti-theoretical" imaginative writing so much at odds with those poetries that foreground their materiality and social construction. I bring this up as a way of noting that fears associated with computer media, including the often-stated concern about a loss of materiality, are often in the service of an intensively antimaterialist, which is to say idealist, assertion of cultural authority and legitimacy.

In his essay in *Reimagining Textuality*, Eaves shows that a continuing value of Blake's work is the anxiety it has caused over issues like this, issues we are just now, it sometimes seems, confronting for the first time. Swinburne's book on Blake was instrumental in gaining recognition of Blake's significance and, as a result, preserving his work. But Eaves has another story to tell, one that in many ways brings to mind Harold Bloom's thesis in *The Anxiety of Influence*.[4] For Blake's work is designed to be misread, but its singular value is manifest only when we come to recognize the misreading, albeit with yet another misreading. Eaves's discussion of Blake points to our culture's need to assimilate an artist's work into a well-established art medium: painter or poet, but not, as Blake insisted, painter and poet. Swinburne the poet claimed Blake for poetry, inducting him into an insurgent literary tradition at the apparent expense of adequately acknowledging the graphical body of his work. The burden of Swinburne's *Critical Essay*[5] was to associate Blake with Whitman and Baudelaire, and implicitly with Swinburne's own poetry—all aesthetically revolutionary projects marked by a refusal to be absorbed into the norms of the contemporary moral order. Blake's verbo-visual excess is Swinburne's exalted example of a visionary art unconstrained by the shackles of propriety (including the constraints of genre). Yet because Blake's project involves redundancy and contradiction, both within and between the layers of his work, much of the force of his aesthetic is evident even in monodimensional samplings. Nonetheless, the

---

the copyeditor, who provided a new URL: http://www3.isrl.illinois.edu/~unsworth//mla-94 .html.

4. *The Anxiety of Influence: A Theory of Poetry* (New York: Oxford University Press, 1973).

5. *William Blake: A Critical Essay* (1868; rpt. New York: Benjamin Bloom, 1986).

full complexity of his work can be experienced only cross-sectionally—not as a synthesis or flattening of levels but, on the contrary, in the clash of levels. Blake's work is not a singular whole, a totality, but a complex of incommensurable layers.

It has never been easier than now to find graphical reproductions of Blake's work, which can be downloaded from the web as JPEG files. These files allow for a viewing that in some ways exceeds what is possible with the originals because of the ability to enlarge small sections of a page in order to see more clearly the ravishing details that comprise these works. In the past, the cost and accuracy of color reproduction limited access to the pictorial dimension of Blake's work, at least in comparison with the ubiquitous text-only dubs. Yet even as these images become more available, they will not replace those textual dubs. For who among of us has not secretly read our paperback, graphics-expurgated, Blake with the glee of a schoolchild high on Cliff Notes, even after many professions of born-again faith in the only truth of his visualized hypermedia? Not to mention giving one too many lectures starting "You haven't read it at all if you've read it without the pictures"—the most recent, in my case, pressed on one of three Japanese tourists asking for directions to Niagara Falls, whom I stopped with just this message on a foggy night not long ago, only to be spurned—"Now get thee hence, though grey-beard Loon! / Or my Staff shall make thee skip."

The question of misleading editions of Blake (or Dickinson) turns us all into loons, whether we hold out for extralexical meaning or tenaciously insist that words are words. Or if not loons then cormorants, diving into the inky waters of our deep blue amnesias. As if we could be woken to words while asleep to language. If we imagine (begin to reimagine) that works of poetry always exist as versions, that there is no singular original but an array of realizations, then the relations between versions is not a moral one of right and wrong but an ethical one of reciprocity. Versions become translations in the sense that all works of poetry are translations, which is to say that writing itself is a form of translation and transformation, spinning and respinning, positioning and repositioning, transcribing and eliding. Editions may redress the wrongs of previous editions, but they also address the songs those editions set in time.

It's not that words exist prior to or independently from the world, but rather that we know the world through the words that initiate us into it. Just as we know words through the world in which we learned them. Poets actualize these potentialities: the worldness of words, the wordness of the world. This is why poetry is not a matter of "understanding": one does not wish to stand under, and in that sense outside, but to move into, within; or perhaps move back and forth: under, inside, on top.

Translation implies a conversion from one set of terms to another. This is a process that is continuous within one's own language and its many layers as well as between different languages. The process is less atomic than contextual: not a matter of identifying individual words or even individual meanings but a matter of attuning oneself to systems of meaning, clusters of signs, contexts of utterances: to scale and shape as much as format and configuration; to sounds and sights as much as lexicon.

In his *Critical Essay*, Swinburne writes, "All that was accepted for art, all that was taken for poetry, [Blake] rejected as barren symbols, and would fain have broken up as mendacious idols" (3). Much the same could be said of Arakawa and Gins, the focus of Mary Ann Caws's essay in *Reimagining Textuality*. Arakawa and Gins have resisted, with increasing scale, the ability of readers/viewers to absorb their work as painting or poetry—or indeed as art. While they may be described as architects of the "Reversible Destiny" projects, the point is not to make aesthetic objects to be appreciated but to construct "stations" that will transform perception. Caws details the temporal modeling of Arakawa and Gins's visual and architectural projects, showing how they are configured to warp and reform the space-time continuum. Language is embedded into these works not as something to be read, as on a page or even a screen, but as something to interact with in an unfolding/enfolding web. The constructed "landing sites" of Reversible Destiny challenge rote perceptual patterns and activate underutilized cognitive paths.

The idea that genres, if not the aesthetic itself, are a barrier to perceptual transformation connects the projects of Arakawa and Gins and Blake to a range of practitioners from Mallarmé and Williams to Duchamp and Cage, all of whose antifoundational investigations have a visual and verbal component. In retrospect, we might say that these artists do not so much abolish the aesthetic as extend and transform it, partly because the boundaries of the aesthetic—our willingness or ability to see something as a work of art—are surprisingly mobile. But if the aesthetic is not a static category, then it may be possible for the "same" object to be viewed, alternately, as aesthetic and not aesthetic. Indeed, aesthetic oscillation is potentially a rhythmic dynamic in a work; that is, a work may be configured in a way that pops out of the aesthetic and then is sucked back in, creating a "hyperaesthetic" environment, to extend an idea of Miško Šuvaković's.[6] Such a work would be as far from the heightened aestheticism of Mallarmé as from the postaesthetic of Conceptualism. In the case of Reversible Destiny, the goal is neither to aestheticize the nonaesthetic nor to deaestheticize the aesthetic, but rather to create a zone that is no longer subject to this oscillation. But this is no more possible than transcending the textual condition, which turns and spins us every which way . . . but loose.

6. *Pas Tout: Fragments on Art, Culture, Politics, Poetics and Art Theory, 1994–1974* (Buffalo: Meow Press, 1994).

THE ART OF IMMEMORABILITY

In the January 1999 issue of the almost unreadably hyperdesigned *Wired* magazine, a quote from the poet and Zen abbot Norman Fischer is splashed across three full-color pages: "The real technology—behind all of our other technologies—is language."[1] This useful motto, echoing as it does the sense of language as *tekhne* suggested by Jerome Rothenberg in his preface to *Technicians of the Sacred* thirty years ago, appears in a paperbound journal of the new electronic communications technologies, a strangely amphibian publication with one foot firmly planted in the print past and the other ready to kick the ball into a digital future. But what ball? What past? What future?

And anyway, who invented language? While that question may have to be left to anthropologists and theologians, the question of the invention of writing in the West is quite a different matter, with a long and well-documented prehistory of inscriptions on rock faces and cave walls, an opening act consisting of Sumerian cuneiform and Egyptian hieroglyphs (emerging about 5,000 years ago) and a second act of North Semitic, Phoenician, and Hebrew consonantal scripts (as early as 3,700 years ago) followed by the Greek alphabet (2,700 to 2,800 years ago).

The technological significance of each of these phases of writing cannot be overestimated. North Semitic, Phoenician, and Hebrew (proto)alphabetic scripts, consisting of twenty-two letters, all consonants, eliminated the need to memorize the hundreds of characters necessary to decipher earlier writing and created a means of representing the sound of spoken language that remains fundamental to Western conceptions of literature. The Greeks built upon and improved this already revolutionary system, creating a set

A Book of the Book: Some Works & Projections about the Book & Writing, edited by Jerome Rothenberg and Steve Clay (New York: Granary Books, 2000). Thanks to Tan Lin, Jerome Rothenberg, and Thomas McEvilley.
1. "The Wired Diaries," in *Wired* 7.01 (January 1999), http://www.wired.com/wired/archive/7.01/diaries.html?pg=15&topic=&topic_set=, 15, accessed July 4, 2010.

of twenty-four letters, of which seven were vowels. The Greek alphabet was easy to form, decipher, and pronounce. In *The Muse Learns to Write: Reflections on Orality and Literacy from Antiquity to the Present*, Eric Havelock tells the story of the evolution this alphabet, noting that the civil society of classical Greece controlled its own transition from primary orality to writing by using a system that they had invented and that was particularly suited to represent the sounds of spoken Greek.[2] The genius of the Greek alphabet was the invention of subsyllabic units that break sound down into "atomic elements" that can be combined to represent "any linguistic noise" (60). This was not quite *wysiwyg* (what you see is what you get), but close—what you see is what you hear; and the alphabet's simplification and supersession of previous systems of writing is not unlike the transformations from Fortran to DOS to Windows. Never before had writing been able to so efficiently represent the full sound sensorium of spoken language. The Greek alphabet was, in Havelock's words, the "first and last instrument to reproduce the range of previous orality" (60).

For those accustomed to rating computer technology in terms of storage memory and processing speed, the alphabetic revolutions can be measured in analogous terms: a remarkably accessible user interface and an enormous capacity to store retrievable information. In the West, Greek-style alphabets would dominate writing technology until the present; though no doubt there is a value in "thinking different," as the current Apple computer ads insist. The Hebrew alphabet showed a remarkable resiliency when revived midcentury as the official language of Israel. And the Chinese written character remains the longest-running show in the writing business. But just as current digital technology is eclipsing the alphabet, it is also forcing changes in Chinese writing as Asian language users converge on the Internet and try to find ways to adapt to the limitations of the alphabetic computer keypad.

While the Greek alphabet, and Greek verbal art, has had an enormous influence on the subsequent Western literature, it is not necessary to argue for the uniqueness of classical Greek literary culture or for the cultural supremacy of the Greek alphabet when considering the value of Havelock's claims. Havelock provides a richly suggestive case study of the effect of writing technology on poetry. In Havelock's view, the greatness of the verbal art in the period from Homer to Plato is significantly the result of the major technological shift that occurred during this time, when alphabetic writing

2. *The Muse Learns to Write* (New Haven: Yale University Press, 1986).

was emerging in an a/literate culture. Thus Homer, Hesiod, and Euripides are not the product of a fully literate culture; rather, they capture by alphabetic technology the existing and dominant oral culture. Yet to capture is also to misrepresent (all representation is also misrepresentation) and to misrepresent is, of course, also to change.

Havelock's perspective runs counter to transcendental humanist claims often made for classical Greek "literature," since he argues that the greatness of this work is partly the result of its *not* being the product of a fully literate culture and partly the result of technological innovation. While early Greek oral and performance art had an aesthetic and entertainment value, Havelock sees the primary function of such works as encyclopedic and memorial: to store for reuse the customs and manners of the culture. For a/literate verbal art to have this capacity, listeners must be able to memorize, remember, and echo. As a result, the language must be memorable. And, indeed, the works whose function is (at least in part) to store cultural memory are repeated over and over again, like children's stories, to allow memorization. The word games and songs of children preserve in our contemporary culture several of the features of such analphabetic verbal art.

Havelock argues that Greek alphabetic writing provided a new and better means for the storage and retrieval of cultural memory by providing a highly supple means to record the aural textures of performed language, thus preserving in writing the modes of information storage deployed by the oral culture of the Greeks. According to Havelock, and in this he echoes the findings of Albert Lord and Milman Parry, the oral (or pneumonic) forms of language storage employed by the Greeks relied on a range of mnemonic techniques that are preserved in a remarkably full-blown way by the Homeric epics. That is, the Homeric epics embody in writing analphabetic modes of language storage. The earliest Greek writing, marked by the emergence of a new alphabetic technology within a culture in which oral technology remained dominant for a few hundred years, takes from a/literate verbal performance the form of rhythmic verse, with much of the emerging "literature" written for the holdover medium of performance. Much of the new alphabetic writing, then, was an aid to memory, taking the form of scripts to be memorized for subsequent performance. As result, the prosody was, to some extent, carried over from analphabetic verbal art. In such scripted writing, the page is not the final destination but a preliminary stage, prompts for final presentation elsewhere.

Such holdover writing practices might be contrasted with more distinctively textual features of writing, ones that are less bound to transcription and scripting—less bound, that is, to "transcriptive" functions of writing. If you write something down, then you don't have to remember it and you don't have to write it in a way that will help you to memorize it. The writing takes on the work of memory rather than being an aid to memory, and this function is not compromised by writing that is difficult or impossible to memorize. On the one hand, it's the difference between the *Odyssey* and the *Encyclopaedia Britannica*; on the other, between a counting game and a poem by Jackson Mac Low.

The distinction I am suggesting here is not unlike one that Marshall McLuhan makes in *Understanding Media* between the received and the new content of the emerging medium. The initial content of television was the product of the previous moving-image medium, film (which, in turn, not only shaped the TV but also changed movies). In contrast, "live" TV (initially broadcasts of sporting events but epitomized by live news broadcasts) is the best example of a distinct genre particular to the medium of television.

If "live" TV suggests a formal essence for the new medium of television, we might look at non-oral, non-speech-based forms of writing in order to identify the distinctly textual, rather than holdover or transcriptive, features of writing.

Greek alphabetic writing, because of both its ingenuity in phonetic reproduction (transcription) and its use as scripts for subsequent performance, may obscure the emergence of specifically textual forms. The almost immediate use of the Greek alphabet for inscribing epitaphs (a quintessentially memorial function of writing and one of the earliest uses of any kind of writing) is an important exception, since, like epigrams, epitaphs are neither transcriptions of, nor scripts for, performed verbal art. Greek prose, in the sense of nonrhythmical, non-performance-scored writing, emerged later, with Plato and Herodotus.

In contrast to the phonic agility of Greek writing, earlier nonalphabetic writing systems had a more marked separation of speech and writing, since such writing systems were less insistent on (or less effective in) invoking a phonemic reality outside the written characters. In such nonalphabetic writing, there are numerous examples of codes, laws, accounts, and other catalogs and compendia that appear to dispense with the mnemonic formula of a/literate verbal art and begin to mine writing's textuality. These writing systems may have potentiated the textual and immemorial functions of writing more fully than alphabetic writing, which bears the trace of its phonetic transcription. The very effectiveness of the Greek alphabet's apparent ability to "capture" speech may have resulted in the appearance of speech "capturing" alphabetic writing. Except that, according to Havelock, the Homeric epics are not transcriptions of speech as such, but rather the translation into writing of the performed verbal art of the period. This suggests that the "transcriptive" process was twofold: notating the oral performance and creating scripts for subsequent performance.

The distinction between textual and transcriptive functions of writing is by no means clear-cut, since the definitions of each are recursive. On the one hand, my speculation about the greater textuality of nonalphabetic or early alphabetic writing is undermined by the possibility that what now appears as textual rather than scripted writing was performed or incanted, as is the case with biblical Hebrew texts. On the other hand, the alphabet provided novel, nonprosodic, means of textual organization, from alphabetization to the numerology of gematria. While not an opposition, a certain divergence can be noted: Writing as transcriptive retains the mnemonic features of a/literate verbal art either as reproduction or to facilitate memorization for subsequent performance. Textualized writing, in contrast, is not an intermediate stage to a performance elsewhere. The immemorial possibilities of textual writing put the memory in the text rather than using the text as an aid to memory.

Writing not only records language, it also changes language—and consciousness. Once some of the memory functions of language are shifted from oral to alphabetic technology, then language may be freed up from these tasks—or in the darker semiotic economy of Walter Ong or David Abram, it loses bodily touch with them. In other words, alphabetic writing makes its own particular marks on language, allowing for greater levels of abstraction and reflection, which has often resulted in diminishing the amount of action and "doing." For example, descriptions of acts of seeing give way to the idea of sight; or consider, as another example: "Toronto-Hatted McLuhan exhorts his minions" versus "Language reveals truth." Indeed, abstraction and reflection are two qualities that typify later classical Greek writing, but, contrary to much received wisdom, these qualities may be less truth-effects than media-effects. The rest, in other words, is history.

The means of language and cultural reproduction always become a means of production and variance, as what is "stored" is transformed by the means of its imagined storage—so that it is a matter of morphing more than storing.

Writing read in this way tells us more than what it purports to tell, since it embodies the story of its mode of telling alongside any tales it tells. However, it's not the tail wagging the dog, as much literary criticism has assumed, but a tale of the dog; though if the dog could talk, would we understand its bark or only its plight?

My speculative model here is not of one technology replacing another, nor am I suggesting that changes in the technology for language reproduction create social or cultural improvement. Alphabetic technology does not replace oral technology any more than cars replace walking. But it does shift the balance, and writing registers the change. After all, poetry precedes prose, but prose does not abolish poetry. Indeed, prose is as agonistic to poetry as it is complementary. Prose has killed poetry many times, but poetry doesn't seem to get the message. But maybe that's because poetry is the vampire medium, sucking the blood from other modes of writing and leaving them lifeless, while itself living on into an eternity at the cost of its mortality. This is why poetry often metamorphoses into prose—to regain its historical existence by casting aside its ghoulish triumph.

In any period, some poetry will discover that which can only be done as writing using new technical means, while other poetry will bring over into the present of writing the forms and motifs of previous technological and historical moments. Neither approach is invalid, just as neither is surefire, but evaluating one approach by the criteria derived from the other is misguided.

Havelock goes on to theorize that Greek lyric poetry is the product of the alphabet, which allows for the abstraction of the "I" and for the development of the individuated lyric self—a claim that modifies Bruno Snell's earlier Hellenophilic argument for the Greek invention of the lyric and the concomitant emergence of *polis* (the city-state).[3] No sooner does the Greek alphabet appear than the "I" of writing also appears. And with the lyric so the satiric—Sappho and Archilochos—and also (the Greek version of) the civic. While early Greek lyrics were composed to be sung with musical accompaniment, early satiric verse was not. Lyric and satiric were the formally innovative poetry that emerged with the new Greek alphabet and with a new civic society; epic persisted, transformed by the new medium and by the company, if not rivalry, of the new genres.

This is not to say that the self was invented by the alphabet, but rather that the Western literary genre of the lyric (and also the satiric) might have been. By making possible a semblance of the speaking voice of the poet, the

---

3. Bruno Snell, *The Discovery of the Mind: Greek Origins of European Thought*, translated by T. G. Rosenmeyer (Cambridge: Harvard University Press, 1953); see especially chap. 3, "The Rise of Individuality in the Early Greek Lyric" (1941).

alphabetic lyric took possession of (or was possessed by) the "other" of that vexed double sense of "lyric"—words to be sung and words spoken by an individual. In this way, the alphabet facilitated the creation of a more stable author identity—the signature, a prerequisite for the lyric as literary genre. The lyric utilized the signature-effect of writing in ways not accessible to (or perhaps even desirable for) analphabetic verbal art. Various forms of self-expression, and of signature, certainly existed in the West prior to the Greek alphabet, and there are a number of precursors to lyric poetry in earlier Western writing as well in Greek verbal art prior to the invention of the Greek alphabet. Gregory Nagy has argued that the metrical patterns and possibly the phraseology of Greek lyric poetry predate the metrics of the oral epics associated with the names Hesiod and Homer and have their origins in far more ancient Indic religious hymns and prayers, such those found in the Rigveda, the oldest parts of which go back 3,500 years (though the means for any such possible transmission remain obscure).[4] Such archaic meters may themselves be derived from earlier fixed phrases or "charms," providing a means for intact preservation over time. Moreover, the Hebrew "Song of Songs" (written about 400 years before Sappho) is often cited as protolyric verse. These examples notwithstanding, the Greek alphabet opened a set of particular possibilities for poetry, including a modulation in the effect of using the "I," which were immediately and brilliantly exploited by the secular early Greek poets in a way that had an indelible impact not only on the medium of poetry, as we know it in the West, but also on writing.

In his comparative study of Greek and Indic meter, Nagy notes that Alfred Lord defines "a truly 'oral' tradition as one in which every performance generates a new composition" (16). In contrast, writing has often been misunderstood as fixing texts. Transcriptive writing has its end not in a fixed and final text but rather in a series of alphabetic and performative versionings—a dynamic that carries over into textual writing as well. Contrary to the received wisdom of textual and bibliographic theory, based on a biblical model that seeks to recover the immutable scriptural original, textual "transmission" should be understood not only in terms of "corruption" but also as new alphabetic performances.

All early Greek writing bears the stamp of a/literate verbal art, and the metrics of both lyric and epic retain features of the mnemonic systems essential to that art. The question is what effect Greek alphabetic writing had

4. Gregory Nagy, *Comparative Studies in Greek and Indic Meter* (Cambridge: Harvard University Press, 1974).

on these archaic modes, both epic and lyric. To what degree did lyric and epic poetry take on distinctly new textual attributes after the introduction of the Greek alphabet into an a/literate culture with a long history of both epic and protolyric modes? The Greek alphabet did not create the lyric out of the blue; nor did a particular technology determine a particular literature. Nothing is ever entirely new. But the "same thing" takes on new meanings in new technological contexts. Writing technologies affect poetry in ways that are often hard to explicate but nonetheless become part of their meaning. In this particular circumstance, it might be more fruitful to focus not on intrinsic features of lyric verse but rather on the "reading effects" that the alphabet created for the lyric, including those that took place over long periods of time, such as the possibility that a lyric might be read and not sung. That is, the lyric takes on a different quality in the new medium. While the lyric initially may have been a script for performance or song, it led to a newly textualized form of poetry.

After the invention of the alphabet, the next most significant Western technological revolution in the reproduction of language occurred in 1451 with the invention of the printing press (the Chinese were printing books eight hundred years earlier). There were other important technological developments between the Greek alphabet and the printing press, including the invention of the Roman alphabet and other scripts, the fabrication of new and more efficient surfaces to write on, and the development of codices and manuscripts and books. But none of these was quite so far-reaching in its impact as Gutenberg's press.

The printing press occurs very late in the history of the book; nonetheless, it ushered in what well might be called the Age of the Book, a period of unprecedented circulation for writing. If the stage epitomizes the transcriptive or memorial functions of writing, the book epitomizes the immemorial storage function of writing. The book is writing's own stage, not a prompt to some other stage. Insofar as literary works appear in books they make possible a circulation distinct from presentation in theatrical performance. The book is the place where writing as writing comes into its own, has its own "place," finds its own forms.

Many of the effects we associate with literacy were not yet dominant in the medieval Europe of Gutenberg, which held fast to many characteristics of analphabetic culture. Writing remained an aid to memory, and oral forms were still part of its infrastructure. Indeed, medieval poetry, scripted to be performed—that is, heard not read—retained many of the rhythmical and rhyming qualities of oral poetry. Augustine of Hippo's 400 CE citing of silent reading is a crucial signpost along the road to changing the user interface with writing technology, since the emergence of silent reading is generally thought to begin only post-Gutenberg and with the advent of prose. As Wlad Godzich and Jeffrey Kittay note in *The Emergence of Prose*, prose in medieval France emerged from verse and gradually replaced a number of the functions of verse, simultaneous with the rise of a middle class.[5]

According to H. J. Chaytor, in *From Script to Print: An Introduction to Medieval Vernacular Literature*, during the script period of medieval Europe, reading was word for word, out loud, and not fluent. Poems were written for recitation.[6] There was no uniformity of grammar or spelling because scripts were to be performed and were only rarely read; except for the case of Latin, only with printing did uniformity even become possible. Before Gutenberg, it was assumed that vernaculars were in flux in terms of pronunciation and vocabulary; the rise of uniform national languages as standard bearers for states was, in part, a media effect. Language stabilization and stylistic idealization (manuals, grammars) are the blowback of the printing press.

According to Chaytor, the first French prose appeared in the late twelfth century; before that, the literature that was produced for public entertainment and education was in verse. This first prose was for legal documents, Bible translations, and, subsequently, historical accounts. Prose was written for individual readers and it was reserved for "matters of fact, not fancy" (85). As part of an emerging, ultimately massive, deversification process, poetry was translated into prose (much as print databases are now being digitalized). The earliest prose by nonpoets or literary artists in France comes from 1202 in an account of the Crusades written in an unembellished, factual style. From the twelfth century on, Chaytor notes, all "important" households in England and Europe had at least one person who could read. By the late 1300s, the first "reading public" emerged in England, with the production of secular literature licensed by universities for students. By the 1400s, prose was preferred for erudition and instruction, while at the same time there was a gradual rise of literacy; but just being literate didn't mean you could read books. According to Irving Fang and the Media History Project's "Timeline," the first paper was used in England

---

5. Wlad Godzich and Jeffrey Kittay, *The Emergence of Prose: An Essay in Prosaics* (Minneapolis: University of Minnesota Press, 1987).
6. *From Script to Print: an Introduction to Medieval Vernacular Literature* (Cambridge: Cambridge University Press, 1945).

in 1309 and the first paper mill was established in 1495.[7] In the fourteenth and fifteenth century books were scarce and expensive and were willed to heirs. Educated men learned to read (women did not)—possibly one-half of the population of England was literate. Indeed, there were more schools in the 1400s than in 1864, suggesting the intensity of interest in literacy in the fifteenth century (Chaytor, 111). By 1450, the first newspapers began to circulate in Europe.

Four hundred years after Gutenberg, the next technological revolution for language reproduction began. For the purposes of defining this ongoing technological vortex, I would point to the telegraph (first invented in the 1830s, with the first transcontinental service becoming available in the 1860s), photography (invented in 1827, popular by late 1830s), the telephone (1876), the phonograph (1877), magnetic audio recording (1899), the loudspeaker (1898), wireless telegraphy (1894), the movie camera (1890–1895), radio (first regular broadcasting around 1907), television (first network TV broadcast 1949), photo-offset printing and "cold type" typesetting (late 1950s), photocopying (first plain paper copier 1959), and, finally, in the last two decades, digital writing and imaging (via computer, the Internet, and the web). Writing in this age of photographic and electronic reproduction is fundamentally postalphabetic in that it no longer relies on scripts to store and transmit information: cultural memory is becoming digital, more image than letter. At the same time, just as the Greeks lived through several hundred years of simultaneous alphabetic and oral culture, we are now living in a period of overlaid oral, alphabetic, and photo/phono electronic culture.

One crucial mark of the overlay of alphabetic and electronic technologies is the emergence of radical modernist art in the late nineteenth and early twentieth century. Just as some of the Greek literary art of the period immediately following the invention of the alphabet formally reflected in the new writing the forms of an oral culture soon to be eclipsed, so radical modernism formally reflects the alphabetic culture soon to be eclipsed (but not replaced) by photographic, electronic, and digital media.

The other crucial marker of the overlay of the oral, alphabetic, and photo/phono electronic is the fact that in North America and Europe, the rise of

7. Media History Project, "Timeline," http://www.mediahistory.umn.edu/timeline/, accessed July 6, 2010. The media history that follows is largely based on this timeline.

mass literacy in the late nineteenth century occurs just as the new era of photographic and electronic communications is beginning, making mass literacy and postliteracy intertwined historical developments. Indeed, the culture of literacy reaches its technical apotheosis in the mid-nineteenth and twentieth century, not only with the rise of a mass readership, but also with invention of nonelectronic and nonphoto/phonographic devices that made language storage and retrieval by writing even more efficient and accessible than ever; for example, carbon paper (1806), the typewriter (first manufactured by Remington in 1873), the mimeograph (invented in 1875 and retailed in 1890), linotype (1886), the Waterman fountain pen (1884), and the ballpoint pen (1938). (The pencil was invented in 1565 and the eraser in 1770, while steel pen points began to replace quill pens in 1780.) The nineteenth- and twentieth-century boom in the production of lyric poetry is coincident with the rise of mass literacy, since many more people were able to become authors. The ability to write and sign something as yours—the signature effect—remains culturally viable until literacy is fully distributed in the society, an event that has yet to occur.

This rise of mass literacy, late in the history of writing, has had the effect of putting the printed and bound book front and center, as the cathected object of the alphabetic unconscious. From the perspective of 1999, the printed book is the best picture we have of alphabetic textuality. As we enter into a postliterate period, we can begin to see the book as the solid middle ground between the stage (performed poetry) and the screen (digital poetry).

In making this broad overview of language reproduction technologies, I want to reiterate that one medium does not conquer another. It is not a question of progress but rather of a series of overlays creating the web in which our language is enmeshed. The alphabet did not prescribe the emergence of lyric poetry as a medium of art but rather created the possibility. Technology determines neither art nor politics, but politics and art are never free from the effects of technology. Technology informs, but it does not determine.

Havelock speculates that perhaps he and McLuhan were alerted to the importance of understanding media by hearing Winston Churchill's "blitz" speeches on the then relatively new and popular medium of the radio. The sheer oral force of the speeches, he says, helped him to reconsider the effects of centuries of silent reading and of the contrasting possibilities for oral performance in early Greek culture. Indeed, radio, and later TV, marked a turn to a/literate modes for transmission and storage of cultural information, and, as we turn to the twenty-first century, analphabetic media are the primary source of information for most people: you are more likely to hear or see the news than to read it (even while newscasts continue to rely on alphabetic scripts). Yet, while audio and video reproduction have eclipsed both alphabetic and oral technologies, they have qualities in common with both. Postliteracy brings us back to preliteracy. In particular, the emergence of the World Wide Web in the 1990s has awakened a sharper appreciation for the medium of writing and for the visual and acoustic elements of language. Similarly, hypertext theory has reopened consideration of the achievements of radical modernist writing.

My interest in the technoformalist criticism of Havelock and McLuhan as well as Walter Benjamin, Clement Greenberg, and Stanley Cavell is not only that they draw attention to what it means to work within a medium, but also that they acknowledge the value of using a medium to do what can only be done in that medium. While humanist literary criticism naturalizes the medium of the art, just as it neutralizes its ideology, technoformalist criticism recognizes the medium (and by extension ideology) to have qualities of its own that some art within this medium will choose to foreground, which is to say, bring to consciousness. In poetry, this approach is at the heart of radical modernism composition, with its focus not only on what is conveyed, but also on the specific conditions of the conveyance. Perhaps the motto for this project can be taken from Jerome McGann's "Imagining What You Don't Know: The Theoretical Goals of the Rossetti Archive": "To treat all the physical aspects of the documents as expressive features."[8]

Writing is a storage medium. It stores verbal language. But the various technologies (hieroglyphs, scripts, printing, hypertext) literally score the language stored.

In other words: Writing records the memory of language just as it explores the possibilities for language.

In a formalist emphasis on the medium, we do not escape the question—a medium of what, for what? Can the medium be emptied out, so that it is just the medium, the pure medium? In that case what does it transport but the *contexts* (contents) in which it is placed, like a crystal ball reflecting the hands that (be)hold it.

---

8. "Imagining What You Don't Know," http://chnm.gmu.edu/digitalhistory/links/pdf/chapter3/3.24b.pdf, 6, accessed July 6, 2010. Collected in part 2 of McGann's *Radiant Textuality: Literature after the World Wide Web* (New York: Palgrave Macmillan, 2004).

A medium cannot be in and of itself, autonomous, for only readers or listeners or viewers bring a medium into use. In this sense, a medium is a mediation, constituted by what it does, for whom, and how.

The "medium" is a metaphor, as Jack Spicer and Hannah Weiner demonstrate when they insist that their poems are mediums, receiving language from a place outside themselves, north of intention.

A medium is an "in-between" in which you go from one place to another but also the material of that in-betweenness. Metaphors are mediums of transformation, in Greek the bearer (*phor*) of change (*meta*). Metaphor involves transference/transport/transfer. A medium is the means of transport, the conveyance, and also the material or technical process of art, like brass or silver. But only use makes something a medium of art. Materials by themselves are inert. Yet sometimes one finds the use of a medium by relying on the resistance of the materials that constitute it.

If poetry in analphabetic culture maximizes its storage function through memorizable language (formulaic, stressed), then poetry in the age of postliteracy (where cultural information is stored orally, alphabetically, and digitally), is perhaps most fully realized through refractory—unmemorizable—language (unexpected, nonformulaic, dis-stressed). This is why apparently nonliterary writing—catalogs, directories, dictionaries, indexes, concordances, and phone books, as well as printing errors, textual variations, holograph manuscripts—have become so important for poetry. And this is also why the textuality of contemporary poetry is so often tested in performance. For the performance of a textual writing, refractory to memorization, creates a new-old *frisson* that is rich with structural meanings and acoustic resonances.

But what of the age between the two—the age of ascendant literacy? It is commonplace to say that photography freed painting from the burden of pictorial representation, as for centuries paintings and drawings had been the primary means of pictorial and image storing (morphing) and transmission. (The trope of being freed from a burden should not obscure the fact that pictorial representation goes on happily ever after in painting; the point is that the meaning of images change in painting because their use value changes.) Alphabetic writing ultimately freed poetry (though never completely) from the necessity of storage and transmission of the culture's memories and laws—*poetry's epic function*. In the age of literacy, this task was ultimately assumed by prose. Poetry, released from this overriding obligation to memory storage, increasingly became defined by the individual voice, *poetry's lyric function* (the persistence of epic notwithstanding, since epic in the age of lyric becomes less infrastructure and more art). In this speculative schema, the lyric is contrasted to the impersonal authority of (nonfiction) prose, constituted by such subjects as law and philosophy.

With the advent of the photo/phono electronic, postliterate age, the emerging function for poetry is neither the storage of collective memory nor the projection of individual voice, but rather an exploration of the medium through which the storage and expressive functions of language work. That is, the technological developments of the past 150 years have made conceivable, in a way hardly possible before, viewing and reproducing and interacting with language as a material and not just as a means. Poetry's singular burden in a digital age is to sound the means of transmission: call it *poetry's textual function*, making audible/visible the ethos enacted in and by the fabric of writing. Textuality does not erase poetry's epic and lyric functions; rather it supplements and transforms, and in so doing aestheticizes, these increasingly vestigial modalities of the medium.

Another way of saying this is that photography and phonography loosened the grip of representation not only on painting but also on poetry.

Humanist literary criticism cannot and will not recognize the necessity of a poetry of textuality in which "memorable language" is just one among many tools of the trade, and not an end in itself. The persistence of the criterion of "memorable language" as a primary category for evaluating poetry is a throwback to an actual social function poetry once had, but which has become in our age largely ornamental and nostalgic except when it is used to tap into the deep fissures of poetry's past, to locate sonic geysers that erupt in the surface of our verses.

A textual poetry does not create language that is committable to memory but rather a memory of the analphabetic that is committable to language. This is why so much textual writing seems to return to a/literate features of language, not only in other cultures but also in our own. This is what I mean to suggest, in part, by the term *a/orality*—the acoustic or aural dimension of language within a postalphabetic environment. The significance of speech for textual poetry is fundamental because such poetry is able to foreground features of speech that do not contribute to the memory function essential for poetry in cultures where oral art is the primary technology for language storage and retrieval.

In the early part of the twentieth century, Gertrude Stein discovered her own version of a/orality through a process of close listening to the vernacular—the African American vernacular in "Melanctha," the broken German

English in "The Gentle Lena."[9] In the context of a postliterate writing, the transcription of speech looks very different than it did at the dawn of the alphabetic age: static, noise, and other microtextures loom large when the art of memory is not at stake. Repetition without memorability uses the features of oral art for textual ends: it is not memory that is being stored but texture that is being exhibited. The result is not a poetry in the service of memory but a poetry, in Stein's phrase, of "the continuous present."

Textuality, sounded, evokes orality. Conversely, orality provokes textuality (polymorphously), albeit the virtual, aliterate materiality of woven semiosis. This is orality's anterior horizon, its acoustic and linguistic ground, embodied and gestural. The *stuffness* of language, its *verbality*, is present in both writing and speech, but it is particularly marked when language is listened to, or read, without the filter of its information function. (The material stratum that weaves together speech and writing provides not only the means for language's information function but also information in its own right.) Textuality is a palimpsest: when you scratch it you find speech underneath. And when you sniff the speech, you find language under that.

Poetry's social function in our time is to bring language ear to ear with its temporality, physicality, dynamism: its evanescence, not its fixed character; its fluidity, not its authority; its structures, not its storage capacity; its concreteness and particularity, not its abstract logicality and clarity.

To say we are in an age of postliteracy does not mean that literacy is no longer necessary, but rather that it is no longer sufficient; perhaps the better term would be hyperliteracy. Poetry in a digital age can do more than simply echo the past with memorable phrases. It can also invent the present in language never before heard.

9. Stein, *Three Lives* (1909), http://www.bartleby.com/74/, accessed July 4, 2010.

MAKING AUDIO VISIBLE: POETRY'S COMING DIGITAL PRESENCE

I originally presented this talk as part of a panel on "Textuality and Visual Cultures" at the Society of Textual Scholarship (STS), immediately following presentations more obviously related to the topic by Marjorie Perloff and Johanna Drucker. Perhaps it found a more expectable home in its next incarnation, a collection of essays on "writing environments," since sound recordings are a crucial environment for poetry. Monaural recordings of voice coming from a fixed location are as monodimensional as the alphabetic transcription of voice. The next frontier for poetry sound environments may involve new sound installation technologies, such as those pioneered by Janet Cardiff, that permit multidirectional and multifocal acoustic projection. In such environments, the sound not only changes as you walk through the space but also has a 3-D effect: you hear sounds emanating from different parts of the environment. For example, a voice sounding as if it is coming from right in front of you is overlaid by a whispering voice that seems to come from immediately behind you.

My topic this morning—the digitalization of the recording of poetry readings—would seem, on the face of it, remote, a stretch at best, perhaps even a stubborn refusal to stick to the topic that would not exactly be uncharacteristic for me. But the more I delve into my subject, the more I see how difficult it would be to extract the topic of digitalized sound files of poems from either visual culture or textuality.

Let me start with a highly reductive history of language-recording technologies.

The first great technology for recording the sound of spoken language was the phonetic scripts of about 2,500 years ago. The phonetic (literally "spoken voice") alphabet created a simple visual notation system that was

Presented at the annual meeting of the Society for Textual Scholarship (STS), March 21, 2003, in New York, and published in STS's journal, *Text* 16 (2006). Subsequently published in the "Writing Environments" feature, edited by William Watkin, in *Textual Practice* 23.6 (2009).

used, in many instances, as a transcriptive device: that is, as a script for performance, the letters serving as cues to prompt oral recitation. The significance of a visual technology for the notation of an aural phenomenon is profound; its implications for our way of understanding language, and indeed for our perception of both reality and its others, is incalculable, and, as a result, has been the subject of many learned treatises, very few of which were composed for the tongue. Curiously, the significance of visual language on the semantics of literary works has been less widely acknowledged. From the point of view of aesthetics and literary criticism, the works, over the past twenty years, of Drucker and Perloff, are signal exceptions. In contrast, from the point of view of bibliographic scholarship, the significance of visual coding has remained central, even as the field itself has become more marginal in an age of cultural studies and theorization.

But, back to my abbreviated history—with a two-millennia jump.

In 1877, Thomas Edison made the first recording of the human voice—a short recitation of the first verse of Sara Josepha Hale's 1830 poem "Mary Had a Little Lamb." Edison's recording was made just two years before the poet's death at the age of ninety-one. The first sound recording was of a poem, though not in the author's own voice. Edison stumbled upon his "speaking machine" while working on a device to speed up telegraphic transmission—the telegraph itself being a device for the audio transmission of visual (alphabetic) code. Edison's sound-recording device was variously called a talking machine, a speaking machine, and a phonograph. *Phonograph*, the word Edison chose for his company, suggests something of the visual/verbal paradox that is my topic today, meaning, as it does, something like sound writing or sound drawing. We don't, literally, read a sound recording but play it. And while the sound recording is able to capture far more acoustic data than phonetic script, "sound writing" shares with alphabetic writing the ability to retrieve recorded verbal data. This combination of inscription and retrievability marks recorded sound as a new form of textuality, new, that is, for the past century. Indeed, as I note in "The Art of Immemorability," sound recording is inextricably linked to modernist poetry and its specific textual forms.

The most famous image of the phonograph, "His Master's Voice," pictures a dog—Nipper by name—listening to a gramophone. The first version of the image was made in 1898 by the British painter Mark Barraud and called "Dog Looking at and Listening to a Phonograph" (see figure 1). Later the specific machine depicted was changed and the image became famous as the logo for the Gramophone Company in England and for RCA Victor

FIG 1   Mark Barraud, *His Master's Voice* (1898).

in the United States.[1] Barraud's work is iconic of the uncanniness of the human voice emanating from a machine unattached to a body. Dogs, beloved by their owners for their ability to distinguish specific human voices from other sounds in the environment, are the adequate symbol of transhuman voice recognition. As Gertrude Stein puts it, "I am I because my little dog knows me."[2] If the dog hears it, it must be Memorex. For Stein, that is, the dog wags its tail when it catches the scent of human nature but not human mind. And since dogs don't talk, but only listen, the dog represents the ideal audient for a talking machine that, like a text, speaks but cannot hear.

Barraud's original title, emphasizing the combination of looking and listening, is telling because one of the most striking features of the image is Nipper gazing affectionately into the Victrola's large horn, sometimes imagined to be an ear, but which more pertinently can be imagined as a

1. Significantly, Barraud's original painting has the dog's head at a greater distance from the horn. For a history of the paintings, along with images of the original (still owned by a Gramophone Company's successor, EMI), go to http://www.designboom.com/history/nipper.html, en.wikipedia.org/wiki/Nipper, and http://www.emiclassics.com/aboutusnipper.php, accessed July 8, 2010.

2. "Identity a Poem," in *A Stein Reader*, edited by Ulla E. Dydo (Evanston, IL: Northwestern University Press, 1993); see also Stein, *The Geographical History of America; or, the Relation of Human Nature to the Human Mind* (New York: Vintage Books, 1973). I comment on this essay in "Stein's Identity," in *My Way: Speeches and Poems* (Chicago: University of Chicago Press, 1999).

mechanical throat and mouth. Nipper is looking into the horn as if this were the most natural and comforting thing in the world; as if, that is, there were something to see inside the horn, in its dark interior. In other words, the dog (I keep typing this, dyslexically, God) is sniffing out the ghost in the machine. Indeed, with his nose almost entering into the cavity, it looks like Nipper's head would fit snugly into the device, which might be something of a textual womb; or, alternately, as if Nipper might be swallowed up into the voice machine, as Jonah into the whale. Nipper, a dog who is the fantasy of visual culture, is looking straight into the production of a human presence that can call his name but doesn't know he's there.

Much has been made of the ghostly presence of the disembodied phonographic voice, the novel possibility, with this new invention, of the voices of the dead speaking to us. But I am interested in a quite different cause for the uncanniness of grammaphony. Talking machines merge two usually separate cognitive phenomena: speech-mode perception and non-speech-mode perception. As Reuven Tsur explains it, we cognitively process speech sounds differently from other sounds.[3] Consider, though, that the talking machine produces mechanical sounds that we process, against our typical automatic response, as if they were speech. With early recordings, just as with radio with bad reception, we actively search for the voice in the static, as if it were a figure to be differentiated from the ground: the mechanical semblance of voice has become the signal in a medium whose material base is sonic, not vocal. In such a phonic economy, noise is sound that can't be recuperated as voice. Tsur, following Roman Jakobson, defines the poetic mode of cognitive perception as the perception of speech as if it were sound. The grammaphone reverses the Jakobsonian definition of poetry: it incites the perception of mechanical sound as if it were speech. *The grammaphone is a reverse order poetry machine.* This is what fascinated Nipper, our ideal audient. The master at whose voice he stares is not his human owner but the machine that produces a voice without body. We are all Nippers now.

The conjuring of voice unattached to body is a kind of disappearing act to which we have grown so accustomed that we need a little dog to remind us of what's not seen. To accept a link between sound reproduction and visual culture, you would have to allow the conceit that invisibility is a part of visual culture. Voice-reproduction technologies undermine intuitive distinctions not only between sight and sound, but also between space and time.

3. *What Makes Sound Patterns Expressive? The Poetic Mode of Speech Perception* (Durham: Duke University Press, 1992).

As the story is told, the earliest playable sound recording, from 1878, is
Frank Lambert's "Talking Clock." Lambert had the idea of marking time in a
temporal medium: the new "speaking machine" would provide an alternative in real time to the visualization of time in previous clocks. The recording has four basic sections: 21 seconds of indistinct speech, 11 seconds of
Lambert clearly calling out hours (five o'clock, six o'clock, seven o'clock,
eight o'clock, nine o'clock, ten o'clock, eleven o'clock, twelve o'clock). There
follow 36 seconds of silence and then the most extraordinary thing of all:
29 seconds of voiced but illegible sound. Evidently, Lambert cranked the
cylinder in reverse, producing, for the first time, the human voice played
backward. The first distributed sound recording was not just of a human
voice counting numbers but also the first sound poem. Indeed, it is impossible to imagine Lambert's "Talking Clock" as having any practical import at
all: it is nothing less than the first work of grammaphonic sound poetry.[4]

Mechanically reversing the flow of a recorded voice breaks down the perceptual distinction between space and time: it can be both disorienting and
mesmerizing. The fact that, with the cranked gramophone, the recorded
voice can be played back in two directions is something that puts the earliest experiments with the plasticity of the reproduced voice in a conceptual
tape loop with the rhythmic use of vocables in the sound performances of
analphabetic cultures. Voice becomes text, just as with phonetic scripts text
becomes voice.

But not so fast. Is sound, is the performative dimension of the poem,
really textual? We typically associate textuality with the woven texture of
written language, and, indeed with visual inscription. Within the context
of literary criticism or textual scholarship, the performance of the poem
has not been generally recognized as part of the work, a designation that is
reserved for the text understood as the scripted incarnation of the poem.
Nonetheless, in alphabetic and postalphabetic visual cultures, the a/oral
dimension of the poem can't be split from the text "itself," even if it threat-
ens to undermine the coherence of the poem by adding possibly new and
incommensurable textual layers, to echo a point of Jerome McGann's about
the multiplex nature of the textual condition.[5] The audio text may be one
more generally discounted destabilizing textual element, an element that
undermines our ability to fix and present any single definitive, or even

4. "Talking Clock," http://writing.upenn.edu/bernstein/syllabi/readings/lambert.html, accessed July 6, 2010.
5. *The Textual Condition* (Princeton: Princeton University Press, 1999).

stable, text of the poem. Grammaphony is not an alternative to textuality but rather throws us deeper into its folds.

To say that we don't literally read a sound recording, but play it, is itself to trip on the distinction between the graphic letter and the interpretive moment. Perhaps we could call this grammaphonic enunciation the sound of one hand clapping, whether that one hand is the stylus or the digital decoder. But the nonliteral sense of reading crosses the sound barrier: for to read a poem out loud is to give a reading of it just as to listen to a poem recited is to have to read it with your ears. The paradox, to say it again, is in the words we have given to these machines: for example, *gramophone* (or *phonogram*), which might be translated as *texted voice*, suggesting, as it does, that the lettered word—gramma—is made invisible so that it can be heard. The process of inscription and retrieval is shared by both the grammaphonic and, if we want to invent a new word for writing, the grammagraphic.

One hundred years ago, a wax cylinder inscribed with the human voice stored two minutes of sound. At present (an ever shifting term), a CD inscribed with compressed sound files can store ten hours of sound, and a portable MP3 player, at less than six ounces and smaller than a wax cylinder, can store "10,000 songs," as the ad tells us. The revolution in our ability to record and store sound has had a huge impact on many areas of the culture; not the least of these, though perhaps the least remarked on, is poetry. In the business press, it is common to hear about the disruptive effect of MP3 music file exchange on the pop-music recording industry. Dire pronouncements are made about theft of intellectual property by the very same companies that sell the hardware and software to record and play these files. Certainly, we are seeing a great change in the mobility of recording, playing, and, crucially, distributing, sound recordings. The change is quite significant, but I think the greatest significance may well be not for pop music and its financial base but for poetry and its grammaphonic status. And that's a prediction you won't be hearing on *CNNMoney*.

In the era of print, from which we are slowly emerging, the alphabetic version of a poem was supreme, unchallenged. While poems were sometimes produced in nonalphabetic contexts, within alphabetic cultures, literary production has been synonymous with writing understood as a visual system of notation. Poetry readings, while significant, have been regarded largely as extensions or supplements of the visual text of the poem. Indeed, there has been very little critical work on the poet's performance of a poem; at least up until very recently, literary criticism has pretty much been confined to the printed text.

The reason for this is practical as much as conceptual. While archives of poetry recordings exist, they are largely inaccessible. Very few editions of poets' sound recordings have been published. As a result, basic principles of textual scholarship have not yet been applied to the sound archive. But the times they are a-changin'.

With the advent of file compression and broad-band web connections, it is now possible for individuals to exchange sound files of recorded poetry. The digitalization of the archive of recorded poetry is just now getting started, and it is this digitalization that is my primary focus this morning.

At the University of Pennsylvania, we have started a project we call PennSound, which extends the work I have been doing with Loss Pequeño Glazier and Martin Spinelli at the Electronic Poetry Center in Buffalo (http://epc.buffalo.edu) and builds on the foundational work of Kenneth Goldsmith at Ubuweb (http://www.ubu.com).[6] Pennsound is a collaboration between the Center for Programs in Contemporary Writing (Al Filreis) and the Annenberg Rare Book and Manuscript Library (Michael Ryan). For this project, we intend to develop protocols for the indexing and tagging of sound files of poetry readings. At this time, there are no such standards, and relative chaos exists at every basic level, from file-naming conventions to formatting to file-format choices to relevant bibliographic coding to copyright questions to storage and preservation issues.

I believe that the availability of compressed sound files of individual poems, freely available via the Internet, offers an intriguing and powerful alternative to the book format in collecting a poet's work and to anthology and magazine formats in organizing constellations of poems. Imagine for a moment that you had on the hard drive of your computer a score of MP3 files of poems by fifty of your favorite twentieth-century poets. I would bet that no matter how involved or committed any of you may be to twentieth-century poetry, none of you have such a collection readily available. But with poetry's coming digital presence you will, or anyway, you easily might. What would be the implications of such a collection?

In my focus on the recording of the unaccompanied voice and more specifically on poets reading their own work, I am not unaware of the importance of sound recording technology for music; and I have been told that there has been quite a lot of material produced and distributed, over the past hundred years, with either just musical instruments or with musical instruments accompanied by singing. Quite a bit of fuss has been made

6. PennSound, http://writing.upenn.edu/pennsound, officially launched on January 1, 2005.

about this and it is evidently today a multibillion-dollar worldwide industry. But I wouldn't want this aspect of sound recording to overshadow what is for me, thinking in terms of the art of poetry, a crucially significant feature of sound recording technology: the reproduction of the unaccompanied human voice. In other words, I want to remain archly formalist and even purist on this issue, at the risk of seeming to direct way too much attention to what for most people is at best an epiphenomenon, a footnote to the larger story.

For teachers, one obvious implication of the archive of recorded poetry becoming more available is that listening to the poem read by the poet might become a commonplace feature in any course, since such recordings would be able to be assigned in much the same manner as the visual or alphabetic text of the poem. The sound file would become, ipso facto, a text for study, much like the visual document. The acoustic experience of listening to the poem would begin to compete with the visual experience of reading the poem. Many of us, of course, ask students to read poems aloud, or we read the poems aloud in class. But the textualization of the sound as an object of study radically changes this dynamic.

How about for readers of poetry? What effect would the collection of poetry MP3s have? For one thing, the experience of listening to poetry would be far more mobile and portable than it has been, rivaling, though not exceeding, the portability of the book. Now, however, those interested in poetry performance mostly access it live and in person, where the visual element of the poet reading, the theatricality of the presentation on stage, and the social element of exchange in many ways equal, or surpass, the importance of the merely acoustic dimension. Despite the long-time availability of poetry recordings, very few people have anything more than a passing relation to this archive in comparison to their experience of reading poetry in visualized formats (writing) or going to live readings. Indeed, it is hard for me, and probably hard for any of us, to imagine that possibility—that someone would have their primary relation to poetry via audio recordings.

In poetry's coming digital presence, the poem, understood as a recorded performance of thirty seconds or three to five minutes or even ten or twenty or thirty minutes or more, may take on an integrity that it presently does not have in the era of book collections of poems. Poems, that is, might find themselves liberated from books, free-standing, available to combine with other poems in one's collection to play in the car or at the health club or on the plane or walking around the city or sitting at the beach or dancing on the head of a needle, a virtual phonograph needle that is. Imagine digital files of discrete poems as individual leaves in an anthology of one's own creation. Poems, set adrift from their visual grounding in alphabetic texts, might begin to resemble the songs from which, for so long, they have been divided.

A widely available digital audio poetry archive will have a pronounced influence on the production of new poetry. In the coming digital presence, it becomes possible to imagine poets preparing and releasing poems that exist only as sound files, with no written text, or for which a written text is secondary. Orally composed, or nonscripted, poems have already been realized by bpNichol and Tracie Morris, among others, but greater access to digital sound editing opens other doors. In the coming digital presence, poets will compose the text of their poems by dictating and editing sound files much the way we now compose and edit alphabetic writing. In this sense, the production of poetry will come closer to film or radio—works that are produced in the cutting room. The result will not necessarily be sound poetry or poetry with accelerated variations of performance affect or number of performers, but possibly an audio-textual poetry akin to the modernist and contemporary work, extending the formal possibilities of language worked as a virtually physical material for making the poem.

Consider also, dear listener, the effect of easily available sound files on critical writing published in digital media. It might become as common to include sound clips in an essay as it is now to include an image; and the clips could themselves be subjected to a microanalysis, via a sound editing program, that we presently do strictly by visual parsing. And I can only here mention the possible transformation of our sense of the poem when we consider the acoustic record along with the visual marking; or when we look at the visual print or sonograph of a performed poem, as becomes possible with any sound editing program. The sound shape would not be merely a metaphor for acoustic or rhythmic analysis, but also an image created through processing the sound in ways that give it a visual trace.

Moreover, the kind of "deformative" criticism advocated by McGann and Lisa Samuels,[7] or my own set of "wreading" experiments at the Electronic Poetry Center, which mostly involve visual markup and coloration and erasure or transposition/translation of visual linguistic elements of the text,

---

7. Lisa Samuels and Jerome McGann, "Deformance and Interpretation," in *New Literary History* 30.1 (1999): 25–56; collected in part 2 of *Radiant Textuality: Literature after the World Wide Web* (New York: Palgrave Macmillan, 2004).

could be done via acoustic processing: dropping sound levels, increasing speeds, changing timbre, repeating phrases.

For the fact is that the sound file exists not as a pure acoustic or sound event—an oral or performative event outside textuality—but as a textual condition, mediated by its visual marking, its bibliographic codes, and the tagging we give to it to mark what we consider of semantic significance.

Another central issue is the effect that sound files might have on scholarly editions. Or should I say the havoc that they might wreak. What, for example, is the relation of the recordings of a poem to the printed text of the poem? How might this relation be articulated in different types of editions, print and digital? Just as there are often multiple alphabetic versions of a poem, there are also multiple performed versions. Indeed it is likely that for a poet for whom we have an extensive archive of recordings, there are likely to be more variations of the poem than produced by print forms. We might have the same poem read at very different points in the poet's life and there might be lexical variations in each performance (or not).

The types of variations of a poem found in audio recordings are substantially different from those in visual culture documents. To what extent to "authorize" such variations as credible versions of the poem is itself an issue. But what about different approaches to the performance: timbre, speed, rhythm, temporally marked lineation, emotional valences. Perhaps of greatest significance is the paratextual framing of a poem in a reading. For one thing, there are the introductory, peripheral, and explanatory remarks made before, during, and after the reading of the poem per se. At this year's annual meeting of the Modern Language Association, Kenneth Sherwood presented an elaborate transcription of remarks of this kind made by Amiri Baraka in a reading in honor of Robert Creeley in Buffalo.[8] For another, there is the context of the reading itself, which is akin to the context of publication in a magazine or by a specific publisher. Finally, there is the order of the poems presented in a reading, which will often offer a distinct and significant setting of the work.

A poem, to paraphrase Jerome McGann from a talk he will be giving this afternoon,[9] is not a converging system of coherent signs but—now

8. Ken Sherwood, "Elaborate Versionings: Characteristics of Emergent Performance in Three Print/Oral/Aural Poets" (Amiri Baraka, Kamau Brathwaite, and Cecilia Vicuña) in *Oral Traditions* 21.1 (2006), http://journal.oraltradition.org/issues/21i/sherwood, accessed May 1, 2009.

9. "Texts in N-Dimensions and Interpretation in a New Key," presented at the Society for Textual Scholarship, March 21, 2003; published in *Text Technology* 12:2 (2004).

this is me again—a diverging environment of incommensurable sights and sounds—"a dimension of mind. You're moving into a land of both shadow and substance, of things and ideas. You've just crossed over into . . . the Twilight Zone."

Within the coming digital environment of a poet's work, the sound file is at this time the orphan, something that if included would disrupt even the most expansive conception of versions, all based on different print versions.

I realize my proposal invites as many questions, and raises as many problems, as it answers. This is as it should be at this stage. From the point of view of textual scholarship, it still remains to be seen what kind of tagging within the sound file would be valuable, not to say useful. One obvious issue would be search capabilities, how the conception of searching might be translated into recorded sound of poetry, beyond the obvious tagging of line and stanza breaks, titles and subtitles, key words, or even every word. Certainly, there is much to be learned from the far more advanced work in this area with various spoken word archives, from radio to oral histories. But the bibliographic issues for poems would be different. The term "bibliographic" is yet another reminder of how sound itself will be mediated by visual—graphic—tools. I might call for bibliophonic tagging, but I can't say what that would mean.

I have emphasized the importance of the recordings of the poets' own performance of their work. I realize that some will object that this valorizes the author function in a way apparently at odds with what many of us have argued for in terms of the active role of the reader. My choice is based on a clear aesthetic preference for poets reading their own work, but of course it is imaginable that performances by others might become significant. I address this issue in *Close Listening*, where I state my preference for audio recordings over video or film recordings of poets reading their work.[10] On a practical level, the visual quality of taped readings is usually very limited in comparison to other moving-image productions; sound recordings do not have the same comparative problem. Then again, like most people,

10. My remarks at STS, and in the previous essay in this collection, "The Art of Immemoriability," extend my work editing *Close Listening: Poetry and the Performed Word* (New York: Oxford University Press, 1998). *Close Listening* remains the only overview by scholars and poets that addresses the significance of the contemporary poetry reading for literary studies and poetics. The book came out simultaneously with a related collection of essays, *Sound States: Acoustical Technologies and Modern and Postmodern Writing*, edited by Adelaide Morris (Chapel Hill: University of North Carolina Press, 1998).

I prefer sound recordings of most music in comparison to straight "head shot" or concert video versions (there is at present nothing comparable to music videos for poetry, though this is a form that might well develop). In any case, my claims of value for poetry audio are tied in to the particular formal significance that unaccompanied voice recording has for the grammaphonic imaginary.

"His Master's Voice," the voice on a record, is invested with the aura of invisible presence. It speaks to us as through a wrinkle in time. The recorded voice only speaks; the possibility for dialog or response always present at a reading—where the presence of an audience intimately affects what is being presented—is illusory, making our close listening across the electrostatic barrier all the more our own private affair. The recorded reading re-enacts the conditions for dialog without its actual presence, unless we want to consider the presence of the imagination. For the imaginative projection solicited by close listening to the grammaphonic poem is the one writing has required all along. Here we go again: it's déjà vu one more time.

Let me end with a brief manifesto for the PennSound archiving of recorded poetry:

1. *It must be free.* Ideally, all the sound material we put on the web should be cleared for copyright to be distributed free. Users of the site will be able to download the MP3s to their own computers or players or play them in a streaming fashion. Teachers could make course CDs or add the MP3s to their online syllabi. Other websites and libraries could recollect the material. Credits for digitalization and copyright release would also be embedded into each file. One of the advantages of working with poetry sound files is that we don't anticipate a problem with rights. At present and in the conceivable future, there is no profit to be gained by the sale of recorded poetry. There is, however, considerable expense involved in preserving, cataloging, and distributing such material.

2. *It must be MP3 or better.* RealAudio is a proprietary format with sound quality that will not stand the test of time. We need to use open formats that reproduce reasonably high-quality sound, for a listenership that is used to astoundingly good sound quality from commercial sources.

3. *It must be singles.* At present, the vast majority of poetry recordings are for entire readings, typically thirty or more minutes, with no tracking of individual cuts or poems. While these full readings have great literary and archival value taken as a whole, few but the most devoted listen to full recordings of readings, or if they do, fewer still listen more than once. The

more useful format is to break readings up into individual poems and to make MP3s of each poem available. MP3s of song-length poems could become a very appealing format for poetry. The implications for audience, listenership, critical thinking, poetics, and poetic production are great.

4. *It must be named.* Presently, downloaded poetry sound files tend not to have informative names. Looking at a directory of such files, it is impossible to determine what the file contains from the visual information available. File sharing for music employs a simple system of the name of the singer and the song, but the P2P system is not compatible with FTP, especially in terms of blank spaces between words, which need to have dashes or underlines. In addition, song MP3 file names start with the first name of the singer, but for the poetry files I think we need to move to the more conventional last name first and give the date and place of the performance as well. For poetry file names I propose: lastname-firstname_cut-number_title_place/series_date .mp3.

5. *It must embed bibliographic information in the file.* It's important that basic bibliographic information be embedded in the MP3 sound file itself, so that when someone downloads the file they get the right file name and also they get a full range of "ID3"-type information—all in the same file. This is basically a consumer-oriented MP3 file exchange approach. The goal is to make these sound files available for users to have readily accessible for play and replay. Since downloaded files will be separated from their home library website or catalog, information on that website or in a catalog will not necessarily be retrievable (although the URL for the catalog can also be embedded).

6. *It must be indexed.* This will ensure that it is retrievable both from a library catalog under the author's name and via web search engines.

THE BOUND LISTENER

The alphabet is frozen sound.

In *Dialectic of Enlightenment* (1947), Theodor Adorno and Max Hork-heimer focus on *The Odyssey* as foundational to what they call the Enlight-enment thinking of Western Civilization. While they don't comment on the performance history of the text, their reading helps us understand the significance of the epic's historical movement from open and variable in performance to a fixed, authoritative text; the movement, that is, from oral culture to alphabetic inscription. (Revising Pound's definition that the epic is a poem including history, we might now say that an epic is a poem fabri-cating history.)

With phonic writing, a strata of spoken language appears to lie under the alphabetic script (this is indeed the lie or *geist* of the spoken). This ghost of speech (what Jack Spicer calls "low ghost") would have been all the more acute during the several hundred years that the oral epic was transcribed through the newly invented Greek alphabet. As Eric Havelock emphasizes, the significance of classical Greek literary art is that it provides a record of the transition from an oral to an alphabetic means of cultural reproduction and storage. The new technology of phonetic writing could be said to have rationalized, or dominated, speech, and this form of rationalization is expe-rienced, in retrospect, as a kind of fall, a break from the unity of word and thing that music and poetry *may be felt to* reverse.

The rupture of word and thing is the repressed trauma of writing-as-rationalized-speech. In the act of recording speech, writing cuts its umbilical chord to sonic embodiment. The verse line is the scar of this cut. In every account of the history of sound, one finds, consciously or not, the projection of a prelapsarian—a *prior*—state, whether by means of a neoprimitivism or a psychoanalytic presymbolic. This is the ontological illusion of the ratio-nalization of language, it is as imaginary (and as palpable) as the mirage of

Textual Practice 23.6 (2009).

water in a desert. It is this repressed ontology that literally (and literarily) underwrites teleology.

For Adorno and Horkheimer, the story of Odysseus's triumph over the Sirens through cunning is a key to the ontological status of song in Western culture. In this view, interior to any song is the memory of the traumatic breaking of the unity of speech and things, and, indeed, of the sacrifice of the Sirens on the altar of rationalization. Odysseus, like a modern day Professor of Literary-Cultural-Historical-Transnational Studies, stuffs the ears of his charges with wax, so they will not succumb to the irresistible power of the Sirens' song. They may look but not hear, nor can they communicate with one another. Odysseus, in turn, is bound to the mast so that, while he may be ravished (enraptured) by the call of the Sirens, he will be unable to respond. (This is what has come to be called mastery.) Later, he will report what he hears to his charges, who must take him at his word. But when the ship of Enlightenment sails by those enchanting voices, Odysseus's men will be oblivious to his pleas to set him free. In the end, Odysseus will be free, the lord of his newly dominated dominion; while the Sirens, spell broken, are forever more bound in those special cages reserved for fallen creatures of the wilderness, in the sideshow of literature.

In hearing the Sirens' song without abandoning himself to it, Odysseus rehearses the conditions of language reproduction, whether alphabetic, magnetic, or digital, in which one hears voices but their sources are necessarily out of bounds, unreachable.

> Odysseus recognizes the archaic power of the song even when, as a technically enlightened man, he has himself bound. He listens to the song of pleasure and thwarts it as he seeks to thwart death. The bound listener wants to hear the Sirens as any other man would, but he has hit upon an arrangement by which he as subject need not be subjected to them. . . . The Sirens have their own power, but in primitive bourgeois history it is neutralized to become merely the wistful longing of the passer-by.[1]

1. *Dialectic of Enlightenment*, translated by John Cumming (New York: Continuum, 1972), 59–60.

HEARING VOICES

What's the difference between the alphabetic text of a poem and its performance? So much depends upon whether one imagines the poet's performance as an extension of an authorized and stable written work or as a discrete work in its own right. While the first view might allow the performance as a variation of the original, the second implies that textual and vocal instances of the poem offer discrepant versions of the work.

Any reader can perform the written text of a poem and indeed many poems need to be read out loud in order to make tangible the rhythm and sound patterning. But a poet's reading of her or his own work has an entirely different authority. The poet's performance, both live and recorded, poses an arresting issue for poetry, for the differences among the alphabetic, grammaphonic, and live are not so much ones of textual variance as of ontological condition.

But why this focus on the poet's performance? Isn't this just another way of fetishizing the author and the author's voice? The facts on the ground are these: the archive of recordings, as well as the live performance, of contemporary poems is almost exclusively composed of poets giving voice to their own work; in the first instance, the claim for the significance of poetry performance is less theoretical than an acknowledgment of actually existing poetic practice. Nonetheless, I would welcome an outpouring of cover versions of contemporary poems, let's say William Shatner reciting Leslie Scalapino's *Considering how exaggerated music is* or Harold Bloom declaiming John Ashbery's *Girls on the Run*.

The closest thing we have to this in contemporary poetry might be Kenneth Goldsmith's highly rhythmical and markedly accented recitations of

Presented at the Presidential Forum, "The Sound of Poetry/The Poetry of Sound," Modern Language Association Annual Convention, Philadelphia, December 28, 2007, and published in *The Sound of Poetry / The Poetry of Sound,* edited by Marjorie Perloff and Craig Dworkin (Chicago: University of Chicago Press, 2009).

signature moments of Western aesthetic thought.[1] In a voice that some-times sounds a bit like Danny Kaye, Goldsmith reads Wittgenstein with Stravinsky in the background, performs Adorno over a sonic bed of Satie, and does Barthes layered with the Allman Brothers. *He Do the Theorists in Voices*: Goldsmith's New York accent gives a local, not to say ethnic, flavor to what might otherwise sound like deracinated ideas, reminding us that poet-ry's all about accent while theory has a tendency to sound the impersonal.

Striking an altogether different note, Caroline Bergvall, in a 2006 perfor-mance, samples, warps, and not so much rearticulates as reaccents Geoffrey Chaucer, bringing the putative godfather of English poetry into a multilecti-cal and ideolectical sound spectrum that includes Middle and contempo-rary English, French, and Latin. Bergvall's "Shorter Chaucer Tales" is Jack Spicer's "low ghost" in the flesh: a glossolalic ghost looking for a medium.[2]

For the contemporary poet, though not necessarily for her or his reader, performance is the ultimate test of the poem, both stress test, in which the rhythms are worked out in real time, and trial of the poet's ability to engage listeners. At least this is true for those poets for whom performance is a central part of their practice. For poets so engaged, there are as many modalities of poetry performance as there are styles of poems. While most of the performances archived at PennSound involve poets reading scripts, some poets, as different as David Antin and Tracie Morris, work without prior texts, while other poets, usually associated with "spoken word," pre-sent memorized versions of written poems.

Today's memorized recitations should not be conflated with the non-scripted poetry of analphabetic cultures nor with the use of memory as part of the poetic process. The poetry of analphabetic cultures used prosodic formulas both to aid meaning and to goad composition. Since there were no scripts, literal memorization was inconceivable. Memory, as a poetic practice, involves an active exploration of the unknowable in ways that im-part an evanescent presence. Memorization is a postscript technique that requires precise, literal reproduction of a prescribed source. In contrast, the oral poetry of analphabetic cultures is a technology for the storage and re-trieval of cultural memory that involves variance, repetition, improvisation, elaboration. In this sense, memorization in poetry is a theatricalization of orality rather than an instance of it. So it's not surprising that, currently,

---

1. "Kenneth Goldsmith Sings Theory," http://writing.upenn.edu/pennsound/x/Goldsmith .html, accessed April 1, 2010.
2. "Shorter Chaucer Tales," http://writing.upenn.edu/pennsound/x/Bergvall.html, accessed April 1, 2010.

memorized spoken word is the most marked "performative" style of poetry presentation, which often resembles an actor's performance (motivated character and all). Spoken word's opposite number—the chamber music performance of the words in more antitheatrical styles of poetry reading—is no less a performance. Moreover, the performance of virtually unmemorizable, nonformulaic scripts is one of the signal features of a postalphabetic poetry in an age of photo/phono/digital reproduction. And when such scripts are performed from memory, and by actors, as in Mac Wellman's *Terminal Hip*, Fiona Templeton's *You—The City*, or Olivier Cadiot's *Colonel Zoo*, it is uncanny and exhilarating.[3]

If live performance of poetry can be, as Antin once titled a talk, "a private occasion in a public space," then recorded poetry might be thought of as a public occasion in a private space.[4] Indeed, one of the fundamental conditions of the grammaphonic voice of the poet is its ghostly presence. Listening to such recordings, we hear a voice, if not of the dead, then one that sounds present but is absent, a voice that we can hear but that cannot hear us. Perhaps this touches on the reason poets read the work of their contemporaries almost only at memorial gatherings, as a space of mourning in which we keep the poet among the living for one last time.

And so yes, I do fetishize the acoustic inscription of the poet's voice, or at least I find it aesthetically significant, partly because doing so returns voice from sometimes idealized projections of self in the style of a poem to its social materiality, to voicing and voices. In that sense, though, any performance of a poem is an exemplary interpretation, that is, one that imagines itself as rehearsal rather than as a finalization.

The alphabet, with its thirty or so marks, offers a remarkably agile technology for noting speech sounds, which, in our digital environment, makes it remarkably easy to cut, paste, and transmit. In contrast to alphabetic writing, the grammaphonic inscription offers an immensely thicker description of the voice, making explicit many vocal features that need to be interpolated when a poem is read from an alphabetic script.

---

3. Olivier Cadiot, *Colonel Zoo*, Ludovic Lagarde's production presented by Act French, New York, in 2005; English version published as *Colonel Zoo*, translated from French by Cole Swenson (Los Angeles: Green Integer, 2005). Fiona Templeton, *You—the City*, independently produced in New York in 1988; script published in 1990 by Roof Books, New York. Mac Wellman, *Terminal Hip*, PS 122, New York, 1990; script published in *Performing Arts Journal* 40 (1992).
4. "A private occasion in a public space," in *Talking at the Boundaries* (New York: New Directions, 1976).

There are four features, or vocal gestures, that are available on tape but not page that are of special significance for poetry: the cluster of *rhythm* and *tempo* (including *word duration*), the cluster of *pitch* and *intonation* (including *amplitude*), *timbre*, and *accent*. The first two of these features can be visually plotted with waveforms; the gestalt of these features contributes to *tone*.

The performed rhythm and tempo of a poem are not identical to its meter, and as Reuven Tsur has suggested, dynamic performances of metrical poetry may work against the implied metric of the text. For Tsur's perception-oriented cognitive poetics, performance comes after and rearticulates prosody. If performed rhythm trumps idealized meter, tempo can be used to telescope or attenuate articulated rhythmic patterns.

Nonmetrical and polymetrical poems will have rhythms and shifts of pitch that are not necessarily apprehendable on the page even while they are foregrounded in performance and visible in waveform graphs. Rhythm and pitch/intonation are not something inherent in the alphabetic script of the poem, but are extended, modified, improvised, invented, or enacted in performance.

In his far-ranging discussion of the sounds and senses of Coleridge's "Kubla Khan," Tsur contrasts two cognitive modes of literary criticism, Negative Capability and Quest for Certainty.[5] For Tsur, critics who tend toward a Quest for Certainty display an intolerance of ambiguity, uncertainty, and multiple interpretative possibilities; a resistance to symbolism in favor of allegory; a perceptual dependence on the concrete and an inability to process multiple abstractions; a tendency to reduce a poem's meaning to a single level (a form of what I call frame lock); a propensity for "extreme" and "polarized evaluations, namely, good-bad, right-wrong, black-white" (18); "a greater insensitivity to subtle and minimal cues and hence a greater susceptibility to false but obtrusive clues" (18). Ambiguity intolerance is also associated with a desensitization to the nonthematized emotional dynamics of a poem, the very kinds of dynamics that are intensified in performance. Tsur notes that his categories are related to psychological studies of dogmatism and the authoritarian personality. I would add that they resonate with Wittgenstein's analysis of "aspect blindness" and George

5. *"Kubla Khan"—Poetic Structure, Hypnotic Quality, and Cognitive Style* (Amsterdam/Philadelphia: John Benjamins, 2006). See especially chap. 1, " 'Kubla Khan' and the Implied Critic's Decision Style." Tsur provides waveform analysis of pitch, amplitude, and intonation in chap. 4, "Vox Humana: Performing 'Kubla Khan.' "

Lakoff's distinction between the cognitive framework of the "strict father" and that of the "nurturing parent."[6] What distinguishes Tsur's study is its detailed critique of examples of literary criticism and its stress on the sound of poetry and poetic performance as a prod to interpretive uncertainty and emotional intensification.

Performance allows the poet to refocus attention to dynamics hidden within the scripted poem, refocusing emphasis and overlaying immanent rhythms. The performance opens up the potential for shifting frames, and the shift of frame is itself perceived as a performative gesture. The experienced poetry performer can't help but loop this experience back onto the compositional process. The implied or possible performance becomes a ghost of the textual composition, even if the transcriptive pull is averted, just as a reader can't help but hear an overlay of a previously sampled voice of the poet, a ghostly presence steaming up out of the visual script.

No consideration of the poetry reading can leave out the significance of the timbre of the poet's voice, yet the subject tends to elicit little more than a blank, if knowing, nod. Like the face of the poet, timbre is both out of the immediate control of an author and the best picture we have of the poet's aesthetic signature or acoustic mark. Camus is said to have remarked that after a certain age each person is responsible for her or his face. After a certain age, each poet is responsible for his or her voice. If timbre is a given dimension of a poet's performance, accent is a technical feature that can be used to perform and deform social distinctions and variations. For the modernist poetics of the Americas, the artifice of accent is the New Wilderness of poetry performance, that which marks our poetries with the inflection of our particular trajectories within our spoken language.

While script permits the poet to elide (if not disguise) accent, performance is an open wound of accentual difference from which no poet escapes. This is not the accent of stress but accents of distressed language, words scarred by their social origins and aspirations. The tension of iambic stress against the accents of the vernacular is one of hallmarks of Claude McKay's Jamaican dialect poems and a legacy of Paul Laurence Dunbar. In those cases, orthography was bent in service of the sound of the spoken language; but words spelt according to the standard can still be pronounced slant.

6. Wittgenstein, *Philosophical Investigations*, translated by G. E. M. Anscombe (New York: Macmillan, 1958), part 2. Lakoff, *Moral Politics: How Liberals and Conservatives Think* (Chicago: University of Chicago Press, 2002).

T. S. Eliot's "The Waste Land" might, at first or even second blush, appear to be the epitome of modernist impersonality. Eliot's own performance of his poem, originally called "He Do the Police in Voices," can be described as having as its baseline a deaccentuated voice that is haunted by the often sudden intrusion of accented voices:

> Marie, Marie, hold on tight.
> When Lil's husband got demobbed, I said—
>
> Speak to me. Why do you never speak?[7]

One answer is that when poetry does speak, those too enmeshed in the literary tradition either refuse to listen or just may be unable to hear, partly because it's not the speech they are accustomed to hearing; indeed it may not sound like voice or speech at all. Accented voices are easily dismissed as unrefined, crude, even ignorant, just as accented or deformed syntax may register as just noise.

Performance always exceeds script, just as text always outperforms audibility. The relation of script to performance, or performance to script, is necessarily discrepant, hovering around an anoriginal center in a complex of versions that is inherently unstable. Poetry readings proliferate versions of the poem, each version displacing but not replacing one another. As such, close listening presents an ongoing challenge to readings that, in their intolerance of ambiguity, associative thinking, and abstraction, reduce the poem to a single level of meaning, banishing from significance—as stray marks or noises—all but the literal or concrete.

Recognizing that a poem is not one but many, that sound and sense are as much at odds as ends, makes the study of poetry's sound a test case for midrashic antinomianism, a new approach to critical studies that I am launching here, and one that I am sure will take a prominent place in the general field of Bent Studies.

> Which is to say, to come to some conclusions
> A work of art always exceeds its material constructions
> As well as its idealizations

7. "The Waste Land," http://town.hall.org/Archives/radio/IMS/HarperAudio/011894_harp_ITH.html, accessed April 1, 2010.

Physical or digital instantiations
Anterior codes or algorithmic permutations
Experiences while reading or viewing are no more than weigh stations
And any number of interpretations, contexts of publications, historical
    connections—
All these have a charmed affinity
Clustering around a center that is empty

That empty center or blank space is the possibility of freedom.

OBJECTIVIST BLUES: SCORING SPEECH IN SECOND WAVE MODERNIST POETRY AND LYRICS

1. How Strange the Change from Major to Minor

Since I am interested in the conflict, as well as the interconnectivity, among poetic forms, the modernist period has drawn me again and again. I find the proliferation of new styles in the first decades of the twentieth century particularly interesting in the context of the more traditional styles that also flourished. I like to think of the period as having produced an epic collage poem of innovative and traditional poetry, popular verse, newly emerging styles of song lyrics, from blues to Tin Pan Alley, and also the linguistically accented talk forms emerging from vaudeville.

Perhaps the best representation of this collage is *American Poetry: The Twentieth Century*, the Library of America's two-volume anthology, which covers poets born from 1838 to 1913.[1] In a dialog published in *boundary 2* with Geoffrey O'Brien, the anthology's lead editor, I noted that one of the remarkable facets of this period is the reversal of fortune for many poetic forms and styles.[2] Some considered marginal and eccentric not only in their

Ward Phillips Lecture, Notre Dame, November 28, 2006. *American Literary History*, 20th Anniversary Issue, 20.1–2 (2008). Thanks to Gordon Hutner.
1. *American Poetry: The Twentieth Century*, 2 vols. (New York: Library of America, 2000). The advisory board for the anthology consisted of Robert Hass, John Hollander, Carolyn Kizer, Nathaniel Mackey, and Marjorie Perloff. Geoffrey O'Brien, the editor in chief of Library of America, coordinated the editorial team. The first volume goes from Henry Adams (born 1838) to Ezra Pound (born 1885) to T. S. Eliot (born 1889) to Dorothy Parker (born 1893); the second volume goes from e.e. cummings (born 1894) to May Swenson (born 1913).
2. This section is adapted from Geoffrey O'Brien and Charles Bernstein, "A Conversation," in *boundary 2* 28.2 (2001).

time but until relatively recently now seem the most influential, while lots of the presumed majors now look more like held-over corporals from the previous epoch. But perhaps even more intriguing is how the players with the smaller parts now look so indispensable.

The whole period, as presented by the Library of America anthologies, has an ensemble feeling, rather than a set of star turns or continuous highlights. It insists that poetry is for reading, and if all you want to do is skip to the so-called good parts, you are missing the story. This, in turn, strikes a blow against a still prevalent reading value for poetry—that the only thing that really matters is masterpieces, those precious few. To read poetry filtered in that way is to take it out of the social field, to deanimate not only poetry but also individual poems.

The spirit of poetry, not to say what matters about poetry, can only be experienced if one reads around in it, checking out not only the different types of work but also the different orders and measures of success. And this is because many readers will disagree about what is the best, accusing each other of perpetrating minors as majors, so that one never will really be able to come out with consensus on just exactly who those elect might be. The problem is with the idea of the "few" itself: poetry is a social field whose meaning comes, in part, from the relationship among poems. To remove that social field is to strip poems of the cultural context that lends them meaning. Yet you can only acknowledge this social field by very precise selections; indeed, judgments of quality not only are a required part of this activity but also are given a more active role. More, rather than less, judgment, articulation of preference, is required. If anthologies are something of a shell game, the point is not just to uncover the peas but to present the shells as well; otherwise you may find the dish ran away with the spoon.

Maybe you remember this story? A couple of critics were speaking of their ideal anthology. The first critic compared two anthologies. The first anthology was described as containing only the most perfect works, sublime content married to consummate craft. The other anthology was described as a ragtag and noisy affair of the good, the bad, and the promising, the overstated or too ambitious, the utterly discountable, and the at-best-OK. Finally, the second critic got up to speak and said she agreed completely with the first critic, that the two anthologies were accurately described. The one anthology was indeed very crowded and boisterous and, no question, the other was pristine and solitary, unmarred by imperfection. The only problem was that it was blank: there wasn't a single poem in it.

I read modernist American poetry in a comparatist frame that emphasizes technical invention. One of my persistent interests is the interplay between the vernacular, the colloquial, the ordinary, and the self-constructed syntax and vocabulary of the ideolectical; that is, the ideological play of dialects—real and imaginary—in American poetry. One way to trace this is to take the representation of speech in Paul Laurence Dunbar's African American and Claude McKay's early Jamaican dialect poems and run that against Oscar Hammerstein II's lyrics for *Show Boat* ("Ol' Man River") or DuBose and Dorothy Heyward and Ira Gershwin's more supple lyrics for *Porgy and Bess* ("Summertime" and "I Loves You Porgy"), James Weldon Johnson's early song lyric "Under the Bamboo Tree" and his later sermonic textualizations in *God's Trombone*, Fanny Brice's Yiddish schtick monologues (or Groucho Marx's Euro-ethnic ones), the virtually "Objectivist" blues of Robert Johnson or Charlie Patton, and the transcriptive works of Sterling Brown; or contrast these with the more fluid poetic vernacular of William Carlos Williams, Jean Toomer, and Langston Hughes, and the rebarbative anti-assimilationism of Louis Zukofsky's "Poem Beginning 'The,'" or Melvin Tolson's *Harlem Gallery: Book 1, The Curator*. Or then again jump to the other side of the Atlantic and look to Tolson's and Zukofsky's immediate contemporaries Basil Bunting and Hugh MacDiarmid, both of whom wrote major works in reinvented (or synthetic) local dialects, Northumbrian and Scots, respectively. From there, we might be able to consider, under the sign of sound poetry—that is, not as a matter of influence but of Second Wave Modernist refinement/revision—Cab Calloway's scat "Hi-De-Ho" as an ideolectical descendent of Velimir Khlebnikov's *zaum*, Kurt Schwitters's "Ur Sonata," and Hugo Ball's Dadaist "Karawane." My mix is certainly odd by most accounts. But there is something at the least fascinating in considering McKay and MacDiarmid and Groucho Marx, or Cole Porter and Patton and Brice, not to say Walter Benjamin and Ludwig Wittgenstein, all born in the first four years of my putative period.

I give this list not to be exhaustive—it's only the tip of the tongue—but to suggest the tensions between the oral, transcriptive, and textual, not to say popular and rebarbative, that gives so much resonance to the poetry of this period. Underlying the range of approaches is the formidable technical achievement of these literary artists, a technical achievement that needs to be read within the context of the emergence of mass literacy, the prevalence of second-language speakers of English, the new presence of sound reproduction technologies, and a generation of poets for whom poetry was as much an arena to resist cultural and linguistic assimilation as a place that marked such assimilation. In a sense, this period represents a reaccenting of English, but not by the English. Indeed, one of the primary sites of poetic invention in this period involved novel ways of alphabetically representing, or refusing, accentuated speech. In other words, identity is not so much constructed as performed.

2. Objectivist Blues

238 If horses could but sing Bach, mother,—

239 Remember how I wished it once—

240 Now I kiss you who could never sing Bach, never read Shakespeare.

. . . .

251 Assimilation is not hard,

252 And once the Faith's askew

253 I might as well look Shagetz just as much as Jew.

254 I'll read their Donne as mine,

255 And leopard in their spots

256 I'll do what says their Coleridge,

257 Twist red hot pokers into knots.

                        —Louis Zukofsky, "Poem beginning 'The'" (1926)[3]

In "Poem Beginning 'The,'" a very young Louis Zukofsky (born in 1904) writes of the temptation to assimilate into the "historically valued"[4] English literary tradition. "Assimilation is not hard," he tells his mother; but the burden of the poem is to register both the difficulty of resisting assimilation and the unexpected and irreparable costs of not resisting. The "The" of Zukofsky's poem is Eliot's "The Waste Land." Zukofsky's critique provides a very early and profound recognition of that poem as establishing a fault line for high culture that is self-defeating in its exclusion of the minor keys that Zukofsky's poem ludicly enumerates, from Bolsheviks and Broadway to Bach's horse play, from accented speech to unaccented meter. Zukofsky recognized that Eliot's poem, great as he undoubtedly thought it was, created an impasse for poetry in its wake, at least for those, talented or not, who found themselves on the outside of Eliot's brand of literary tradition.

3. "Poem beginning 'The'" in *Selected Poems*, edited by Charles Bernstein (New York: Library of America American Poets Project, 2006), 7–8.
4. To echo business theorist Clayton Christensen, quoted above in "Invention Follies."

Zukofsky grasped that radical modernism was, like racial modernism, inevitably connected to the multiplicities of spoken sounds. The burden of modernist composition was to articulate the range of sounds into fugal patterns, not purify the language. In his 1940 study for "A"-9, Zukofsky creates one of the wittiest and most trenchant dialect poems of Second Wave Modernism. "A foin lass bodders," his translation of Guido Cavalcanti's thirteenth-century poem "Donna mi prega" into Brooklynese (itself a foil for Yiddish dialect). The poem begs performance:[5]

> A foin lass bodders me I gotta tell her
> Of a fact surely, so unrurly, often'
> 'r 't comes 'tcan't soften its proud neck's called love mm . . .
> Even me brudders dead drunk in dare cellar
> Feel it dough poorly 'n yrs. trurly rough 'n
> His way ain't so tough 'n he can't speak from above mm . . .
> 'n' wid proper rational understandin' . . . (*Selected*, 152)

Zukofsky's dialect, one might even say schtick, translation of Cavalcanti is noisy, disruptive, brilliant, and unacceptable all rolled into one. Zukofsky is here responding to First Wave Modernist Ezra Pound's 1928 "traduction" (as he called it) of "Donna mi prega":

> Because a lady asks me, I would tell
> Of an affect that comes often and is fell
> And is so overweening: Love by name.
> E'en its deniers can now hear the truth,
> I for the nonce to them that know it call,
> Having no hope at all
> that man who is base in heart
> Can bear his part of wit . . .[6]

Pound's commentary on Cavalcanti, and in particular on "Donna mi prega," together with his translation of the poem, appeared first in *The Dial* (with the subtitle "Medievalism") in 1928; in 1934 it was collected in *Make It New*.

---

5. You can hear my performance of the poem at http://writing.upenn.edu/ezurl/5/ and Zukofsky's performance at http://writing.upenn.edu/ezurl/6/.

6. *Pound's Cavalcanti: An Edition of the Translations, Notes, and Essays*, edited by David Anderson (Princeton: Princeton University Press, 1983), 171.

Pound praises Cavalcanti as being more modern than Dante and also characterizes him as a radical and indeed "dangerous" figure, a "natural philosopher" in the sense of an atheist (he connects Cavalcanti to Averroes as well): proof by experience ("natural demonstration") not preordained authority.[7] This perhaps explains Cavalcanti's place in Zukofsky's "A"-9, in which his words and his canzone form are put in fugue-like arrangement with Marx and Spinoza, twin figures of radical Jewish secular thought. While Pound's transduction makes Cavalcanti come alive in quasi-idiomatic English rhythms that play to, while transforming, historically mediated standards of high lyric sonorousness, "A foin lass bodders" is obtrusively antiassimilationist, not to say dissident or antiabsorptive, both culturally and poetically. It is this twining of ethnic and aesthetic resistance, in both "A Poem beginning 'The'" and "A foin lass" that makes Zukofsky's work of such signal importance for the politics of poetic form in Second Wave Modernism.

Nowhere are the innovations of both assimilation and disruption more compelling than among the Second Wave Modernists, poets and comics, lyricists and blues artists born between 1889 and 1909. The dates are somewhat less arbitrary than they might at first appear, since they cover the first wave of response to many of the radical and disruptive innovations of the modernist poets and artists of the previous generation. You could call this postmodernism *avant la lettre*. Indeed, Second Wave Modernism may be the most profound critique we have of modernist art—not in theory but in practice. One element of this critique is certainly related to ideology and politics, and this is in a sense how we often receive these writers of the " '30s generation," as they may sometimes be called. In contrast, I want to point to how modernist art practices were both refined and deepened, questioned and extended. The work may sometimes seem less bold than its immediate forebears, and it is often less celebrated, but I would propose that the subtle and intensely technical innovations of the period remain foundational for present work.

One of my interests in focusing on Second Wave Modernism is to trouble the distinctions made both within and between high and low culture and to focus on a key category, the *in between*. The literary artists of this period were witness to, even participants in, the movement from folk and popular culture to mass culture and the culture industry. Distinguishing between popular and mass culture encourages a scrutiny of how mass culture was forged out of—both extending and betraying—popular and folk culture,

7. See Pound's 1928 essay "Cavalcanti" from *Make It New* in *Pound's Cavalcanti* (203–51).

though it also needs to be acknowledged that common concerns for the vernacular, as well as immediacy of experience, cut across these lines. By considering transitional works of popular and folk culture in the unfamiliar context of the radical technical innovations of Second Wave Modernist poetry, it's possible to recognize how the diction and form of these works resist or embrace, invent or reconceptualize, assimilation, that always vexing virtual horizon of American culture.

Let me start with a few comments on Second Wave Modernist Cole Porter's "You're the Top" from the 1934 show *Anything Goes* (Porter was born in 1891).[8] In his forging of the prewar American popular song, a precursor to, but not identical with, the American mass culture song of the postwar period, Porter's innovations included an exquisitely effervescent use of colloquial language that never marks itself as vernacular in the literary sense but passes by means of its urban wit. At the same time, Porter engages in a range of juxtapositions that take something from the Pound-Eliot paratactic playbook but with a distinctly anti- (or a-) canonical twist. Porter's heteronomous juxtapositions are renowned of course, but their charm should not detract from the marvelous, even devilish, cultural aggressiveness of their high/low conflations: an old Dutch Master with Mrs. Astor with Pepsodent, Dante with Durante, a Bendel bonnet and a Shakespeare sonnet or, outdoing himself one more time, the National Gallery—and what could be a more explicit symbol of the canon?—with Garbo's salary and then, in perhaps Porter's most memorable example of the nonpareil par excellence, cellophane, which he identifies, barely a beat away, as the sublime. Then again, consider the Red 1930s conflations of the political and its others in the rhyme of Mother Russia with a Roxy usher or Mahatma Gandhi with Napoleon Brandy.

If Frank O'Hara and John Ashbery can be credited with the "postmodern" inclusion of popular culture in their poems, it's hard to take in the history of such poetic peregrinations without a nod to Porter, even if it turns the distinction on its head given that Porter incorporates not the low in the high but the high in the low, or really leveling or parodying the distinction.[9] Indeed, Porter's collages of discrepant materials represent a shifting,

8. The Library of America anthology, vol. 1, includes three Porter lyrics—"I Get a Kick Out of You," "Anything Goes," and "Just One of Those Things." "You're the Top" is collected in *Reading Lyrics*, edited by Robert Gottlieb and Roger Kimball (New York: Pantheon, 2000).

9. This also makes Porter a precursor for Pop art. And with Porter's double entendres, the "homotextual" dimensions of his work are as startling and revelatory as those of his fellow Second Waver, Hart Crane (1899–1932), both Porter and Crane leading, after a fashion, to

an opening, of American social space as much as any poetry of the period, and his cosmopolitan élan might just be the medium or tone that allows this to be not polemical but intoxicating, even as it risks apolitical depolarization. On the one hand, "You're the Top" can be read as a refinement of the modernist innovators (and not only in terms of collage but also in the use of vernacular, or perhaps to say in a more Porteresque lingo, slang). On the other hand, the work is a form of disruptive innovation, since it brings into being a new, and ultimately dominant,[10] model for popular music, affecting production, style, and distribution at the same time, exploiting the new technologies for sound reproduction, including the phonograph record, the radio and voice amplification through the microphone. Invented just nine years before *Anything Goes* opened on Broadway, the microphone was used to magnificent advantage to create a new intimate sound—often with

---

Ashbery and O'Hara. "Love for Sale" is only the most emblematic of Porter's charting of "Love that's only slightly soiled"—"the wayward ways of this wayward town":

> Let the poets pipe of love
> in their childish way,
> I know ev'ry type of love
> Better far than they. (*Reading Lyrics*, 117)

The song is from the 1930 show *The New Yorkers*. According to Roger Kimball's *The Complete Lyrics of Cole Porter* (Cambridge: Da Capo Press, 1992), Porter at one point said "Love for Sale" was "his favorite Porter song." Kimball also reports that to get around objections to the song's propriety, the setting was changed from outside a white nightclub to Harlem's Cotton Club, and a black singer was substituted for a white singer (145). That singer, Second Waver Elisabeth Welch (born in 1904), was the child of a Scots mother and a father of "African and Native American" descent, according to the African American Registry, http://www.aaregistry.com/african_american_history/2268/She_could_Do_It_All_Elisabeth_Welch, accessed August 8, 2007. One of the most recent covers of the song intensifies, more than any other I know, the foreignness at its heart; perhaps it is not that surprising that the Brazilian musician and vocalist Caetano Veloso would—like Billie Holiday—bring out just how haunting and desolate "Love for Sale" is. Veloso includes the song on his album of American standards, *A Foreign Sound*, a 2004 Nonesuch release. Veloso knows just how to make the familiar strange.

10. The sexual image of a top and a bottom might also be thought of in terms of the newly emergent dominance of mass culture (one of Porter's tops is the Tower of Babel). At the same time, Porter's works suggest that the major and minor, the dominant and the submissive, master and slave are as much a psychosocial erotic continuum as terms of positive valuation. In Irving Berlin's "parody" version, written for his friend Porter, Berlin is nothing if not explicit in his rhymes for top: King Kong's penis, self-abuse, the starch in a groom's erection; in contrast to the bottom as "a eunuch / who has just been through an op." The parody is attributed to Porter in *Complete Lyrics* (171); Roger Kimball makes the correction in Porter's *Selected Lyrics*, edited by Kimball (New York: Library of American, 2006), 56.

songs by Porter—by such Second Wavers as Fred Astaire (born in 1899), and such younger singers as Frank Sinatra (born in 1915), and Billie Holiday (also born in 1915), among many others. All were "swooners" who swerved from the style of such "crooners" as Rudy Vallee (born just two years after Astaire).

American mass culture is founded (and founders) on a streamlining, not to say mainstreaming, of vernaculars, in order to forge a synthetic mass slang that is the antithesis of dialect, which remains marked by the local and unassimilated. Mass culture entails the absorption of dialect by refinement, assimilation, and ultimately standardization. The precarious distinction between popular (or folk) culture and mass culture retains force within the cultural field of mass-mediated culture even today, when bluegrass music can interpose itself as exemplary of folk or popular culture, in contrast to mass culture, as, for example, in the 2002 Grammy Awards with Ralph Stanley walk-on to Britney Spears's party. The backstory of that cultural hiccup, or momentary malabsorption, would require that I introduce into evidence Harry Smith's epic *Anthology of American Folk Music* (1952), a Homeric project, collecting and conceptualizing recordings made primarily in the late 1920s, the works of a set of singer/lyricists of a then-thriving American oral culture, almost all of whom are part of the Second Wave Modernist generation.

Before taking up Smith's anthology, I want to turn to a song I mentioned briefly, "Under the Bamboo Tree" (1902), composed by the First Wave Modernist team of Bob Cole, J. Rosamond Johnson, and James Weldon Johnson (born in 1871). "Under the Bamboo Tree" was a megahit of the day.[11] The song is notable for its setting "down in the jungles," featuring, "a Zulu from Matabooloo," who every morning sings to his beloved from under a bamboo tree. For those of you who may not be familiar with the location of Matabooloo—it's just a few miles from Passaic, right by the Orientalist Mall's Bamboo Court, which has only recently been renamed Bantu Court; the Voodoo Lounge is no longer open. What drove this song up the charts before the hit parade was even a glimmer in Dick Clark's mother's eyes is the catchy, just about unshakable refrain, reprised most famously by Judy Garland and Margaret O'Brien in *Meet Me in St. Louis*. Listen to Harry

11. See Thomas L. Morgan, "Bob Cole, J. Rosamond Johnson, and James Weldon Johnson" at http://www.jass.com/c&j.html, accessed November 26, 2006. The 1902 recording was made by Arthur Collins.

MacDonough and John Bieling's version of the song, recorded on February 27, 1903, by Victor Talking Machine (for a sound clip of "Under the Bamboo Tree" go to http://writing.upenn.edu/ezurl/1):

> Down in the jungles lived a maid,
> Of royal blood though dusky shade,
> A marked impression once she made
> Upon a Zulu from Matabooloo;
> And ev'ry morning he would be
> Down underneath the bamboo tree,
> Awaiting there his love to see,
> And then to her he'd sing:
>
> If you lak-a-me, lak I lak-a-you
> And we lak-a-both the same,
> I lak-a say, this very day,
> I lak-a-change your name;
> 'Cause I love-a-you and love-a-you true
> And if you-a love-a-me.
> One live as two, two live as one
> Under the bamboo tree.
> . . . .[12]

In this song, so much the prototype of the American popular song, we get a sort of undifferentiated pan-culturalism, which nonetheless is unmistakably African and whose refrain is a bepidginonated or perhaps nonsensicalized version of black dialect, invented, at least in part, by the author of *God's Trombone* (1927), perhaps the greatest translation, or transposition, of the African American oral sermon into modernist American poetry. "Under the Bamboo Tree" is a quasi-sound/scat poem accompanied by teasing eroti-

12. The lyric is included in the 2004 Library of America edition of James Weldon Johnson's *Writings*, 811–12; note that there is a typographical error in this printing: "One [not *once*] day he seized her" is correct. A website, *John Kendrick's Musicals 101*, provides an image of the cover page of the sheet music (as published by Jos. W. Stern & Co in New York in 1902) as well as a transcription of the lyrics, http://www.musicals101.com/lybambootree.htm, accessed Aug. 17, 2007; however, Kendrick misreads the attribution "By Cole and Johnson Bros" to mean Bob Cole and J. Rosamund Johnson rather than the Johnson brothers J. Rosamund and James Weldon.

cism, not to say exoticized racial fantasy (though this verse does not make it to the 1903 recording):

> And in this simple jungle way,
> He wooed the maiden ev'ry day,
> By singing what he had to say;
> One day he seized her and gently squeezed her . . .

Seized and squeezed is exactly the linguistic action of the poem: seizing the vernacular into Victorian song form so that it can be titillatingly squeezed—a formula that mass culture hasn't so much overcome as capitalized.

None other than the Ol' Possum heself, Mr. Thomas Stearns Eliot, seizes and squeezes this song in his 1932 unfinished poem "Sweeney Agonistes":

> SONG BY WAUCHOPE AND HORSFALL
> SWARTS AS TAMBO, SNOW AS BONES
>
> Under the bamboo
> Bamboo bamboo
> Under the bamboo tree
> Two live as one
> One live as two
> Two live as three
> Under the bam
> Under the boo
> Under the bamboo tree[13]

Rachel Blau DuPlessis discusses "Sweeney Agonistes" in terms of black and Jewish minstrelsy and vaudeville, with particular reference to Vachel Lindsay's "The Congo" in "'HOO, HOO, HOO': Some Episodes in the Construction of Male Whiteness."[14] Her essay charts the First Wave Modernist

13. T. S. Eliot, *The Complete Poems and Plays 1909–1950* (New York: Harcourt, Brace & World, 1971), 81.

14. *Genders, Races, and Religious Cultures in Modern American Poetry* (New York: Oxford University Press, 2001). In a subsequent chapter, "Wandering Jews: Melting Pots and Mongrel Thoughts," DuPlessis discusses the passage of Zukofsky's "Poem Beginning 'The'" cited here. Cultural mongrelization and miscegenation is a keynote of Second Wave Modernism; DuPlessis adeptly sets the stage in a discussion of First Wave Modernist Mina Loy's antiseminal poem "Anglo-Mongrels and the Rose" (1923–1925).

use of "hoodoo" and "voodoo" to mark racialized projections of the primi-tive, let's call it *jungleification*. Responding to Michael North's discussion, in *The Dialect of Modernism*, of Eliot's pastiche of "Under the Bamboo Tree," DuPlessis notes that the poet from St. Louis "acknowledges the power of Af-rican American popular culture in relation to other powerful theatrical tra-ditions" (193). *Hoodoo* and *voodoo* would melt into pop in the Second Wave lyrics of Johnny Mercer and Cole Porter, where the spondaic beat is not of the jungle but of the human heart. Consider Mercer's 1939 "Day In—Day Out"—"The same old hoodoo follows me about / The same old pounding in my heart / Whenever I think of you" (*Reading Lyrics*, 437); and Porter's ver-bally acrobatic charm-melos in his 1929 "You Do Something to Me"—"Let me live 'neath your spell, / Do do that voodoo that you do so well" (*Complete Lyrics*, 117). "Do do" secularizes and pragmatizes "voodoo." The charm of slang absorbs (sublimates?) the sting of dialect; the spell works. Or is it sub-lates, as the sharp demarcation of the discourse of master and slave seems to vanish before our ears? Porter shows perfect cultural pitch for the process: "You do something to me, / Something that simply mystifies me. / Tell me, why should it be / You have the pow'r to hypnotize me?"

It's not, then, such a huge jump from this First Wave Modernist era song to the modernist classics, Oscar Hammerstein II and Jerome Kern's *Show Boat* (1927), and Dubose and Dorothy Heyward's and George and Ira Gershwin's *Porgy and Bess* (1935).[15] (While Kern was born in 1885, Hammerstein was born in 1895, Ira Gershwin in 1896, and George two years later.) In "Ol' Man River," Hammerstein essentially took on the task of setting dialect vo-cabulary into the rhyming, metrically and tonally unified song form of a new musical genre emerging from the operettas of Victor Herbert and the

15. A smaller jump from "Under the Bamboo Tree" would be to a contemporary song, "Under the Matzos Tree: A Ghetto Love Song" (1907) by Alexander Carr and Fred Fisher, which was reissued on *Jewface*, a CD of comic, sometimes self-deprecating songs and schtick by Jewish performers, recorded from 1905 to 1924. Perhaps the most famous song on the album is Irving Berlin's 1916 "Cohen Owes Me 97 Dollars." Many of these songs used Yiddish dialect, or, if this is a difference that makes a difference in the context of dialect comedy, travesties of it. The 1906 "When Mose with His Nose Leads the Band" includes its own scat/vocable refrain: "Oy, oy, oy, oy / Mazel tov!"; *Jewface*, curated by Jody Rosen (N.p.: Reboot Stereophonic [RSR 006], 2006). The contemporary poet Thomas Fink takes up this tradition, with an idiolecti-cal twist, using Yiddish syntax and, in performance, intonation and accent, in his "Yinglish" poems—"We'll have snow April. Did / you ever have here April snow?": "Yinglish Strophes" 8, in *Clarity and Other Poems* (East Rockaway, NY: Marsh Hawk Press, 2008), 24; see also his *Yinglish Strophes 1–19* (New York: Truck, 2009).

American parlor songs of Paul Dresser ("On the Banks of the Wabash") and Stephen Foster before him. The setting of African American dialect into a familiar-sounding English verse prosody—into the stadium of a metrical, not to say Euclidian, acoustic space—bears a relation to the iambic pentameter (and hexameter) dialect poems of Dunbar and McKay. Hammerstein and Kern perform both a translation and transposition of this material. "Ol' Man River" is an explicitly heterogeneous, not to say dysraphic, work; indeed its hybridity, uncomfortable for and even offensive to some contemporary audiences, is prominently figured in the plot. *Show Boat* is, after all, about racial passing, about the status of miscegenation, about a person, who, like the show itself, is one-eighth black and seven-eighths white. But it is only in the soaring, projective operatic performance by Second Wave Modernist and noted African American political activist Paul Robeson (born in 1898) that the social formalism of the song is fully articulated.

Take a look at the reproduction of the facing pages on which this lyric appears in the Library of America anthology (see figure 2). (The anthology is sequenced by author's date of birth.) The verso page, from Abraham Lincoln Gillespie's marvelous post-Joycean collection of constructed words, could not be more fortunate from my point of view, especially since I discuss Gillespie in the context of McKay's dialect poetry in "The Poetics of the Americas" (this essay is the sequel). The lexicon on both pages is immediately odd, unfamiliar, estranged. In the case of the Gillespie's ideolectical, nonidentitarian language, this is the intended effect. Taken by itself, Hammerstein's lyric, written as a part of a score to be sung, not as a poem to be read on its own, suffers from a fundamental paradox: the closer we get to transcribing the actual sound of speech, the odder the transcription may appear. The dialect spelling looks strained if not condescending: if it gestures at a spoken language that is unselfconscious and fluid, it presents at the same time an ethnographic distortion or slur in the very method of its means of reproduction. In performance, however, much of this strangeness, though by no means all, disappears. And it is significant that the musical appears at a time when writing has been suddenly and radically replaced as a medium for reproducing and storing local speech and local song by the invention of a means of mechanical reproduction of sound—the tape recorder and the phonograph.

Listen to Robeson singing "Ol' Man River" in 1932, the exact same time as the recordings that Harry Smith collected were being made (for a sound clip of an excerpt from "Ol' Man River" go to http://writing.upenn.edu/ezurl/2):

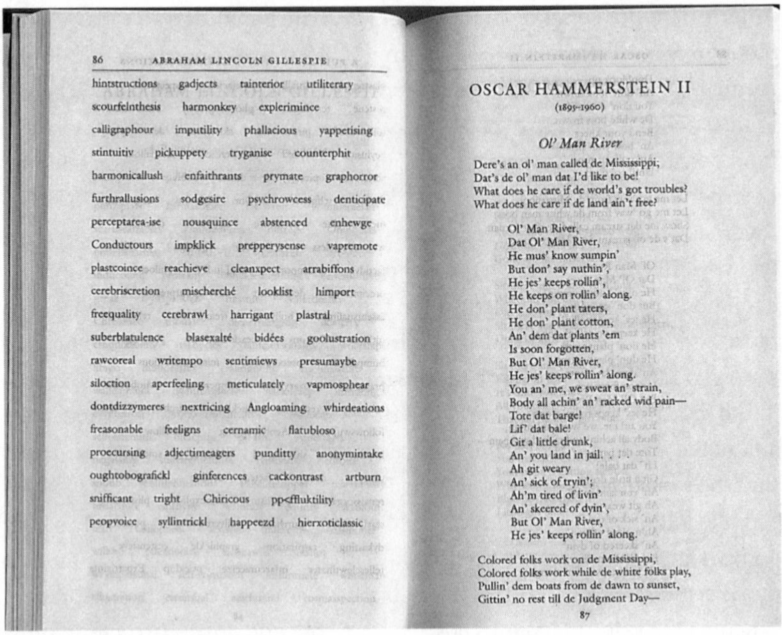

FIG 2   Gillespie and Hammerstein from Library of America's *American Poetry: The Twentieth Century* (New York: Library of America, 1993), 2:87–88.

Dere's an ol' man called de Mississippi'
Dat's de ol' man dat I'd like to be!
What does he care if de world's got troubles?
What does he care if de land ain't free?

Ol' Man River,
Dat Ol' Man River,
He mus' know sumpin'
But don' say nuthin,'
He jes' keeps rollin,'
He keeps on rollin' along.
. . . . .
You an' me, we sweat an' strain,
Body all achin' an' racked wid pain—
Tote dat barge!
Lif' dat bale!
Git a little drunk,
An' you land in jail. . . .

Ah gits weary
An' sick of tryin';
Ah'm tired of livin',
An' skeered of dyin' . . .
. . . .

—Library of America anthology (88–89)

Nowhere in *Show Boat* is the contrast stronger between the lexical markings of dialect and the very nonvernacular, highly enunciated singing style demanded by Kern and Hammerstein's score. The dialect is strictly in the words, not in their pronunciation, an odd but highly significant reversal, given that in speech the main mark of dialect is accent, not lexicon. In the 1932 studio recording, Robeson modifies Hammerstein's dialect lyrics, changing "git" to *you gets*, "land in jail" to *lands in jail*, "ah get" to *I gets*, and "jes" to *just*.[16] This oscillation among dialect, standard, and new standard dialect underscores both the fluidity and the incommensurability of the social layers that are dysraphicly fused together in the birth of popular song.

Robeson went on to use "Ol' Man River," over the following decades, as a theme for his radical racial and social politics, but not without turning the lyric on its head, in a collaboration *involuntaire* with Hammerstein. In a 1952 performance at a civil rights meeting in Chicago (and also at other concerts), Robeson sings just the initial four-line stanza and the twenty-four-line refrain, expeditiously eliding the reference to "Colored folks" that starts the next stanza. In the quatrain, he blows away Hammerstein's spirituals-inflected, let's-forget-our-troubles-and-watch-the-river-flow-there's-a-better-world-on-the-other-side-of-the-River-Jordan fatalism by negating the identification with the river in the second line—"Dat's de ol' man dat I'd like to be!"—singing, in its place, "That's the ol' man I don't like to be!," while

16. There are similar differences between the "official" Hammerstein lyric published by Library of America and *Reading Lyrics* and the 1928 vocal score of the London production that first featured Robeson: "Don'" is *don't*, "git" is *gits*, and "skeered" is *scared*; see Jerome Kern and Oscar Hammerstein 2nd, The Theater Royal Drury Lane Production of *Show Boat*, vocal score (London: Chappell; New York: T. B. Harms, 1928), 53–64. There are a number of recordings of Robeson singing "Ol' Man River," and innumerable versions by a vast array of singers, from Ray Charles to Rosemary Clooney to Frank Sinatra, most of whom modify the dialect. The first recording of the song was by Bing Crosby, with the Paul Whiteman orchestra, in 1928; Crosby, in his thin and jaunty version, averts Hammerstein's dialect. Judy Garland, performing the song on her early 1960s TV show, had mainstreamed (not to say whitewashed) the song to such an extent that it retained almost no hint of Hammerstein's dialect.

at the same time standardizing the pronunciation of the definite article in the final two lines of the stanza, singing *the* not "de."[17] In place of one of the troubling stereotypes in the lyric, "Git a little drunk / An' you land in jail," Robeson sings, "You show a little grit / An' you lands in jail." He completes his call to action by replacing "Ah git weary / An' sick of trying" with—

> But I keeps laughin'
> Instead of cryin'
> I must keep fightin'
> Until I'm dyin' . . .[18]

. . . and that old person river . . . well, it just keeps roiling along . . .

In his concert programs, as they evolve over his career, Robeson lifts his material up and out of its initial context, creating a panethnic and multinational—in short internationalist—frame for the many folk and popular songs he performs. For Robeson, the operatic voice, with its deep bass resonances, is the vehicle of internationalism, while the local accents of individual songs are—in Ezra Pound's sense—luminous details. Enormous respect—not to say affection—is given to the particulars, and yet the transcending grandeur of Robeson's voice marks something beyond the particulars, something utopic. Robeson performs spirituals not as a re-creation of the direct, heart-rending, expression of an enslaved group but as art songs, as a classically trained singer might perform Schubert lieder. This is why his singing is so inspirational but at the same time unsentimental. In a late concert, Robeson can segue directly from a Russian folk song ("The Song of Volga Boatman") to a spiritual ("Deep River") to "St. Louis Blues" to "Kaddish" to Beethoven's "Ode to Joy" to a Chinese children's song to an American folk song ("John Henry") to a militant labor anthem ("Joe Hill") to a

---

17. According to Robeson's son, Paul Robeson, Jr., Robeson began altering the lyrics "during the civil rights struggle of the 1940s." See Robeson, Jr.'s liner notes to *The Odyssey of Paul Robeson*, a CD compilation produced by Seymour Soloman and Robeson, Jr. (New York: Omega Classics [OCD 3007], 1992). Martin Duberman, in his biography *Paul Robeson* (New York: Alfred A. Knopf, 1988), dates the first changes to 1935, at the time of the film version of *Show Boat*, and, in part, at the suggestion of his lifelong friend, leftist Freda Diamond (604–5).

18. Duberman documents Robeson's introduction of this change at a concert in support of the anti-Fascist Spanish Republicans at Albert Hall (in London) in December 1936 (213–14). He quotes Hammerstein's 1949 response: "As the author of these words, I have no intention of changing them or permitting anyone else to change them. I further suggest that Paul write his own songs and leave mine alone" (604).

Broadway standard to a recitation from Shakespeare's *Othello*.[19] The result is a virtually Poundian montage, but with a Popular Front ideology: discrepant particulars—radically mixing high, folk, and popular culture—are connected both through the medium of Robeson's elegiac voice and through his strongly articulated aesthetics of musical relationships through contrast and conflict. Robeson's concerts construct a utopian space in which solidarity and struggle move us closer to imagining a just world. And such struggle begins with an abiding, unbreachable, commitment to "historical and contemporary particulars," to use a phrase of Zukofsky's.[20]

The act of rearticulating—translation through performance and transmission through resounding and replaying—is fundamental to the process initiated in Robeson's performance as well as in the work of a number of jazz musicians and vocalists in their performances of versions of "standards" (as they are still called) with lyrics by Hammerstein, Gershwin, Porter, and other Tin Pan Alley writers. Consider, for example, Nina Simone's signature performance of "I Loves You Porgy," in which she restandardizes the lyric to "I Love You, Porgy," as indeed Billie Holiday does in her own performance of the song. Consider too that the Gershwins refined themselves by Anglicizing their names, which in their school days were Jacob and Israel Gershvin, an assimilationist practice that was common at the time. The translation of Jake and Izzy to George and Ira certainly makes for a fascinating rhythm. *But youse certoinly cain't get vehry far on duh greht vite vay with ah noime like dat.* Indeed, many of the songs we call jazz standards are just such reinscriptions, though translation and improvisation, of songs by Hammerstein and Gershwin and Porter, not the least of which are the re-versionings of

---

19. Speaking of the segues in one of his concerts of the late 1950s, Robeson notes "the likeness of the music of various peoples": *The Odyssey of Paul Robeson*, track 23. This echoes similar comments Robeson made starting as early as 1929 (Duberman, 121). The next *Odyssey* track (24) introduces Robeson's lamentation of Jewish oppression, Levi Yitzhak of Berditchev's "Hassidic Chant," an eighteenth-century rearticulation of "Kaddish" that is also known as "Din Toyre mit Got" ("The Lawsuit with God"). Robeson says that it is "very much like the sermons in the Negro church." Robeson's pancultural commitment to folk songs was in full evidence by 1934 (Duberman, 176–78). Robeson's 1958 Carnegie Hall concerts are the best-known example of his late-style concert organization, which can usefully be contrasted to Harry Smith's folk anthology of the same period. For a discussion of "Hassidic Chant," as well of Robeson's concert programs, see Jonathan D. Karp, "Performing Black-Jewish Symbiosis: The 'Hassidic Chant' of Paul Robeson," in *American Jewish History* 91.1 (2003): 53–81.

20. Zukofsky uses this phrase in "An Objective," collected in *Prepositions* (Middleton, CT: Wesleyan University Press, 2001), 12.

Porter's "Night and Day" (1934), with its opening spondaic verse, simply dropped by Billie Holiday in one recording:[21]

> Like the beat beat beat of the tom-tom
> When the jungle shadows fall (*Reading Lyrics*, 118)

Just how far this Second Wave lyric is from the crude but mold-breaking First Wave jungleification of Vachel Lindsay's 1914 "The Congo: A Study of the Negro Race" is the measure of Porter's exquisite assimilationist aesthetic of cultural absorption.[22]

The American songbook "standards" of Second Wave Modernism have the peculiar history of rearticulations (aka covers) across the political and aesthetic spectrum, from bebop to Mantovani. (The British conductor Annunzio Mantovani, whose rigorous practice of taking out the highs and lows of lowbrow and highbrow music alike to create a smooth and sedating sonic wash that is the ultimate symbol of Cold War middlebrow culture, was himself a Second Waver, born in Italy in 1905.) Unlike language standards that are models of correct articulation, the American standard songs are open invitations to radical stylistic otherings. They are virtual tokens of Emersonian moral perfectionism, a constellation of interchanging variations that together suggest the unfinishable possibilities of community.

But now it's time to return to St. Louis, or at least to the "St. Louis Blues" by W. C. Handy (born 1873), which is often considered to be the first blues song. The song was published in 1914, the same year as Lindsay's "Congo." I want to contrast Handy's foundational First Wave Modernist song, and especially his performance of it, with Charlie Patton's paradigmatic Second Wave Modernist work, "High Water Everywhere," which, like Robeson's performance and Smith's recordings, were recorded in the late 1920s. In Handy's performance of his "St. Louis Blues," he incorporates many of the harmonizing elements of the Victorian parlor song: voice is projected over the melody; melody exists as separate from the lyric rather than as an extension of the lyric; tone, melody, and lyric are harmonized, subordinated

---

21. According to Michael Steinman, John Hammond produced the 78 rpm recording on December 13, 1939; Steinman notes that the opening lines might have been cut, at Hammond's suggestion, due to the time limitations of the disc (personal communication, September 23, 2008).

22. PennSound has made available a recording of Lindsay reading "Congo," http://writing.upenn.edu/pennsound/x/Lindsay.html, accessed May 1, 2007.

to one another. The figure of the words is set off against the ground of the music. In the Library of America anthology, the lyrics look like this (for a sound clip of "St. Louis Blues," go to http://writing.upenn.edu/ezurl/3):

I hate to see de ev'nin' sun go down,
Hate to see de ev'nin' sun go down,
'Cause ma baby, he done lef dis town,

Feelin' tomorrow lak ah feel today,
Feel tomorrow lak ah feel today,
I'll pack my trunk make ma gitaway. (vol. 2, p. 89)

"St. Louis Blues" creates a song form that is unified, prosodically consistent, and sonorous. It creates a Euclidian or proscenium space that is projective in its centripetal force. The setting is formal and reproducible. Handy sings in a melodic falsetto that is projective in the way of trained singers. (Robeson's performance of "St. Louis Blues" is structurally similar to Handy's, but Robeson is even more operatic than Handy.) The metrical structure exists independently of the performance, suggesting a continuum with the setting of dialect or vernacular within a received metrical structure in Dunbar, McKay, Johnson, and Hammerstein.

In contrast, the work of Second Wave Modernist Charlie Patton (1891[?]–1934) breaks drastically from almost all of these features, in ways that make his songs resonant with radical developments among other Second Wave Modernists. His sound is not separable from his words but emerges from them and returns to them. The timbre or grain of voice is foregrounded over both the tune and enunciation of the words. Patton actively works to collapse the separation between figure and ground, between lyric and melody, between song and singer, and between voice and projection. The acoustic equivalent of perspective is thwarted. The effect is of a radical acoustic flattening—a feature sometimes noted as "muddiness." Listen to Patton singing "High Water Everywhere" (sound clip at http://writing.upenn.edu/ezurl/4). During his second recording session in October 1929, Patton literally inscribed his song by means of a needle writing directly onto a wax master, singing into a sixty-centimeter wide, eight-foot-long plywood horn that was attached to the needle.[23]

---

23. Keith Briggs and Alex Van Der Tuuk describe the session in the booklet that accompanies *The Definitive Charley Patton* (UK: Catfish Records, 2001). (Patton's name is frequently

The song is not projected by convex force into the Euclidian or three-dimensional space of the proscenium theater but resonates within the body; it is almost as if the sound-shape is two-dimensional or concave. Body and voice are one; or, to put it in more formal terms, Patton plays the body as an instrument—typically against the grain, emphasizing the artifice of noise over the fluidity of voice. The song has no inner or outer; it starts in the middle and stays there. The singing is inwardly directed in constructing the song out of its vocal materials; as such it is nonprojective or introjective. The melody is not detachable from the words, does not accompany the words, but rather comes out of the words. Its musical shape is created primarily by rhythm, making the work, formally, as close to sound poetry as to the emerging styles of popular and folk song. At the same time, its rhythmic base also marks the origins of this style in African American field shouts, work songs, and chants of the nineteenth century, with their rhythmically intoned vocables serving as acute temporal markings. Patton's words also oscillate into vocables, which is to say become indecipherable, as he plays the signal-to-noise ratio almost as one would play an instrument. Indeed, there is a kind of sonic Fauvism or brutism emerging here.

Patton's nonprojective singing is not a matter of reduced volume, as it is, for example, in the emergent informal and intimate singing made possible by the introduction of microphone amplification in 1925. Patton's volume can be substantial, but the vocalization emanates from the body and is not separated out into a vocal stream; the sound is contained and suffused. Patton's guttural soundings are by now highly influential. He sings in and through his throat not, as with a conventionally trained voice, up from his diaphragm and out from his mouth. Like Robert Johnson, he overlays his singing with various noise effects that interrupt any continuous melodic production: talking, grunts, inhalations, interjections, improvisatory rather than formulaic repetitions, variations, extensions, and rephrasings, incommensurable switches of tempo, pitch, volume, and tone.

In his foundational study of Patton's work, John Fahey notes a stunningly innovative use of disjunctive, recombinant lyric patterning in which Patton improvisationally samples and recombines phrases and lines without apparent reference to conventional narrative or grammatic continuity or

---

given as "Charley.") A transcript of the improvised lyric is included in vol. 1 of the Library of America anthology. The visceral subject of "High Water Everywhere" is the catastrophic Great Mississippi Flood of 1927.

coherence.[24] Such nonlinear, or serial, lyric composition bears a close resemblance to the collage technique of radical modernist poetry, creating a body of work as inventive in its ludicly inchoate, disruptive force as any of its poetic counterparts.

No metrical structure exists external to the song's unfolding. The rhythm and acoustic patterning is dominant but also irregular from the point of view of conventional prosody, emerging from the poiesis, from the materialization of the song, out of the active, inventive, wording process in a practice of errant wandering and acoustic probes. The music doesn't take the words on a flight of sound but rather brings the words home, back to themselves, to ourselves. Here, I see an affinity between this work and Zukofsky's poetics, particularly his conception of sincerity and objectification, articulated for the first time in an essay published within a couple of years of the recording of "High Water Everywhere": sincerity—song as an extension of its poiesis of self-making; and objectification—structural solidity of the singer/song intertwined into a single figure.

To transpose my account of Zukofsky's poetics, "objectification" marks an insistence on "the detail, not mirage" of hearing ; the desire is to represent not the appearance of nature but its conditions—autonomy, completeness, self-sufficiency, particularity. "Sincerity" is not an affect but the truth in the materials: "thinking"—and here say "singing"—"with things as they exist," where things are not only objects but also persons. Sincerity and objectification are means of grappling with the structures and conditions through which things come into perception and by means of which we come into contact with them and live alongside them.[25]

"High Water Everywhere," then, is a form of sprung or informalist, if not to say Objectivist, verse. Patton's vernacular is not something set to music but is infused with it, far from what James Merrill has praised as the felicitous iambic pentameter of Handy's "St. Louis Blues."[26] I use the term "informalism" advisedly, thinking of Bruce Andrews's extension, in his

24. *Charley Patton* (London: Studio Vista, 1970).

25. This passage is adapted from my foreword to Zukofsky's collection of essays, *Prepositions*, cited above. See "An Objective" and its 1932 source, "Sincerity and Objectification: With Special Reference to the Work of Charles Reznikoff."

26. Merrill's "The Education of the Poet" is cited in Raymond R. Patterson, "The Blues," in *An Exaltation of Forms: Contemporary Poets Celebrate the Diversity of Their Art*, edited by Annie Finch and Kathrine Varnes (Ann Arbor: University of Michigan Press, 2002). The quotations in the next paragraph are from this essay, 191.

essay in *Close Listening*, of Adorno's idea of "constructivist noise or athematic 'informal music.' "[27]

In "The Education of the Poet," Merrill takes on the ideolectical/free verse issue directly, by contrasting Handy's pentameter to the "new measure" of Pound, Williams, Ashbery, and Allen Ginsberg. "The pentameter—so went the argument—wasn't a truly American line. I had to wonder if these patriots had ever heard the blues. 'I hate to see the evening sun go down'—wasn't that an effortless and purely native music?" Handy, in his own account of the origin of this song in the recording, is at great pains to show the effort and resistance embedded in the song, and specifically those lines, which evoke the pain of a homeless man facing another cold night on the streets. But Merrill is certainly right to associate Handy with that aspect of African American poetry that wedded itself to the pentameter, from Paul Laurence Dunbar to Claude McKay's early Jamaican poems to Countee Cullen.[28] This, though, is only one part of the blues, and surely one of the bluest parts. It's as if one associated jazz with swing rather than "free" jazz or Dadaist noise music. In poetry, in the broadest terms, the contrast is Dunbar and Cullen versus Sterling Brown, on the one hand, and Jean Toomer or Langston Hughes, on the other. In political terms, Booker T. Washington versus W. E. B. DuBois. In any case, what is native to America is always synthetic, not to say syncretic. The pentameter is always a device, and its meaning has to be not read, but heard, socially, in terms of its aesthetic motivation.

In looking at the Patton lyrics in the Library of America anthology, it is important to note that the text is not Patton's creation; his inscription was with a needle on a wax master, not a pen on a blank page. Patton is a pioneer of the new age of phonographic reproduction. The Library of America creates a place marker in its collection; its transcription uses the alphabet, an earlier form of language reproduction technology that is clearly not up to the task at hand. The significance of its inclusion in the anthology is in part to mark that writing has been superseded in its function of scoring speech. Indeed, this is not a script to be performed, but a transcription after the fact of performance. It is documentation that supports the primary work, which is not the lost "live" performance but the fabricated acoustic recording.

---

27. "Informalism," in *Close Listening: Poetry and the Performed Word*, edited by Charles Bernstein (New York: Oxford University Press, 1998), 73.
28. I outline this in "The Poetics of the Americas," in *My Way: Speeches and Poems* (Chicago: University of Chicago Press, 1999); this essay is a sequel to "The Poetics of the Americas."

3. Get Ready for Saints

Cole Porter's "How strange the change from major to minor" could be the theme song of Second Wave Modernism, where minor keys struck major chords.[29] If Porter, in his songs, included the high in the low, then Danny Kaye's and Second Waver Louis Armstrong's rollicking (and deliriously scripted) version of the African American spiritual "When the Saints Go Marching In" in the 1959 movie *The Five Pennies* is the ultimate anthem of such cultural miscegenation, here brought to a crescendo by the Jewish Kaye singing side-by-side with Armstrong, the icon of African American classical music.[30] (Kaye, born David Daniel Kaminsky in 1913, is four years too young to be a full-fledged Second Waver.) At one point, the younger Tin Pan Alley crooner impersonates the classic jazz singer (including the famous handkerchief-on-mouth), to which Armstrong remarks, in an aside, "Is this cat digging me, face and all?" (See figure 3.) In this (Levinasian?) moment, Kaye dialogically redefines by refining—*yet without redeeming*—Al Jolson's blackface "Jazz Singer."[31] Armstrong and Kaye riff on popular figures of European classical music—"Chopin—*solid man . . .* Mozart—*with the symphonies and operas and all that jazz . . .* Rimsky—*of coursikov . . .* Ravel and Gustav Mahler—*but don't forget Fats Waller . . . put Liszt on that list . . .* Haydn [pronounced Hidin']—*well let him come out! . . .* Khachaturian—*gesundheit . . . ,*" ending the performance with an ecstatic dose of ideolectical, aka scat, mayhem.

"Who's gonna play on the day when the saints go marching in?" Armstrong sings, envisioning a messianic, not to say apocalyptic, moment of judgment and redemption in which Western high culture marches into paradise side by side with jazz and Broadway. "I want to be in that number": elect but more profoundly, *company.* Being in the number does not elevate the "other" but rather democratizes the "high," brings the "high" and "low"

29. "Ev'ry Time We Say Goodbye," *Complete Lyrics*, 362.

30. *The Five Pennies*, directed by Melville Shavelson (Paramount, 1959).

31. In *Mandy Patinkin*, his 1989 debut CD (Sony), Patinkin puts Jolson front and center of his pastiche of bathos in American popular song, doing covers of a number of Jolson's signature songs, recontextualizing them within an eclectic range of his characteristic over-the-top performances of classics and novelty numbers. Somewhere over the rainbow, emotional artifice is a covering angel for American bifacial aspiration, tainted by racialist masks but opening toward what Melvin Tolson called "the racial ballad in the public domain." Or isn't it pretty to think so. (Tolson citations from the epigraph to sec. 4 [note 32], pp. 154–55, below.)

FIG 3   Louis Armstrong and Danny Kaye. Still from *The Five Pennies* (1959).

(sacred and profane, standard and aberrant) into the space of the people (*demos*), the commons. Amidst the final scat, the singers exclaim to each other, "Oh too high! Oh too low!," meaning the notes but also the cultural referents. It is an exuberant moment not so much for popular culture (in terms of which this is nothing special), but for high culture.

Cultural miscegenation (the mixing of types) is in dialectical relation to assimilation. Miscegenation, insofar as it is marked by difference, resists assimilation. But miscegenation is also assimilation by means of absorption; call it, the syncretic. Conceptualized as a function, assimilation has as its utopian upper limit Emersonian moral perfectionism, whose horizon is the new or invented, in the sense of emergent or not yet realized (possibly not realizable). The dystopian lower limit is absorption into the dominant culture without a trace of the constituent parts, the fantasy of the total dissolution of otherness into the mirage of the preexisting; call it the *final solution* by other means.

4. Incognegro

I knew
About the split identity
Of the People's Poet—
The bifacial nature of his poetry:

The racial ballad in the public domain
And the private poem in the modern vein.

—Melvin Tolson, *Harlem Gallery*[32]

The social trauma inscribed by accent and assimilation is resolved, in American poetry, only at the cost of repression, a repression that manifests itself in both a celebration of identity and a despair at identity's loss. This remains a fundamental condition for American poetry, one which finds its signature moment in Langston Hughes's identification and distance from the singer of "The Weary Blues." Code switching, from vernacular to standard, from slang to formal, is a part of American life as common as having clothes from the Gap and Brooks Brothers in the same closet. But poetry takes nothing for granted when it sacrifices the ease of the given on the hooks of the difficult. The title poem of D. S. Marriott's *Incognegro* offers both demonstration and instruction in such difficulties.[33] In and around 1990, Marriott published a few startling chapbooks that while identifiable with a kind of Cambridge (UK) style, seemed to eviscerate the very grounds of their own expression. As some of these works resurface in *Incognegro*, their lyric abjection and loneliness swell into unsung song. These poems, revised and collected, become palimpsests, overlaying personal anguish with the social terror of racism, and the historical trauma of slavery. Marriott teaches in Santa Cruz, grew up in England, and has parents from Jamaica. "Incognegro" offers a startling alternation, line by line, of marked black dialect against its lexically standard lyric twin, each line reciprocally mirroring the pain of the other's deformance. The poem internalizes the alternation of

32. *"Harlem Gallery" and Other Poems*, edited by Raymond Nelson (Charlottesville: University Press of Virginia, 1999), 335. The Curator, a central character of Tolson's poem, is speaking of the poem's poet, the Cab Calloway namesake Hideho Heights. In a 1965 radio interview, Tolson comments: "The Curator is of Afroirishjewish ancestry. He is an octoroon, who is a Negro in New York and a white man in Mississippi. Like Walter White, the late executive of the NAACP, and the author of *A Man Called White*, the Curator is a 'voluntary' Negro. Hundreds of thousands of Octoroons like him have vanished into the Caucasian race—never to return. This is a great joke among Negroes. So Negroes ask the rhetorical question, 'What man is white?'" Quoted in Joy Flasch, *Melvin B. Tolson* (New York: Twayne Publishers, 1972), 100; cited in Kathy Lou Schultz, *"In The Modern Vein": Afro-Modernist Poetry and Literary History* (Doctoral dissertation, Department of English, University of Pennsylvania, 2006). *Harlem Gallery* was first published in 1965, but was probably started in the 1930s and then put aside for a couple of decades.

33. *Incognegro* (Cambridge: Salt Publishing, 2006).

dialect and standard in Dunbar, making a Möbius strip of the either/or dynamic of mastering form/deforming mastery that is at the heart of Houston Baker's *Modernism and the Harlem Renaissance*.

> Back-a-yard is wey de fuss is,
> and the moon bright in the scuffed mirror.
> Me nuh see wha a gwan,
> but the glass reflects what is real and what is not.
>
> Dem sey dem feel involve
> even though pity is missing from the gaze,
> a lapse, a density, as the bizzies armlock him,
> so him put up nuh fuss, an dem candemn im to damnashan,—
>
> the thought of calling her mobile
> for our own peace of mind, only.
> Wi look like wi headin back to de grave,
> but the soul is so unlikely a captive,
>
> dem nieda see nor do dem feel
> the smoke above the ash trees, the banks of fog,
> de time incognegro an nat a dyam ting
> but silence at the other end of the line.
>
> Im sit wid us in the dark, de man nuh respec us,
> the fault is in the cold night air,
> in the grim, deep and unsettling form of the mirror.
> Di pathos an disenchantment, undastan, lass beyan rekonin.

"Incognegro" is a fiercely formal study of the poetics of subjection, assimilation, lyric authority, and historical double-consciousness. The particular closed poetic economies of Derek Walcott and J. H. Prynne just part of the background against which Marriott weaves his cries—not just of the heart but of history. "Incognegro" does not permit any settling into a single mode in its unforgiving demonstration of the disguises of voiced voicelessness. The result is both incendiary fire and cold logic.

Radical formal innovation in modernist and contemporary art has, at times, been seen as undermining the aesthetic, but it is more accurate to say that such work reinvents the aesthetic for new readers and new contexts. It's the refrain. We have constantly to reinvent our forms and vocabularies so that we don't lose touch with ourselves and the world we live in. The need for change in art is prompted by changes in the social and economic environment. The responses of the past are not always able to grapple with the present. Second Wave Modernism may be understood in this context as part of a continuing struggle to reinvent modernism for present times and present conditions, often in specific response to challenges posed by First Wave Modernists. Its technical innovations are an ongoing witness and adjustment to the social dislocation and relocations of the contemporaneity, the pressure of reality.[34]

34. Williams Carlos Williams (born 1883), ends "To Elsie," from *Spring and All*, "No one / to witness / and adjust, no one to drive the car": *The Collected Poems*, vol. 2, *1939–1962*, edited by Christopher MacGowan (Princeton: Princeton University Press, 2001), 217–18. In "The Noble Rider and the Sound of Words," Wallace Stevens (born 1879) writes of "the pressure of reality": *Collected Poetry and Prose* (New York: Library of America, 1997), 643–45.

The Fate of
the Aesthetic

It is likewise probable that the pre-ecstatic euphoria constituted one of the universal sources of lyric poetry. In preparing his trance, the shaman drums, summons his spirit helpers, speaks a "secret language" or the "animal language," imitating the cries of beasts and especially the songs of birds. He ends by obtaining a "second state" that provides the impetus for linguistic creation and the rhythms of lyric poetry. Poetic creation still remains an act of perfect spiritual freedom. Poetry remakes and prolongs language; every poetic language begins by being a secret language, that is, the creation of a personal universe, of a completely closed world. The purest poetic act seems to re-create language from an inner experience that, like the ecstasy or the religious inspiration of "primitives," reveals the essence of things. It is from such linguistic creations, made possible by pre-ecstatic "inspiration," that the "secret languages" of all the mystics and the traditional allegorical languages later crystallize.

MIRCEA ELIADE, *SHAMANISM: ARCHAIC TECHNIQUES OF ECSTASY*, TRANS.
WILLARD R. TRASK

You'd never know it
But buddy, I'm a kind of poet
And I've gotta lotta things to say.
JOHNNY MERCER, "ONE FOR MY BABY AND ONE MORE FOR THE ROAD"

Poets are fakers
Whose faking is so real
They even fake the pain
They truly feel
AFTER FERNANDO PESSOA

McGANN AGONIST

At the heart of a crisis in contemporary literary criticism is the systematic use of "text" for "poem." According to Jerome McGann, a *poem* is a social event—a *work* of literature—embedded in a dynamic, multilayered historical and ideological context. In contrast, a *text* is a deanimated linguistic structure—a *document*—removed from sociohistorical context. "What we ought to see," says McGann in *The Beauty of Inflections*, "is that 'text' is the linguistic state of the 'poem's' existence. No poem can exist outside of a textual state any more than a human being can exist outside of a human biological organism. But just as a person is not identical to a particular body, so neither is a poem equal to its text" (22).

This metaphor suggests a parallel between New Criticism and behaviorism; both collapse the operant distinction between a mechanism (*behavior*) and a function (*action*). McGann's polemic takes up the philosophical and political imperatives of Bakhtin, asserting that language is a social act and meaning is interdependent on social context; it offers an alternative to imagining language as a formal system in which meaning is derived by a variety of internal differentiations.

McGann's "historically based critical procedure" represents one of the most comprehensive and sophisticated efforts in academic literary criticism to reverse the dehistoricizing and depoliticizing tendencies not only in New Critical "close reading" but also in structuralist and poststructuralist "textualizations." The goal is not to reject, wholesale, these heterogeneous developments but rather to incorporate them, where possible, into a historical program that would radically alter the practice of literary criticism

Three books by Jerome McGann are discussed in this essay: *The Romantic Ideology: A Critical Investigation* (Chicago: University of Chicago Press, 1983); *A Critique of Modern Textual Criticism* (Chicago: University of Chicago Press, 1983); and *The Beauty of Inflections: Literary Investigations in Historical Method and Theory* (Oxford: Clarendon Press, 1985). *Sulfur* 15 (January 1986).

by redressing the current schism between textual and bibliographic scholarship (investigations of the history of the text and reception of the work) and literary criticism (that is, interpretation). For McGann, textual and bibliographic research is not preliminary and incidental to the interpretation of literary works; it is a basic part of the interpretative act. That is, its function is not simply textual emendation but, more importantly, establishing the significance of the context of publication. As McGann repeatedly shows, the same text has different meanings—*is a different poem*—depending on where and when it appears.

In 1983, McGann published two short books, *A Critique of Modern Textual Criticism* and *The Romantic Ideology*, aimed at making a decisive intervention within the practices of textual scholarship and literary criticism, respectively. Because these books are akin to legal briefs—summarizing major positions and formulating an alternative, ideologically self-conscious program—they emphasize how seriously McGann takes the precedence of historical engagement over "pure theory"; that is, they demonstrate his commitment to sociohistorical *reflection* as an essential part of any meaningful historical engagement. When McGann criticizes his profession for repressing the ideological character of its subjects, his point is that neither poetry nor criticism transcends ideology. (An interesting, and provocatively truncated, appendix to *The Romantic Ideology* argues that Louis Althusser and Pierre Macherey are wrong to suggest that art is not to be counted among the ideologies; however, this crucial point is best understood as a corrective to Althusser's more general formulation of the concept of ideology in his germinal essay "Ideology and Ideological State Apparatuses,"[1] a formulation on which McGann's relies.)

For McGann, it is not just the historical subjects of literary criticism that need to be recognized; rather, and rather more crucially, contemporary criticism's own institutionally based ideological formations must also be explicated. Literary criticism can never be the final arbiter of the fixed meaning of a "text," just as literary or linguistic theory cannot be the ultimate explicator of fixed systems of meaning. In contrast, McGann's two tracts insist that literary criticism is an active participant in the continuing reception—*reproduction*—of *works*. I say "tracts" to emphasize McGann's stylistic extension of his ideological interventions; these pamphlets are in every sense didactic; their virtue is to be repetitive and blunt more often

1. *Lenin and Philosophy* (New York: Monthly Review Press, 1971).

than elusive and elegant. If there can be any doubt that this is deliberate, the contrast with *The Beauty of Inflections* will settle the matter. McGann's expansive, thoughtful readings of works by Keats, Byron, Crabbe, Coleridge, Christina Rossetti, Tennyson, and others are exemplary of the possible fruits of his program. Swimming against the tide of literary theory without literature, McGann anchors his methodological and interpretive craft in close, and contextual, readings of specific poems.

In *The Romantic Ideology*, McGann argues that the criticism of Romanticism, to our own day, has uncritically absorbed the key self-representations of the Romantic movement. Terms like "spirituality," "creativity," "process," "uniqueness," "diversity," "synthesis," "reconciliation," "imagination," "poetic truth" are accepted as fundamental human concepts that need not, and cannot, be analyzed. McGann contends that the belief that Poetry transcends history and ideology (in the sense of false consciousness) is an essential element in Romantic displacement, the "grand illusion" that one may escape the disappointments of history through imagination and poetry: "a sense sublime," as Wordsworth had it in "Tintern Abbey," "Of something far more deeply interfused, / Whose dwelling is the light of setting suns . . . / A motion and a spirit, that impels / All thinking things, all objects of all thought, / And rolls through all things." While the wrecks of history "fade and fall to ruin," McGann comments, "the abbey of the mind suffers no decay. . . . The poem generalizes—we now like to say mythologizes—all its conflicts, or rather resituates those conflicts out of a sociohistorical context and into an ideological one" (87–89). "The polemic of Romantic poetry, therefore, is that it will not be polemical; its doctrine, that it is nondoctrinal; and its ideology, that it transcends ideology" (70).

Romantic ideology has descended to us, says McGann, largely through the lines of thought that have developed from Coleridge and Hegel (the German ideology). But while the Romantic ideology of 1789 to 1824 was articulated, to a large extent, by poets skeptical of many of its features, this ambivalence and self-consciousness largely disappears in the debased forms of Romantic ideology we encounter today. McGann censures his own 1968 study, *Fiery Dust: Byron's Poetic Development*, because of its absorption in Romanticism's self-representations and its presumption of the poet's linear development (a biographic teleology that cripples much critical thinking about art).

The uncritical acceptance of Romantic ideology, however, poses problems for more than the study of Romanticism. The effect is all the more disastrous when, institutionally reified, this ideology continues to be the basis for the reception of post-Romantic poetry by an influential segment of what McGann calls the clerisy, that is, literary academia. In this light, the grotesque, yet systematic, misjudgments about twentieth-century poetry by a critic of Romanticism such as Harold Bloom become more understandable, if no less excusable. McGann's sometimes humorous self-consciousness, true to his own didactic intentions, specifically keeps the focus on "that narrowest and most cloistered of spheres . . . the critical work produced by the literary academy" (59). It would be a mistake to ignore the pervasiveness of the same debased Romantic ideology as it informs much contemporary American poetry. Indeed, a broad range of seemingly antagonistic tendencies in current writing share a conception of poetry as giving a "voice" to unmediated "basic truths" of "imagination" and "feeling" through "direct expression" of human "creativity"; they also share an allergic reaction to any intimation, in a poem, of intellectual or ideological self-consciousness. Absorption in Romanticism's self-representations, then, is not only a problem for critics; it is also a problem for poetry. This is the kind of reciprocal interaction in our own time that McGann sees as central to understanding the ideological context and reception of past and present literature.

I take McGann's various explications of Romantic ideology to be provisional, that is, a stage in the development of a historical criticism informed as much by the contemporary ideological climate as by Romantic "texts." While McGann rejects René Wellek's view that there is a basic unity underlying the various manifestations of Romanticism, he does not quite adopt A. O. Lovejoy's skepticism—Romanticisms, not Romanticism (17). The first step in breaking from the spell of a unified Romanticism is to recognize its particular and parochial ideological formations. McGann notes the fundamentally Christian character of the Romanticism formulated by Coleridge and formalized by Hegel. It is not surprising, then, that Heine—a poet inclined to consciously resist absorption in Christian Romanticism—would write a work McGann finds paradigmatic for historical criticism, *The Romantic School*. Heine "writes between 1833 and 1835 as an expatriate German Jew to a French intellectual audience about a cultural phenomenon, German Romanticism, which is now historically concluded. . . . At every point Heine is concerned with the problem of the immediate relevance of removed cultural resources—in this case, German Romantic literary works. He is qualified to take up this problematic matter because he contains in himself, as it were, a crucial division of sympathies and knowledge" (33). Heine's otherness can serve as a reminder that Romantic ideology was one among many ideological formations present in the early nineteenth century. Which is to say, the history of literary criticism is as much a history of unheard or disregarded voices as it is of the privileged voices able to "dominate" a period (originally or in retrospect). The increased prominence that historical method gives to the history of a work's reception makes imperative that lacunas—failures or refusals of reception or publication—be enabled to speak as loudly as the ideas that flowed unimpeded through official cultural channels. Otherwise we will see, as we have seen over and again, the initially tragic story of marginalized lives told in farcically amnesiac official histories of English and American writing.

In this respect, McGann makes a useful distinction between Romantic works and the Romantic period, citing Austen and Crabbe as non-Romantic writers of the Romantic period. He is particularly irritated at attempts, for example, to reverse the critical "neglect" of Austen by trying to make her out as a closet Romantic. Nonetheless, the kind of critical thinking that McGann encourages will hopefully move more in the direction of Romantic *ideologies* than he presently allows for, without vitiating the polemical edge of his term; perhaps, that is, the non-Romantic ideologies of the "Romantic period" may even erode the legitimacy of that moniker. McGann's position on such problems is basically pragmatic; he wants to develop a historical methodology that will be as *teachable* as New Critical reading. Radical skepticism about periodization and ideological characterizations may be difficult to teach, but it is just this type of institutionally motivated thinking that led to many of the problems with New Criticism. Critical thinking has not fared any better under historical narratives than it has under structural verities. While a historical and ideological dimension needs to be restored to discussions of literature, positivism and reductionism are perennial dangers. McGann is acutely aware of these problems, despite his troubling espousal of the hegemony of the sociohistorical method as "the general *science* governing [the] human context" [*Inflections*, 63; my italics]. (The troubling positivism within the natural sciences is exactly the suppression of this sociohistorical context.) But his intensely reflective example, his consistent reiteration of the tendentiousness and ideological character of his own (or any) historical account, will not necessarily be heeded by those adopting his program.

McGann's method would remove poetry from the pedestal of the purely beautiful and sublime, beyond or above ideology, where it is constantly at risk of dissolving into the "spirit of the age," or worse, "the spirit of the ages"—authorless, contentless. To tar poetry with the name of "false"—that is, historical, partisan—consciousness is to return it to the field of contention and *use*. It is as valuable to take issue with Shelley's "doctrines," as one would take issue with Napoleon or Rousseau, as to savor his "exquisite sensibility." This requires a recovery of the historically specific situations in which poems of the past were written, published, republished, reviewed, and read (all different dynamics). It means we stop reading past works as if they were contemporary or temporally transcendent and start to appreciate their value as culturally alienated and socially estranged.

"We have to recover those traditional philological procedures for putting us in touch with worlds, people, and experiences from the past, and with the media in which these things embodied themselves; for putting us in touch with them in the full range of their pastness and differentials. The ultimate purpose of establishing a structure of such differentials is not to lose one's self in a displaced world, which is certainly a danger in pursuing such methods, but to gain a measure by which our present interests and ideologies may be critically observed. Past worlds, in a historical consciousness, make up points of fixity and finishedness, but not in some permanent and absolute sense. The finished past is constantly being reformulated into new forms of finishedness, forms which answer to the changing needs of the immediate world. Nevertheless, whatever form of finishedness the past may take, it can be—must be—made into an (arbitrary) measure in terms of which the present may be understood and judged" (*Inflections*, 12–13).

In *A Critique of Modern Textual Criticism*, McGann notes that "a hypnotic fascination with the isolated author has served to foster an overdetermined concept of authorship, but (reciprocally) an underdetermined concept of literary work" (122). He argues that the best text of a poem is not necessarily produced by trying to reconstruct the "author's final intentions." He criticizes, for example, the preference for using as "copy-text" an author's manuscript even when an early edition, together with author-corrected proofs, is available. Traditionally, textual scholars have tried to construct a hypothesized "lost original" for classical or medieval works whose earliest extant texts date from long periods after the work's composition. Biblical scholars face the most extreme, and metaphorically interesting, case of lost "originals." As a result, the work of textual scholarship has been defined as purifying the corruption and contamination of the "lost original" that has occurred in the process of transmission through publication, expurgation, augmentation, modernization, and previous scholarly editions.

In modern textual criticism the "ideal text" has become a substitute for the "lost original," and the author's holograph documents are taken to be the source for the author's final intentions, even if the writer never imagined that these documents would be reproduced. McGann disputes the notion that publication necessarily contaminates the text. Poetry, insofar as it is published, is a social form, and the intersection of the text with social institutions is *part of* the work, not a corruption of it. "Having learned the lesson that authors who wish to make contact with an audience are fated, by laws of information theory, to have their messages more or less seriously garbled in the process, textual critics proposed to place the reader in an unmediated contact with the author. This project is of course manifestly impossible, a Heisenbergian dilemma, since some form of mediation is always occurring, not the least in the editions produced by critical editors of various persuasions. Nevertheless, though everyone today recognizes this inherent limitation on all acts of communication, the idea persists in textual studies that a regression to authorial manuscripts will by itself serve to reduce textual contamination" (41).

McGann argues that the overall effect of much textual criticism is to discount the social and historical dimensions of textual production. Certain writers serve as outer limits to his consideration: Blake's self-published editions and Dickinson's manuscripts were specifically produced outside the customary social nexus of publication; however, their work is now known only insofar as, at some later point, it entered into this nexus. Moreover, the collaborative interaction of writers, friends and colleagues, assistants, proofreaders, editors, publishers, and readers is not inevitably pernicious. Almost all writers choose to make some sort of collaborative arrangements, as much because of, as in spite of, potential disagreements. "Sometimes these relationships operate smoothly, sometimes the author will struggle against every sort of intervention, and between these two extremes falls every sort of variation. . . . 'Final authority' for literary works rests neither with the author nor with his [or her] affiliated institution; it resides in the actual structure of the agreements which these two cooperating authorities reach in specific cases" (53–54). The history of publishing is filled with unwarranted and meretricious alterations of a writer's punctuation, spelling, and grammar; such abuses need to be adjudicated on a case-by-case basis. At the same time, the dispute becomes part of the work's meaning, which is suppressed when such problems are resolved, as McGann puts it, in terms of right and wrong rather than "what does this mean?" Ironically, recourse to the ideology of final intentions has often resulted in the circumvention of the writer's actual intentions as expressed by active consent.

The social process of literary production is a constituent component of a work's meaning, not a barrier preventing access to it. In this regard, the visual representation of language—typography and book design—is among the least recognized, and most important, actors in constituting a work's meaning. Furthermore, theories about "ideal texts" do not offer viable methods of resolving problems arising from variant versions of the "same" poem. Variants, McGann points out, arise from different social contexts of publication, changing assumptions about readership, or a poetics that incorporates variants as part of its processes. The contextual nature of variants helps to dispel the illusion that each poem has a perfect and inviolable autonomy that is defamed not only by publisher's changes and printer's mediations but even by author's errors and irresolutions. McGann notes that many writers have been more than willing to dismember and revise their poems, leaving open the issue of finalization. In contrast, the reification of the Poem erases the historicity of its composition, that is, its appearance in the world and the forms its past readers have responded to. Reified timelessness is an effect that some poets may wish to create, but, as McGann says, "an author's work possesses autonomy only when it remains an unheard melody" (51). The theory of final intentions turns out to be thick with Romantic ideology.

Most importantly, McGann argues that just as there is no ideal text of a poem, so there is no ideal—definitive—scholarly edition. Scholarly editions are historical, institutionally motivated documents; yet the scientism inherent in much textual methodology denies this ideological dimension. The implication of this appeal is not to legitimize unwarranted alterations by publishers and scholars but to bring into the open the dynamics of these virtually inevitable interactions. McGann's writing acknowledges the effects that current developments in poetry have on the editing of past poetry. *A Critique of Modern Textual Criticism* will seem relevant to readers familiar with Charles Olson's notoriously indeterminate manuscripts; Robert Duncan's and Robert Grenier's insistence on retaining the typewriter grid in their books; any of a number of recent collaborative poems; and the scrupulous or funky self-publications of many writers, ranging from photocopies of manuscripts with holograph changes to "book art" productions in which the graphic element is foregrounded. McGann's currency will not surprise those familiar with a book he published a baker's dozen years ago, *Swinburne: An Experiment in Criticism*. Cast in the form of a dialogue among a variety of personages who knew Swinburne, the book provides a beautifully realized alternative to the monological voice of critical authority; it also engages many of the questions that have focused discussions of poetics in the ensuing years.

In advocating a sociohistorical approach to the poem, McGann is as wary of biographic reduction (conceiving of the poem as existing primarily in terms of the poet's life history) as of formalist aestheticization (poems are primarily about other poems or the poetic process). Yet it is important to keep in mind that a well-grounded, scholarly reading of a poem is not the only kind of desirable reading. Many poems thrive on wildly ill-informed readings, as anyone knows who has flipped open a book of older texts and read them without reference to author or date. That a poem may have this kind of resilience is a central fact in *any* reading of it. Thinking of poems as *texts* is liberating because it locates their object status within the generic democracy of the written—*a piece of writing*; it undercuts the Romantic aura of the Poem while allowing for an exhilaration in the wordness of all writing. Poems are not necessarily diminished (*or illuminated*) by specialized (partisan, tendentious) readings—Marxist, psychoanalytic, biographic, structural, formal, bibliographic. The problem arises when such readings claim for themselves priority or exclusivity, that is, deny their sociohistorical and ideological character; which, of course, they so often do. Indeed, it was the hegemony of proprietary readings of literature—fixed meanings *executed* by authors and embalmed by textual science—that led Roland Barthes to renounce the notion of the *work* (that which can be "held in the hand") in favor of that polymorphous, heterogeneous, decentered, unauthorized, plural "methodological field" that is the *text*.[2] McGann's work is polemical because he does not ameliorate the dispute between "Dryasdust" philologists and "Skimpole" deconstructionists, as he labels them. On the contrary, he wishes to bring into the open a conflict both sides have chosen to ignore by proceeding, uncontested, on their own *falsely* separate paths. McGann's historical program, paradoxically, supplements, rather than supplants, Barthes's critique (as is apparent in his considerations of "final authority"). Like Marx critiquing Hegel, he wishes to turn Barthes's dialectic on its head, not revert to the state of affairs that led Barthes to write his essay.

2. See Barthes's 1971 essay, "From Work to Text," in *Textual Strategies*, edited by Josue V. Harari (Ithaca: Cornell University Press, 1979); and "Shall These Bones Live," in *The Beauty of Inflections*.

There is no key that unlocks the mystery of how or what or why a poem means or becomes. All readings are partial and distorting, though some more than others; there are many virtues in excess, even if this excess effectively annihilates the object of reference. McGann's view is more sobering, less ludic. He insists that we pay a high price for such transgressions, that they threaten our ability to learn what history teaches. The implicit analogy is to our relations with one another, where a moral distinction can be made between projection and understanding; response based on projection is a form of denial, on understanding, a sign of acknowledgment.

McGann's project is not to curtail the proliferation of approaches to reading, or writing, but rather to ground them. I think he means something like that by choosing as the epigraph to his most *textual* work some lines from Wallace Stevens's "Thirteen Ways of Looking at a Blackbird":

> I do not know which to prefer,
> The beauty of inflections
> Or the beauty of innuendoes,
> The blackbird whistling
> Or just after.[3]

---

3. *Collected Poems* (New York: Alfred A. Knopf, 1954), 93.

POETRY AND/OR THE SACRED

Every time I hear the word "sacred" I reach for my checkbook. Every time I reach for my checkbook I get a warm glow that haunts me with the flow of international capital. In God we trust—all others need a major credit card. I'll give you credit for that—just don't bank on it. Is nothing sacred anymore? Of course nothing is sacred: some things never change. But I'd put it is this way: at least nothing is sacred. That's a start. Either nothing is sacred or everything is. If the sacred is the hot air inflating a poem, it doesn't mean the poem won't fly, though just as likely it may snore. Now is the allusion there to a blimp or to Blimpie's. No more priests—in every sigh of every woman, child, and man. Not something to rise up to but something in which to descend, the gravity Simone Weil talks about that is a condition for grace.

The sacred as opposed to what? Against the priestly function of the poet or of poetry I propose the comic and bathetic, the awkward and railing: to be grounded horizontally in the social and not vertically in the ethers. My motto would be a revision of Cavalcanti: "for the sacred is such a thing that if it is portrayed it dies."

Lately I've been thinking about the distinction between moral discourse and ethical reciprocity. Morality as a fixed system telling you what is good or good for you: the sacred can sound a lot like that, even if it's supposed to be something deeper or more experiential or exceptional. I think of ethics as intertwined with aesthetics, as dependent on context, judgment, shifting situations. Ethical reciprocity involves recognition and acknowledgment— a process of registration—rather than states such as feeling spiritual (as if it were a goal). I'm for conversation not conversion. I would worry—for me worry is the only sacred giraffe—about all the things not sacred . . . Well, that old song—and dance.

"Poetry and the Sacred," keynote panel at the 17th Annual Tucson Poetry Festival, March 27, 1999. Other panel members were Robert Bly, Jane Hirshfield, Ramson Lomatewama, Pat Mora, and David Shapiro. & with thanks to Adrienne Rich. *Salt* 13 / *Jacket* 14 (2002).

In the Jewish mystical tradition, there is the idea that everything is holy—an idea given a particularly forceful spin in the coda to Allen Ginsberg's *Howl* (the spatula is holy, the tuxedo is holy, the mud is holy, the tumescence is holy, the misquotation is holy, the parody is holy, my jacket is holy—but I just bought a patch to fix that). Ginsberg's famous Whitmanian lines extend a crucial tradition in American poetry away from the allegorical and high-literary and religious and toward the ordinary and the detail. William Carlos Williams and Gertrude Stein are the paradigmatic modernist poets of the ordinary. Just as Williams found the poetic, and possibly the sacred, in the back-lot "cinders // in which shine / the broken // pieces of a green / bottle,"[1] so Stein found the poetic in the materials of the poem, "actual word stuff, not thoughts for thoughts," to use Williams's formulation.[2]

This brings to mind again that the crucial focus for Jewish mysticism is on language, in its material form: not what language represents or means or signifies, but what it is in itself.

Poems are no more sacred than the use to which they are made, any more than you or I or Uncle Hodgepodge is. They are scared and looking for cover, scarred by the journey. They may be good company but more likely resemble the man in the train compartment who never stops talking. What time is it *now*? Are we *there* yet? What do they *call* this town?

1. "Between Walls," in *The Collected Poems of William Carlos Williams*, vol. 1, 1909–1939, edited by A. Walton Litz and Christopher MacGowan (Princeton: Princeton University Press, 1986), 453.

2. Williams is commenting, in a letter to Zukofsky on April 2, 1928, on Zukofsky's "Poem Beginning 'The'": "It is thoughtful poetry, but actual word stuff, not thoughts for thoughts." *The Correspondence of Williams Carlos Williams and Louis Zukofsky*, edited by Barry Ahearn (Middletown, CT: Wesleyan University Press, 2003), 544.

THE ART AND PRACTICE
OF THE ORDINARY

—and, by words
Which speak of nothing more than what we are . . .
WORDSWORTH, "THE RECLUSE"

The ordinary is always elusive—"near is / and difficult to grasp"—even as
it is the most present actuality. And my sense, when talking about the ordinary, is always how extraordinary it is. Paradoxically, any attempt to fix the
ordinary pulls it out of the everydayness in which it is situated, from which
it seems to derive its power.

The problem with transparent language is that it aims to create a semblance
of the ordinary, a spectacle of the ordinary. But that is the opposite of what
you may want to achieve. Instead of creating an experience of, or in, the
ordinary, you have created a representation of it. Transparency, in trying to
picture the ordinary, at the same time removes the reader from it.

   In a society of the spectacle, such as American society, much of ordinary
life is constructed by consumer culture. In this sense, the mall is the most
ordinary environment and shopping the most ordinary activity. Yet, this
kind of ordinary may be quite opposite to the everydayness a poet might
want to evoke.

Adapted from "Pour une critique de l'ordinaire: Entretien avec Charles Bernstein" [Toward
a critique of the ordinary: an interview with Charles Bernstein], by Barbara Abad, Thérèse
Tseng, and François Paré, published in Études françaises (University of Guelph, Quebec), 33.2
(1997). Presented at the Séance symposium at the California College of the Arts, Red Cat Theater, Los Angeles, October 30, 2004; published in Séance, edited by Christine Wertheim and
Matias Viegener (Los Angeles: Make Now Press, 2005). My translation of the opening lines
of Hölderlin's "Patmos" is quoted in the first sentence: "Nah ist / Und schwer zu fassen [der
Gott]"; see Friedrich Hölderlin, Hymns and Fragments, trans. Richard Sieburth (Princeton:
Princeton University Press, 1984), 88.

For me the question of the ordinary breaks down practically and philo-sophically into three separate, interrelated, but not entirely commensurate elements. One is the representation and objectification of everyday life, which I have just barely touched on now. Another is ordinary language philosophy (not only Ludwig Wittgenstein but also Michel de Certeau and Stanley Cavell). But there is a third issue, which is crucial in terms of poetry: the transcription of spoken, everyday language, which can be considered as a problem of poetic diction, or of the vernacular, or indeed of dialect.

In the American poetic tradition the question of diction takes several forms. First, there is the insistence that a poetry of the everyday be written in American, rather than British, English—a development most often linked to William Carlos Williams. Vernacular diction is not, however, the same as the transcription of spoken English. In fact, spoken American English has a very complex structure, and there is no simple or single method of presenting it in writing. If you transcribe everything I say, including the pauses and hesitations, you'd get a very dense, Joycean text. Any attempt to reduce speech to a particular literary style of representing speech, in order to claim that style as "ordinary," is always a move away from the ordinary. Indeed, such an "ordinary" poetic diction has fetishized as ordinary what is in fact a literary style. The tension between the spoken—the vernacular or dialect—and the literary representations of it, going back to Dante and ear-lier, produces new poetic dictions but never the erasure of poetic diction, never an absolutely "ordinary" diction. This dialectical movement is one of the most important features of English poetry, not just since Wordsworth's "Preface" to *Lyrical Ballads*, but going back to Old English.

But the relation of the ordinary to speech is not necessarily one of transcrip-tion, idealized or empiricized. Take Gertrude Stein's poetry as an example. Stein is not interested in the transcription of the spoken language, but she is committed to using everyday words. Stein makes a syntax for them; that is, she invents new word orders rather than following the conventions of received grammar. She works with ordinary American words and with ev-eryday objects. She repeatedly uses words like "this," "a," "one," and "the" or "belly" or "button" or "tender" or "shutters," and rarely uses anything but such everyday words—but not as a way of representing anything. Stein is emphasizing the everydayness of the vocabulary rather than emphasiz-ing what the words are used to represent, the everydayness of their refer-ent. If you compare Stein's poetry from the first two decades of the twentieth century with the carefully wrought, eloquent diction of one of Robert Browning's monologues from the middle of the nineteenth century, or more generally, with Victorian poetry, Stein's poetry is stripped of all its literariness, as marked by high poetic diction, a certain set of themes, metrical conventions, even the look of the poem on the page. Indeed, the prose format of *Tender Buttons* is more ordinary than the verse format of a sonnet. So the work is certainly a move toward the ordinary and away from the literary. But because it is not representational in a conventional way, it seems odd or opaque. It does not appear to be ordinary, yet its aim is to present the ordinary. William Carlos Williams is more representational, but often the thinness of his subject matter has a similar effect of grounding the poem in vernacular experience and in stripped down vernacular language (what emerges in Robert Creeley's work as the common fact of each word).

Indeed, we can move toward the use of slang or dialect, especially associated with African American writing and Caribbean poetry in English. The attempt to capture the sounds of dialect by deforming the words has a very political and charged quality. It is ordinary in the sense that this work beckons to the way people speak. But because of the spelling, the poetic text often looks strange, even when a new orthography for the dialect words is established (which itself is a move away from the ordinariness of the sound of the words). That is, there is a tension between the dialect orthography, which may look odd, even to the people who speak the dialect, and the putatively naturalizing effect of the "spoken." For instance, some of the postwar Caribbean dialect poems, say of Michael Smith or Louise Bennett, are highly performative. When they are performed, the sounds produced do not raise the question of the nonstandard orthography, because the audiences do not see them written down. But such works may appear to be incomprehensible for people who are not part of that particular speech community. So my point is that even for the speakers of the dialect, dialect poetry seems odd, because they are not used to seeing dialect in a literary context; and for nondialect speakers, the very ordinariness of dialect is what makes it apparently exotic. Consider for a minute the African American dialect poetry that Paul Laurence Dunbar wrote at the very beginning of the last century. This dialect poetry is written in iambic pentameter. Dunbar creates this strange mélange between nonstandard, "ordinary" uses of the language and high literary form, a kind of stylistic oxymoron. This is also true of much current rap music. I don't think there is any way of getting outside of these tensions. The interest of works like Dunbar's is precisely the tension between the literary form and the live performance (not only of the poem but of the language itself).

The issue of ordinary language—dialect, or the nonstandard, second—remains one of the most politically charged issues of the time. Black English is reviled by the conservative mainstream as deformed English and celebrated by Afrocentrics as the mother tongue. What's sanctified as ordinary for one group is derided as spurious by the other. The very ordinariness of black English is what makes it seem of self-evident value to its speakers (and rightly so), but this ordinariness is a red herring to conservatives because it is not ordinary to them. The problem is that there is no one ordinary language, but many ordinary languages. And all languages are social constructions—black English as much as standard English.

The politics of the ordinary plays a crucial role because of the paradoxical conflict between the ordinary and the conventional, between the dialect and the standard, between the normal and the spoken, between the intelligible and the vernacular. It's the ordinary versus the really ordinary. Conventional, standard English derives its authority from being perceived as the normal, the intelligible, and also the transparent. "It must be ordinary 'cause it's what I understand." Dialect, however, casts the conventional or standard as artificial or other or learned or imposed—"it's not my ordinary"—while sometimes claiming to be authentic or natural or spoken.

What the poetics of the ordinary can hope to show is that authenticity and normalcy both misconceive the dynamic and essentially rhetorical or trop(e)ical social fact of language. Black English is just as rich a language as standard English, just as valid (all languages are equally valid). The point is not to go from fetishizing (or naturalizing) the standard to fetishizing (or naturalizing) the authentic, but to acknowledge the multiple possibilities, and different social valances, of language. And to recognize that the ordinary lies not in any one type of language but in the between.

Charles Baudelaire is a crucial poet in terms of what we could call the modern history of the representation of the everyday. Baudelaire wants to take French poetry down from the lofty subject matter traditionally thought of as appropriate for poetry: the beautiful, the expensive, the royal, the mythological, the important, and, crucially, the uplifting. But the problem is that, in "À une mendiante rousse" ("To a Begging Redhead"), for instance, Baudelaire casts himself as a bohemian—a poet freed from the chains of daily life. He can sit in a café and gaze out at the ordinary folk, as Peter Nicholls notes in

Modernisms: A Literary Guide. In short, Baudelaire objectifies his ordinary subject. He gazes upon her from his own point of detached privilege. The problem of objectification is intimately connected to the problem of representation. Baudelaire is important because he identifies with the ordinariness around him. But he cannot get away from this objectification. This issue of representation as objectification is crucial for any consideration of the poetics of the ordinary: it is the fly in the ointment of transparency. For objectification is antipathetic to the poetics of the ordinary because it removes that which is objectified from the flow of the ordinary, from its location in the everyday. I am interested in a poetics of the everyday that attempts to break down this objectification of the ordinary. That requires a kind of writing that tries to break down the relationship between seer and seen, the observer and the observed. And this is where we can see the great importance of some of the poets with us this weekend.

Like Wittgenstein, we must understand that the everyday is in fact a practice, not a style. It is something in which we are engaged. Take, for instance Michel de Certeau's example, in *Arts de faire*, of a worker putting his or her timecard in backward as a way of creating a small space of her or his own: this is a practice that interferes with the everyday; it is not a literary style, it is not a form of representation, it is a way of proceeding. And this procedure, this practice of the everyday, is where the issues can be most richly and dialectically confronted. As it is by Guy Debord and the other Situationists, such as Asger Jorn, who were interested in creating a method of breaking down the barrier of art and the everyday, where art, in its stylistic fixations, was understood as adding to the spectacle of commodity culture. I want a critique of the ordinary (to echo Henri Lefevre's title) that also is a critique of market value. One wants a practice that counters the alienation from the ordinary rather than that domesticates or naturalizes this alienation.

The relation of Marxism to the poetics of the ordinary is fundamental, but I would suggest that poets such as Louis Zukofsky, George Oppen, Charles Reznikoff, Lorine Niedecker, who are often together called, for all their differences, "Objectivists," offer a path radically different from socialist realism, even while sharing some of its political premises. Oppen and Zukofsky were both committed to socialism. Oppen was working with the Communist Party in the thirties and after, during which time he stopped writing, possibly because he could not reconcile his politics with his poetics. His first book, *Discrete Series* (1934) is very difficult, very abstract at one level.

At the same time, its absolutely ordinary words, its series of concrete observations, are permuted one after the other without any literary flourish at all. In fact, Oppen and Zukofsky are the most radical in their disaffiliation from any sort of literariness and aestheticization, also from a kind of bombastic and hyperpoetic work that might be associated with the European futurists and surrealists. Their writing is extremely low-key. They are both coming out of Jewish immigrant families where English was not the first language spoken, but they are choosing to write in English, to be a part of an international modernism. So there is a strain of secular internationalism in them. But, at the same time, they are committed to the particular, to the detail, rather than to the general or metaphysical. In this way, they are very much against the symbolic or allegorical use of the particular, which is contrary to social realism, or more conventional kinds of poetry of the everyday, where the individual is meant to represent something larger. They want things to be what they are.

Much of Reznikoff's work consists of quite short poems in serial forms about topics that do not even seem to be topics. They approach the ephemeral: like gum stuck to the pavement. These are also intensely urban poems, very much outside a literary ethos that is nostalgic for some other kind of life.

More recently, some of these approaches to the ordinary have been pursued by such writers as Creeley, Larry Eigner, Ted Berrigan, Lyn Hejinian, Leslie Scalapino, Ron Silliman, Robert Grenier, Bernadette Mayer, Hannah Weiner, and Kenneth Goldsmith. In my own practice, which, like my contemporaries, is of course quite different from these older poets I so much admire, there is a very strong critique of the institution of literature and a relentless look at how poetry operates at a social level, so that the everyday becomes an understanding of the social uses of language and the different registers of vernacular language.

I am less interested in talking about the aesthetics of the ordinary than participating in the fight for the ordinary. For the ordinary is always contested ground. For this reason, I have been very interested in understanding the problem of the politics of poetic form, rather than the politics of poetic subject matter. The politics of poetry has partly to do with its character of resistance, its recalcitrance, its awkwardness, understood as a crucial space for reflection and thought on the political realm, on values. Imagine the poem as an ordinary space not in content so much as form: I mean imagine the space of the poem itself, with its stubbornness or its erraticness—which would be odd as a literary style—as actually existing in and as the ordinary. What's ordinary is an enacted process, not the product.

Obviously, with the postwar period, poetry no longer is a medium of mass communication. If, as an artist, you are interested in galvanizing the broad masses, poetry would not be the best choice to achieve that.

By the very process of the ideological critique, the poetic work is flipped out of the context of the ordinary. It may not be standardized; it does not speak with an individual voice; it is abnormal. In fact, normalcy of language (that is to say, standardization) is not a natural fact of human being but a highly controlled social institution to which people are forced to conform. If you wish to unlearn normalcy, you will seek a level of inarticulateness which is very ordinary. Inarticulateness, stuttering, oddness are parts of the most ordinary experience, and in poetic language they may refuse coherence. The right will say that such an abnormal language is decadent, un-Christian, anarchic, or nihilistic; in other words, that it is an attack on logos (or anyway logos according to the ideological state apparatus). If you do not examine the values reproduced through grammatical structures, by diction, and via the norms of exposition, then you will find yourself constantly trapped in a controlled simulation of reality that limits any kind of political transformation. Of course, critique does not change the distribution of wealth, or end racial discrimination or gender oppression. Politics never dissolves at any one level, certainly not simply as a result of artistic work. But art does have a crucial social role to play.

What I am trying to do in my own writing is to produce an experience of language as a social material, evoking, in the process, material facts about language and rhythms within language that each of us knows as well as our own breath or the thud of our heart or the viscosity of our saliva. Such writing is often accused of being obscure, difficult, inaccessible, but this may be because preconceptions about what poetry should be like block out the very real experiences possible with language not tethered to stylistic conventions. In contrast, for poetry that advertises itself as directly or emotionally expressive, the very terms emotion and directness are caught within an ideological web of literary manners, forms, and structures that end up preventing direct expression. If a poet does not confront how these concepts of directness and emotionality are the objects of literary manipulations, then she or he is never able to achieve directness in poetry. Such a confrontation and resistance may be difficult at first because it requires questioning, even breaking with, the norms. In attempting to engage the ordinary it is necessary to explore, from a conceptual point of view, the effect of the structures through which the directness of the ordinary is to be expressed. Unfortunately, the politics of the everyday does not allow simple solutions. Social reality is too complex to be conquered or fully understood, but that does not mean we cannot alter or transform it. Our work is to engage with the complexity without losing contact with an ordinary that is our constant companion, our most trusted guide.

ELECTRONIC PIES IN THE POETRY SKIES

Language reproduction technology—from the alphabet to the printing press to our current systems of photoelectronic reproduction—has a history of democratizing social space while at the same time not democratizing it enough.

Freedom is a relative value, not an absolute. The question is always freedom for what or from what, freedom for whom or from whom.

The utopian vision of the open spaces of the Web may also hold out the false promise that everything, at last, can be heard.

Nonetheless, our ideals for technology may incite greater freedom even if these ideals are not, perhaps cannot be, reached.

Authority is never abolished but constantly reinscribes itself in new places.

There is a virus out there, but it is not trying to get to your hard drive but your outsides and insides.

I founded the Buffalo Poetics list (http://epc.buffalo.edu/poetics/welcome.html) in late 1993, with this poem: "Above the world-weary horizons / New obstacles for exchange arise / Or unfold, / O ye postmasters!" The list faced its share of obstacles, changing in late 1998 from an open (but private and subscription-based) to a moderated list. Portions of this work were published online in 2001. In 2002, Damian Lopes did a three-card shuffle realization, now archived by Coach House Books (http://archives.chbooks.com/online_books/electronic_pies). This version was collected in *The Politics of Information: The Electronic Mediation of Social Change*, edited by Marc Bousquet and Katherine Wills (Alt-X Press / Electronic Book Review, 2003). URLs accessed July 7, 2010.

The greatest contribution of small presses and magazines of the past fifty years has not been that they have been more "open" than the trade or commercial presses but that in many cases they have been more selective.

Every new path to freedom creates new, sometimes even more intractable, obstacles to freedom.

The goal of democratizing the Web, understood as an end in itself, may sometimes conflict with the creation of sites that allow for the articulation of alternative perspectives.

Populism is not the same as market share.

Access is a method, not a goal.

The absence of physical or temporal bars to exchange in various interactive spaces does not necessarily allow for a greater range of exchange.

The group dynamics that hamper exchange in "live" settings have colonized our electronic interactions.

& you can never completely rid yourself of this virus, but you can be a more or less hospitable host.

Decentralization allows for multiple, conflicting authorities, not the absence of authority.

Authority is dead; editing begins.

Mass culture is not the same as popular culture.

Fostering dissent on the Web requires the invention of new formats.

Authority in the defense of liberty is not linear.

The destruction, in the United States, of TV and radio as a space for the articulation of alternative political, ethical, and aesthetic points of view haunts all who imagine that new technologies might serve ends other than those of the market or its ideological underwriters.

For interactive sites such as discussion groups, it is always useful to consider whether the structure precipitates resentment over exchange, the average over the particular, mediocrity over difference, voice over thought, immediacy over reflection, recirculation over invention.

The purpose of supporting unpopular culture is not necessarily to make it popular, but this does not mean that preserving unpopularity is itself a virtue.

In some ways, the intimate space of e-mail discussion lists can leave one feeling more vulnerable to animosity than in "live" settings, where the presence of others serves as a buffer.

Freedom is never free.

The structural problem is how to foster counterhegemonic perspectives, including aesthetic ones, within an environment where accessibility and democratization are often used to erode such perspectives.

The Internet provides new opportunities for rumor, gossip, exploitation, and innuendo.

The lobotomizing of radio and TV has been done under the banner of democratization: Let the Majority Decide! Down with the Authority of Elites!

"This time it will be different" but it never (quite) is and never is not (quite).

Majority rule via market and ratings systems, like our winner-take-all political system, has been far more effective than any state-run censorship in ensuring the minority rule of those with the greatest capital accumulation.

Electronic space is neither free nor unlimited because our lives are neither free nor unlimited.

Corporate America is now constructing elaborate Web on-ramp systems to control the flow of hits; that's why AOL bought Time/Warner and not the other way around.

In some of the new Internet environments, there is a fairly high tolerance for flaming, ad hominem attack, libel, and diatribe, as if resentment is a measure of honesty.

The megacorporate control of the flow of hits, of consumer—not citizen—attention is far more important than short-term profits because the system of preserving profits depends upon it.

& sometimes there is nothing you can do about the virus, and those may be just the times when it seems most urgent to imagine that you can do something.

Not all unpopular culture is equal or equally worth supporting.

What's the alternative?

The very ease of posting to a list may sacrifice necessity (not the same as substance) even while allowing for immediacy (not the same as urgency).

Infrastructure, infrastructure, infrastructure.

The Web necessitates ever more editing, more intensive intervention, lest our alternative spaces be rendered vacuous, or desperate, by default launching people into the official flows of information.

Yet righteous outrage is as likely to shut down exchange as provoke it.

Web space is not so much disembodied as differently bodied. And those different bodies can be as scary as the demons that haunt our dreams for human freedom.

While the proliferation of unmoderated spaces does of course allow for some of the otherwise unheard to speak, in the resultant din it may impossible to hear them.

We remain vulnerable to destabilization by *agent provocateurs* but also by provocative agencies within ourselves, our desire for purification through self-immolation.

Knowledge is constituted by the available information in a particular time.

It's not technology that will change the possibilities for dialogue but politics.

In my own experience as the editor/moderator of a listserv, I found it hard to be as grumpy as I needed to be and hard not to be too grumpy about the results.

The automation of language reproduction and exchange possible with the Internet is very alluring as it seems to save so much labor-intensive work in comparison to print publications or letters; ultimately, this is illusory, since the labor of selection, editing, and involving participants/readers is still the essential ingredient, while the technical work of site and list formation and maintenance are themselves relatively complex and time-consuming tasks.

For alternative voices to make a difference, space must be created and maintained so that they can not only speak but also be heard; and this means creating spaces that earn the trust of their participants.

As much as we may be troubled by the growing concentration of "web-fotainment," we also need to be wary that as many of the most "ungoverned" sites purvey disinformation as offer critique.

Automation of language reproduction doesn't make things simpler but more complex.

If the discussion is always starting from scratch, the participants with greater experience may drop away.

Public space requires protecting rights as much as allowing access.

The contribution of small press publications is that they articulate specific, not general, aesthetic values; that they do not allow market forces to be the primary arbiter of value; and that they provide sharp contrasts with the otherwise available literature of the time.

Some disagreements are too extreme to be articulated politely.

The hardest thing is to create spaces that not only provide information but also allow for exchange.

My own reluctance to impose sufficient restrictions almost allowed those antagonistic to the list to destroy it.

It may be as useful to participate in a conversation "over your head" as "at your level."

The virus is in our systems of social reproduction.

The ideal of civility is as often a ploy to suppress dissent as a means of facilitating dialogue.

But because some things are beyond redress it does not follow that every circumstance is without recourse, nor every case without prospect.

There is a pleasure, also, in delusions: not of grandeur but of agency.

There'll be a pie in the sky when you die.

But not likely.

POETRY PLASTIQUE: A VERBAL EXPLOSION IN THE ART FACTORY

Coauthor: Jay Sanders

In June 2000, Jay Sanders wrote me a note suggesting we work together on a poetry show at the Marianne Boesky Gallery, where he was on the staff. In our first few conversations we discovered that we shared a very specific conception for the show. As our planning grew more intense, we began to see that a distinct characteristic of "Poetry Plastique" was that it would focus on poetry off the page or outside normal typographic constraints. Letters of the alphabet are tenaciously referential (standing for a sound or for the idea of the letter), often at the expense of denying the physical and visual existence of written language, even the possible origin of letters as icons and pictographs. Our exhibition would seek to both open up and explore letter shapes, with the idea that as works move off the page and out of the book, letters are able to repossess their thickness as objects and their presence as sounds. The exhibition opened at the Marianne Boesky Gallery on February 9, 2001. On February 10, we presented an all-day symposium featuring most of the poets and artists in the show. Our two panels were chaired by Marjorie Perloff. In the evening, we screened the films that we selected to be part of the show. Anthology Film Archives subsequently presented a separate "Poetry Plastique" program of films chosen by Jay and the Anthology staff. In addition, Granary Books published a catalog for the exhibition, with extensive reproductions and a statement by each participant (available at http://epc.buffalo.edu/features/poetryplastique). For this essay, we have pulled together various statements we wrote to introduce the show.
CH. B.

Not words and pictures but poems as visual objects (read: subjects). Not poems about pictures but pictures that are poems. Not words affixed to a blank page but letters in time. Not works closed in a book but poems hanging on a wall or suspended from the ceiling or rising from the floor or sounding from inside a figure or embedded with paint on a canvas or written in the sky or flickering on a screen.

"Poetry Plastique" presents the work of thirty-four poets and artists working to move poetry off the page and into sculpture, film, painting, assemblage, photography—even skywriting. Pushing the boundaries of textuality, these literary and visual artists move poetry into a new dimension that emphasizes the concreteness and materiality of the written word. Featuring both collaborations between poets and artists and well as visual work by poets and textual work by visual artists, the exhibition presents some of the most significant poets and artists of the time in a context that promises to change our understanding of poetry and its relation to visual art.

The exhibition includes new work as well as a historical section of works from the 1960s to 1980s that provides a context for understanding the developments charted by the show. Extending from the work of visual poetry and book art, the poem-objects in the show suggest a markedly different approach to language than is often seen. Indeed, while language is a common element in much contemporary visual art, the works in "Poetry Plastique" use language not as a conceptual screen or a set of received ideas but as an active principle for articulation and meaning.

"Poetry Plastique" takes a distinct place in a spectrum that includes visual and concrete poetry as well as book and language art. The precedents hang in the air—from William Blake's fusion of poem-engraving-image to the exquisitely expressive features of Emily Dickinson's hand-inscribed fascicles, from Marcel Duchamp's verbal objects and Kurt Schwitters's collages and Merzbau to the collaborations of the Russian Futurist painters and poets and Len Lye's inscribed film stock. A secret history, but one known to an international array of participants, links the works shown here to a range of poems, sculptures, paintings, and books that have formed the matrix of a previous series of exemplary shows that have mapped out the ground for this exhibition. We hope that the inclusion of a small grouping of classic works from the 1960s and 1970s will help to contextualize the new work presented here. At the same time, we realize that even our "classics" will find a new audience with this presentation, since many of them have rarely if ever been shown in a New York art world context. We are also pleased that "Poetry Plastique" brings to the fore a range of new collaborations between poets and visual artists—a traditional pairing here made new again.

Why aren't poets more central to contemporary visual art? This exhibition makes this question impossible to ignore. For many contemporary poets, the connections and affinities with the visual arts are readily acknowledged. Indeed, today's most innovative poets have challenged traditional ideas of the literary, moving their work into close proximity to the most radical questionings of current visual artists. And, indeed, the proximity of avant-garde poets and artists has a vibrant history that our show hopes to bring up to date.

Take, for example, the crucial recent anthology *Poems for the Millennium*, edited by Jerome Rothenberg and Pierre Joris, which is emblematic of the wide-reaching and multifaceted history that contemporary poetry increasingly considers its own. For Rothenberg & Joris, poetry exists in an active context that includes such poet-artists as Marcel Duchamp, Kurt Schwitters, and John Cage (not to mention Picasso, Cendrars and Delaunay, Marinetti, Stepanova, Kandinsky, Grosz, Klee, Michaux, Tzara, Ball, Arp, Picabia, Breton, Ernst, Artaud, Brecht). In their respective practices, these individuals—most of whom are primarily known as visual artists—and many more, are of real interest as poets, informing the survey, connecting the dots, and giving key insights into contemporary poetic practice.

Poems for the Millennium reminds us that poetry has historically played a central role in most of the key art movements of the twentieth century. Futurism, Dada, and Surrealism were all, first and foremost, literary movements. And while the story is perhaps less known today, contemporary poets continue to produce works that rival any other medium in terms of innovation, variety, and accomplishment. With regard to the relationship between poetry and the plastic arts, we've tried to take poetry out of its expected—but not necessary—contexts, pulling poetry out of the book and throwing it up on the wall or down on the floor. "Poetry Plastique" is a verbal explosion in the art factory. It returns cutting-edge poetry to the center of art culture, a position poetry occupied for much of the last century. It is a celebration of the physical dimensions of the written word and the textual dimensions of art objects.

The exhibition presents an important aspect of the often underrepresented visual works of contemporary poets. We offer a constellation of intellectually compelling, poetically dense, visually dazzling works that represent some of the most exciting efforts in current practice. Additionally, we shed light on an essential gathering of historical progenitors. Known primarily as visual artists (Robert Smithson, Arakawa, Tom Phillips, Carl Andre, Wallace Berman), poets (Clark Coolidge, Steve McCaffery, Jackson Mac Low), filmmakers (Hollis Frampton, Michael Snow), and composers (John Cage), the artists in our historical component each exhibit an understanding of the possibilities of enacting the verbal and visual—centering their concerns on a real exploration of poetry and language—rather than simply "text." Such a grouping, shown concurrently with critical contemporary examples, updates the recent historical crosscurrents of poetry and visual art, and contextualizes the contemporary works in a broad manner that extends beyond the specificities of a single medium.

We have taken a wide, interdisciplinary view of "Poetry Plastique" which looks favorably on convergences, collisions, and corruptions between categories in the arts. For many of the participating artists, this means highlighting lesser-known (but more pertinent for us) aspects of their creative endeavors. One of the common hallmarks of the "historical" artists is an unabashed irreverence for the divisions between artistic mediums. Each artist has allowed her or his practice to transcend disciplinary categories, making vital innovations in more than one milieu. And, as we illustrate here, each has critically explored the limits of language and poetic text in a visual context.

For many of the contemporary poets and language artists (David Antin, Christian Bök, Johanna Drucker, Kenneth Goldsmith, Robert Grenier, Lyn Hejinian, Tan Lin, Emily McVarish, Nick Piombino, Leslie Scalapino, Darren Wershler-Henry), we are highlighting both special projects and ongoing corollaries to their practice as writers. For the most part, these poets also publish less visually intensive poetry, but it is their works that combine visual and verbal sensibilities that are central to our concerns. Additionally, we include key painters (Susan Bee, Mira Schor) whose canvases—in a complementary manner—provide grounds for intensive explorations of poetics and language.

We have also chosen to exhibit important collaborations between poets and visual artists. While some of these pieces were made specifically for this exhibition, we did not organize any of the collaborative pairings. Instead, it was our intent to seek out existing relationships that demonstrate a dynamic synthesis of the physical/visual/material with the poetic/textually-dense. While there are many poet/artist collaborations, each of these (Clark Coolidge/Philip Guston, Madeline Gins/Arakawa, Robert Creeley/Cletus Johnson, Mei-Mei Berssenbrugge/Kiki Smith, Charles Bernstein/Richard Tuttle, Lyn Hejinian/Emilie Clark) has intricately intermeshed the visual and the poetic to the utmost degree.

For our show, we have chosen to include neither artist's books nor poetry that is primarily "concrete" or typographical, in part because these forms have been more commonly exhibited, but also because we are especially interested in works whose visual materiality is not fully reproducible in books, anthologies, or on the Internet. For this reason, we have made every effort to display "originals," even of works designed to be read in reproduction. And we have included a number of works—sculptures, paintings, films, and video—where paper is not the medium upon which the words are inscribed. Not simply poems on the wall, the works in our exhibition share an interest in materials and visuality, and exist as "unique" objects ideally viewed in a gallery setting and best appreciated in person.

To the curators of this exhibition, mounting such a show in a commercial New York gallery is an important component. It annexes these poets and their works into the context of contemporary art, and generally restates the importance of poetry in the realm of the visual arts. In organizing and presenting these works, we have taken every measure to acknowledge them to be as compelling as any grouping of artworks.

Organizing a gallery exhibition full of poetry actively pushes against categorical definitions separating artistic mediums. In their endeavors, the poets involved in "Poetry Plastique" are all consciously concerned with boundaries. The boundaries between poetry and criticism, verse and prose, reading and looking, meaning and material are incessantly pushed to the breaking point. We have endeavored to exhibit an element of that spillage, where creative works extend limits so far, they can potentially turn into something else.

SPEED THE MOVIE OR SPEED THE BRAND NAME OR AREN'T YOU THE KIND THAT TELLS: MY SENTIMENTAL JOURNAL THROUGH FUTURE SHOCK AND PRESENT STATIC ELECTRICITY. VERSION 19.84.

[Note this document is best heard with Quixotic's Tympanic Membrane Firmware bundled to the CNS 98 operating system. Upgrade now.]

A lion, a flinch, and an extraterrestrial were in a lifeboat together and supplies were dwindling. Finally, the lion asked the extraterrestrial, "So what's the big deal about the Internet?" "Speed" said the flinch in a blink of a wince.

No matter how you look at it, speed is a morally coded concept. With its etymological roots tied at the groin to success, to think speed is to invoke a java applet alternating flashing SPEED / All Others Pay Cash.

Is it possible to imagine an ethics of speed to contrast with the moral insistence on speed as success, efficiency, progress? That is, to interrogate speed not in terms of whether it is good or bad but by means of reciprocal values in which rate is one among many factors, gauged for its aesthetic articulation more than as an absolute measure of anything? In other words, to break the moral coding of speed in order to release its many valences for aesthetic experience and ethical consideration?

Speed is always, anyway, relative to background, context, observer, observed, expectation, desire, loss, habit; what Einstein called the Special

Written for "Key Words" seminar (speed, betrayal, healing) at the Rockefeller Foundation, organized by Michael Brenson, June 12, 1998. *Shark* 2 (1999).

Theory of Relativity, as in: the station moves along the tracks looking for the train.

An ethics of speed might begin by noting that human sexual response is often enhanced by prolongation, actively slowing down, what's the rush, it's not a race, it's not the goal but the getting there, getting by, the doing not the done, energia not kinesis, distraction not attention, digression not forward movement.

What Muriel Rukeyser calls "the speed of darkness" (70 beats per minute at rest, doubled in motion).

"Faster than a speeding bullet, more powerful than a locomotive," it's John Henry versus the steam shovel in three rounds at the Garden, with running commentary by Bob, or is it Ray?, Slow Talkers of America, or then again the tortoise beating the hare, Charlie Chaplin deranged by Taylorization, Marinetti writing odes to acceleration, Ozu head to head with Jackie Chan in *Swift Justice: The Bonneville 500 Story*, XT, AT, 286, 386, 486, Pentium 1, 2, *you're out.*

As if the choice were between the assembly line and the verse line.

When I was twelve years old I enrolled in a summer Evelyn Wood speed reading course, lured by the image of the man who read a dozen books a day, itself echoing that mad desire Thomas Wolfe writes about in *Of Time and the River* when as a student at Harvard he wanted to read all the books in Widener library. After getting a hang for the Evelyn Wood system, I was able to read Albert Camus's *The Stranger* in twenty-five minutes. "Mother died today. Or, maybe, yesterday; I can't be sure." I still remember the starting line, and it is the sort of blur Camus evokes here that is the sensation of this kind of speed reading. You might call it virtual reading. But the Wood people made a disclaimer that would be welcome in today's cultural speed-up: You can only read as fast as you think.

When I was in college we made the distinction between books we would like to read and books we would like to have read. Or then again there was the legendary story of the student who writes the best exam of his life on speed, the only problem being that he writes over and over on the same line of the page. SPEED KILLS, the poster said, but it also chills and chills out. Up to speed but off the wall.

Looking at something fast you get the advantage of an overview, you see patterns not discernible up close, but you may lose the detail. Can't see the thread only the weave. Is that a technical problem to be solved, an aesthetic problem to be explored, or an ethical problem to be acknowledged?

Efficiency without reason is desperation.

One wants—I want—to slow reading down and speed it up at the same time. That is, I want to have thick meaning and then accelerate it, as if the reader might download a zipped poem that proceeds to unpack itself in the mind, over time. By this method, one combines quick delivery—*condensare*—with "heavy reason." (Laura Riding, in "By a Crude Rotation": "To my lot fell / . . . A slow speed and a heavy reason, / . . . And then content, the language of the mind / That knows no way to stop.")

Art is the ketchup that loses the race.

The political unconscious of postmodern speed is the transcendence of the body and of history, of the resistance in the materials, of the space between here and there, of the time it takes (that time takes as much as it gives); that is, of our *animalady*, the limits that we live inside of (as Charles Olson put it), our grounding in and as flesh.

(As if you could accelerate the pace of recovery without wounding healing.)

Which is to say that there is in our culture, an intense dissatisfaction with the pace of things, the planned obsolescence now known as obsessive-compulsive upgrade disorder (OCUD), with a culture driven by the values of efficiency, celebrity, market penetration, and disposability. In equal proportion to being beneficiaries of this culture, we feel betrayed by it and beholden to it (as the drug is the master of the addict). We have alternatives, but it is our habit to deride these because they offer resistance instead of assimilation, purposelessness instead of profit, blank spaces in place of demographic rationalization, reflection rather than production, inquiry in place of accumulated knowledge. The alternative is to acknowledge the value of stopping, of derailing, of getting off the machine, in which case we may find that we were not speeding at all, just spinning our wheels without traction. I know I am—and I want to do that some more.

If technology is the answer, what is the question?

Our halls of culture boast newly efficient systems designed to maximize the flow of people through spaces that tokenize the aesthetic experience into voiceover tours with take-home souvenirs, making a trip to some museums more like a walk in a mall than contemplating a bust of Homer. Instead of making ourselves tourists to our own culture, we might create ever more dwelling spaces in which to reflect on art, salons that stop the flow of traffic, that encourage the viewer to rest, to flounder, even to be confused—indeed to be consumed by the art rather than to consume its representations.

Much of the prized and popular writing of our time is written to increase the speed with which it can be read. Our colleges are charged with teaching students a kind of expository writing that emphasizes efficient expression and plainness and that demonizes complexity, ambiguity, contradiction, or anything else that might bog readers down in the writing. Such ideologically blindered writing is governed by the three Cs of Strunk and White *Elements of Style* fundamentalism: Clarity, Concision, Coherence. In this context, it is useful to note how close this ideology of writing is to the moral discourse of speed. Yet there is another kind of writing, a writing that slows you down, that makes space for the reader to think, to respond, to wander, to savor. That takes pleasure in complexity and finds complexity in pleasure, that isn't interested in producing a meaning for the reader to skim off the top but to provide a pool of thought—a sound—in which to swim.

How can we find ways to support that, to support a writing—and more generally noncommercial contemporary art—that does nothing concrete, that is noninstrumental, that raises questions more than providing answers. One way is as simple as could be: direct support for the production of works through those independent presses or writing centers or websites, as well as noncommercial art spaces, that publish and present and distribute art. Without direct support for literary publishing, the small presses will not be able to survive in their present form—and the same could be said for the nonprofit sector of the other contemporary arts. And I am not talking about seed money, or money to build better bureaucratic and promotional structures, which are two favored ways to mime, while actually undermining, direct support for the production of literary works and works in other art media.

When the hare always wins, that's morality—speed as success—not ethics. And it sure isn't aesthetics either.

God speeds but she also brakes for humans.

BREAKING THE TRANSLATION CURTAIN:
THE HOMOPHONIC SUBLIME

Translation is always a form of collaboration: between two (or more) poets and also between two (or more) languages. For me, the most important value is that the poem newly being written is engaging as a poem in its "own" "new" language, not a secondary representation of that which lives primarily elsewhere. Accuracy is the bogeyman of translation; for what can be accurately paraphrased is not the "poetic" content of the work.

Translation can be a goad to invent new forms, structures, expressions, textures, and sounds in the (new) poem being written. This is to acknowledge, but also go beyond, Walter Benjamin's famous comment that the mark of the translator should not be made invisible, or inaudible, in the translation.[1] A certain strangeness from the original must necessarily be embodied in the new poem. When I translate, I want to keep as much of the syntax of the original as possible, especially if it goes against colloquial English: this might mean, for example, translating all the articles and genders that you have in French but not English. I realize this is a kind of mania: it is delirium, in Jean-Jacques Lecercle's sense, induced by the ontological inscrutabilities of translation.[2]

The poet/translator should be free to intervene in the process, assert her or his poetic presence, to let the poem mutate into fruition. I always start

L 'Esprit créateur 38.4 (1998).

1. "The Task of the Translator," in *Illuminations*, translated by Harry Zohn (New York: Schocken, 1969). See also Lawrence Venuti, *The Translator's Invisibility: A History of Translation* (New York: Routledge, 1995); and Steve McCaffery & bpNichol, *Rational Geomancy: The Kids of the Book-Machine: The Collected Research Reports of the Toronto Research Group, 1973–82* (Vancouver: Talonbooks, 1992).

2. Jean-Jacques Lecercle, *Philosophy Through the Looking Glass* (LaSalle, IL: Open Court, 1985). See, for example, Yunte Huang, *SHI: A Radical Reading of Chinese Poetry* (New York: Roof, 1997), which provides, for the first time in English, a character-for-character translation of several classic Chinese poems.

with the idea of homophonic translations, which I take from Louis and Celia Zukofsky's translation of Catullus into English, translating the sound of the Latin over and above the lexical meaning. Letting the sound lead is crucial, or often crucial, for the sound may lead to the sense. Every translator knows that a translation requires doing an interpretation of the poem, for words or expressions ambiguous in the original need to be translated one way or another, while a reader need not make any such decisions. We must be wary of a translation that is less ambiguous than its original: the task of the translator is to maintain an economy of ambiguity or inscrutability, as well as of sonic dynamics, not devalue these features in the process. We have many examples of poems that are translated into a fluent or colloquial English that stand in sharp contrast to the marvelous influidities and resistances to assimilation of the original poem: a boring and reductive way to translate, though I would have to say it is the "official" way, the authorized method.

Yes of course these remarks suggest just one way to translate. Nor do I intend them to apply only to poetry: philosophy in translation suffers perhaps more greatly than poetry if only because its readers are often less conscious of the semiotic cost of translation (roughly 3.1459) and even less willing to cede significance to what is unrecoverable.

And perhaps, too, my remarks reflect an American perspective. Because American English is such a capacious language, incorporating the accents, syntaxes, and manners of speech of both many other languages and many varieties of our own, many translations are unable to bring across the innovative force the originals have for their own language. The originals, often set against a very fixed pattern of poetic practice, have decisive meaning for readers or listeners precisely in the departures from this fixed, or relatively fixed, background. In American English, we have no comparable grid upon which these innovations can play, and as a result many of the poems heralded in the introductions, when translated in the conventional manner, seem like weak versions of any of a number of American poetry styles: one can only imagine what might be interesting about them.

Within this context, one might add a formal criterion to the evaluation of translation, taking translation as its own medium, not merely a genre of poetry: what is the translation doing that can't be done in any other medium?

Perhaps this also suggests the need for new formats for translation, using digital formats to allow, for example, for listening to the work read in the original language while looking at a translation—and for the possibility of extensive supplemental material, including multiple alternate figurative, conceptual, and literal translations, as well as a full range of notes. Indeed, the embedding of a translation with such a dense textual field intensifies the possibilities for cultural exchange that might motivate the art of translation, while refusing a reductive idea of poems as lyric utterances, unfettered to specifics of location, language, style, and historical moment.

Disputes about translation are always a pretext for disputes about poetry. Translation theory is poetics by another name. If I am interested in a certain kind of translation, it is because I am invested in a certain kind of poetry. And if I object to a certain style of translation, it is likely that I would also object to this style if it were written "originally" in the American. Yet under cover of "translation," many things—ideas, forms, contents—can be smuggled into the "target" language that might not be allowed, or validated, if composed without justification in some authoritative original other. Of course, this makes translation a rich and valuable field for literary frauds (from Ossian to Araki Yasusada). At the same time, attacks on translation for "unfaithfulness" are typically pretexts for a rejection of a style of poetry in the translator's own language that the attacker find unacceptable, unfaithful to his or her sense of the proprieties of that language.

One of the most interesting post-Zukofsky homophonic translations is David Melnick's *Men in Aida*.[3] While anything more than the most cursory reading of *Men in Aida* would move to its relation to Homer, the fact that this work is a homophonic translation of *The Iliad* has not been mentioned in the publications of the work. This raises the question of whether such works are meant to stand "on their own" or only in relation to their source. What happens when someone reads *Men in Aida* and doesn't recognize the Homer connection? Is the reading invalid? Doesn't Melnick want to allow for this? Once again, it is the question of the original versus the secondary, for which Andrew Benjamin's idea of "anoriginal" is such a useful alternative.[4] Is this like someone seeing *Clueless* but being clueless about Jane Austen? Us parents like to hope it sends the kids back to the book, but this is also preposterous. What really happens is that we Austenites are sent out to the movie. What is valuable, the original or the reproduction (Lori

---

3. David Melnick, *Men in Aida* (Berkeley: Tuumba, 1983); online at Eclipse, http://english .utah.edu/eclipse/projects/AIDA/aida.html, accessed June 28, 2009.

4. "Translating Origins: Psychoanalysis and Philosophy," in *Rethinking Translation: Discourse, Subjectivity, Ideology*, edited by Lawrence Venuti (London: Routledge, 1992).

Chamberlain's engendering reading of that question intended):[5] the source or the transfiguration of it, the product or the activity, the accuracy or the exchange? Or is what is valuable the relation of the original to the reproduction? Or the first on its own, but not the second on its own (the father and the relation of the father to the child, but not the mother/reproducer)? Homophonic translation is significant because it can symbolize the revenge of the translator: no longer invisible, but through the text's opacity making the "original" invisible (or occluded). (Though as Ben Friedlander has pointed out to me, this symbolic or categorical function can empty out what is actually interesting about any given homophonic or otherwise radically nonstandard translation.)

In reprinting Zukofsky's short poems, Paul Zukofsky, product of the reproductive act of the authors/sources LZ/CZ, prints only the LZ/CZ Catullus poems, dropping the Latin originals altogether, saying they get in the way of reading the work in itself as original (as PZ told me in phone conversation, filtered through / translated by my memory and desire to make this point).[6]

Stand on its own, eh? Just like you and . . .

But I could never do that . . .

Can there be a translation without an original? Interpretation without its object or subject? A beloved without a lover? Child without parent?

What is poetry?

5. "Gender and the Metaphorics of Translation," in *Rethinking Translation*.
6. Louis Zukofsky, *Complete Short Poetry* (Baltimore: Johns Hopkins University Press, 1991).

In November 1999, I got an e-mail from Nick Gallansky, saying he had heard that I was giving a talk on literary frauds at the MLA in Chicago and wanted to share some of his thinking with me on the topic. His return address was "NickGa1133@Gotchya.IOU," one of those e-mail services which anyone can use to style their identity. Normally I would have been wary in a case like this, but, from a few remarks he dropped in his e-mail, I had the uncanny sense that Gallansky was reading my mind (or at least the part of it that wasn't password protected), since he mentioned "a certain Czernin" and that he had written extensively on Wayne Pratt, two subjects I thought I would be the first to introduce into the discussion of literary fraud. Gallansky said he was coming to Chicago for the MLA and wanted to meet; he was on the job market for a creative writing job, and while he was a habitué of the Associated Writing Programs' annual conventions, he had never been to an MLA. I couldn't resist continuing a conversation that promised to help me think through what I was finding an increasingly vexing issue. We agreed to have a few drinks before the night session of the MLA on which I was scheduled to speak. I didn't know Chicago well, but Gallansky recommended a bar in the Loop, saying we could grab a cab back to the big hotels and still make it to the last few minutes of the Pataphysics cash bar, which I never miss, and then go together to the session on fraud.

Gallansky turned out to be an affable, red-faced man of around thirty-five, quite a bit older than I had expected. He has the garrulousness of a Silicon Valley CEO giving the specs on a new operating system, but the gleam just beyond his left iris put me on edge. "Have you read this?" were his first words to me, pointing to an article entitled "The Blood Runs Like a River through My Dreams" from the June *Esquire* by a guy going under the name of

Nasdijj and billed as the son of an alcoholic Navajo mother and an abusive white cowboy. "This is the real thing," Gallansky said. While I had heard the buzz that it was the best memoir of 1999, I explained to Gallansky that my beat was poetry and the last memoir I had read was *Hanta Yo* by Ruth Beebe Hill (though as far as first-hand accounts of native American life I still prefer Carlos Castaneda). But Gallansky quickly jumped to what seemed to be his main point, that I should read a book by Nancy Ruttenburg on the use of specter evidence by Puritan ministers, which reminded me a bit of the Salem witch trials, but seemed very remote from the issue of contemporary literary frauds.[1] In any case, I found it hard to focus and my thoughts kept getting interrupted by flashbacks from our high school production of *The Crucible* ("I saw Giddy Yid in the chicken coop with the skinheads"). The next thing I remember was a singsong, nasal voice saying over and over "Hurry up, please, it's time." As I came to, I realized that Bronx Science had never staged a production of *The Crucible*, at least not while I was there. I looked at my watch: it was after two. Gallansky must have slipped me a mickey. There were no cabs on the near-deserted street so I staggered back to the Marriott on foot. The lobby was almost empty, though in the bar there was a spirited discussion about the under-representation of panels on Canadian poetry at recent MLA conventions, one of the hot-button topics in the literary academy in the late '90s.

I was too embarrassed to ask anyone on the panel how it had gone. In any case, I abandoned my plan to write an essay based on my notes since, when I woke up the next morning, I realized they were missing. Gallansky must have taken them from me, or, then again, perhaps I had forgotten them at the bar.

I was reminded of the story recently when reading about James Frey. Was this another case of a white guy getting ahead by casting himself as victim? The mainstream reviewers and editors and book enthusiasts who had become addicted to memoir and uplift were shocked—shocked—that Frey's story was largely fabricated. But the more intriguing response was not the official condemnations of what was all along condoned, but the idea, floated by a few whose claims to aesthetic seriousness come off as particularly ludicrous, that the deep truth isn't who writes something but what it says about human experience. I have been around long enough to

---

1. Nancy Ruttenburg, *Democratic Personality: Popular Voice and the Trial of American Authorship* (Palo Alto: Stanford University Press, 1998).

know how to duck when I hear the "human experience" used in this way. As I wrote in a poem not too many years ago: "nobody seems to want to hear / About the pain we men feel / Having our prerogatives questioned."[2]

Then, about two months ago, in early 2006, I received a manila envelope with no return address, sent to my home. I asked my thirteen-year-old son Felix to open it for me, out of fear it might contain poison or an explosive (a process I follow with all suspect packages). Felix extracted a garden-variety manuscript from the envelope and assured me there was nothing to worry about. The text purported to be my December 1999 MLA lecture. While I disagreed with many of the key points, and found the rhetorical excesses of the piece objectionable, I nonetheless found the essay of some interest, if only for putting forward a point of view that few respectable scholars would care to articulate. However, I was alarmed to find some inconsistencies in the thinking and also some references to events that occurred after December 1999. That led me to question the authenticity of the work. Despite (or possibly because of) these features, and Gallansky's uncanny ability to mimic my essay style and point of view, few would have guessed, or even now will believe, that this essay was in fact not written by me. I present it here as a way to put this incident behind me so I can continue with my on-going work on poetry and truth.

CHARLES BERNSTEIN
UPPER WEST SIDE, MARCH 21, 2006

PRESENTED AT THE ANNUAL CONVENTION OF THE MODERN LANGUAGE ASSOCIATION IN CHICAGO ON DECEMBER 29, 1999

I am sorry to say that Charles Bernstein is not feeling well and has chosen to stay in his room in the hotel. He sends his regrets. In any case, he has decided to withdraw from the panel, feeling unable to discuss inauthenticity with the rigor and intellectual seriousness the topic demands. A few days ago he asked me to substitute for him, expressing his great admiration for my recent work. While I regret Bernstein's inability to appear here, I am

2. "The Influence of Kinship Patterns on Perception of an Ambiguous Stimuli," in *Dark City* (Los Angeles: Sun and Moon Press, 1994), 133.

delighted to take his place. My name is Nick Gallansky and I hope you will remember it, even if you don't remember anything I say. By the way, due to the oppressive time constraints that Bernstein insisted I observe, no doubt a concession to his obsequious relationship to these kinds of social niceties, I have had to cut a far longer, indeed book-length, piece, to just a few pages. Rest assured, that any objections you may have to what I am about to read are fully answered in the longer version.

FRAUD'S PHANTOMS: A BRIEF YET UNRELIABLE ACCOUNT OF FIGHTING FRAUD WITH FRAUD (NO PUN ON FREUD INTENDED), WITH SPECIAL REFERENCE TO THE POETICS OF *RESSENTIMENT*

On certain days
heart is full of hypocrisy
flowers of gobo are purple
SHIZUKU UYEMARUKO, FROM *MAY SKY*

The representation of an idea can under no circumstances be considered successful unless the whole range of possible extremes it contains has been virtually explored.
WALTER BENJAMIN, "EPISTEMO-CRITICAL PROLOGUE"

> It is simply a lie to say that a story that is applicable to a culture or even a subculture or a subsubsubculture or a molecularly distant, tiny, miniscule, subatomic, barely related neighborhood of circling electrons, is owned lock, stock, and barrel by someone so self-important they OWN events common to us all. They simply don't. . . .
> I don't give a damn where you are from.
> I am from EVERYWHERE.
> **NASDIJJ**

Every act of writing is a forgery in "telling but not showing" or showing principally in its telling. In this sense, the only authentic act of writing is the fraud that articulates its own dissembling—but a fraud, after all, can hardly ever be called genuine goods. In this way, the real poem is constantly hitting its head against the promise of a poem about the real, as in Robert Creeley's

"Was That a Real Poem or Did You Just Make it Up?"—real, that is, by being made, like a bed, to lie in.[3]

If one invokes the artifice of a poem, it may well be to avoid deception, as if publicity is a shield against disappointment. Deception is another matter altogether, a confidence game in which we are lead to believe that one state of affairs exists while our deceiver knows, or thinks she knows, that it does not.

Literary frauds that are not deceptive fall into the category of satires or fictions, and we speak of spoofs and personae. The frame of the poem will typically suffice to tip off, broadly or subtly as the case allows.

A marvelous recent example of this is Wayne Pratt's short collection of poems entitled *Watering the Cactus* (originally published in London by Ship of Fools press in 1999).[4] As Pratt himself writes in his illuminating introduction to his own work—I share with Pratt's widow Wendy Pratt-Sidebottom the belief that Pratt is the author despite clear evidence of the hand of Dr. Robert Sheppard—"A simple trip to the dentist is imagined so vividly that we feel we are under the 'interrogation bullseyes' of the dentist who 'garottes / My gaping tooth with a clamp.'" Pratt illustrates how this same poem situates him both as postmodern in content ("He scribbles master hieroglyphs / in the tomb of my mouth") as well a consummate craftsman in the manner of post-Movement orthodoxicalities.

Here is Platt's poem "Fornication":

Limp now, I turn away.
No longer can I face
The heaving spaghetti

Of your steaming sex, or
My elephant's fumblings
In the bamboo pit of our bed.

Hunching over your foetal back
On the infertile
Gulf of our marriage, I hug

3. Robert Creeley, *Was That a Real Poem or Did You Just Make It Up Yourself*, issued as *Sparrow* 40 (Santa Barbara, CA: Black Sparrow Press, 1976); collected in *Was That a Real Poem and Other Essays*, edited by Donald Allen with a chronology by Mary Novik (Bolinas, CA: Four Seasons Foundation, 1979).
4. Collected as "Blues 62" in Robert Sheppard, *Complete Twentieth Century Blues* (Cambridge, UK: Salt, 2008), 324.

My hottie-wottie-boggie
And say goodnight.
This childhood name

Brings back the muscular arms
Of my mother, hauling
The black-bottomed kettles

Onto our northern griddle
Spanning the rubber flanks
Of the spouting hotties.

My only consolations now
Are these virile images
Tossed up in a spray of old words.

If you notice a close resemblance to Paul Muldoon's "Quoof," the resemblance is intended. For in this publication, the literary fraud is amusingly announced from the opening pages and the whole work is clearly by Sheppard. Here a mock fraud is used as a literary conceit to send up a range of earnest and sincere poems. *Watering the Cactus* achieves this aim by being disarmingly straightforward about the terms of the fraud, so that it probably doesn't qualify as fraud at all, but parody.

Pratt may be a persona for Sheppard, but not a persona used to mine deeper poetic or emotional truths than would be possible for Sheppard writing in his own name. In contrast, many poets have used personae as a probe to produce poems that are not primarily satiric. Fernando Pessoa is perhaps the most famous twentieth-century example, though Jack Spicer's *After Lorca* is a crucial example for postwar American poetry. Let me here briefly note Clayton Eshleman's "Hoorah Pornoff" poems, inspired in part by a negative reaction to a review by Marjorie Perloff that Eshleman felt had challenged him to create works, with a female persona, of "horror and pornography" (thus horror/Hoorah and Perloff-Pornography/Pornoff).[5] For Eshleman, the persona allowed him to create poems "free to be *and* not to be me . . . [poems that were] an expression of the extent to which the feminine aspects of my personality had fought over the years for their rightful place in my work" (190–91). After finishing the series of poems, Eshleman

5. Clayton Eshleman, *Under World Arrest* (Santa Rosa, CA: Black Sparrow Press, 1994).

took out a post office box and sent poems out in Pornoff's name, with the poems soon appearing in *Fag Rag, Momentum,* and as the featured poems in the fourth series of Cid Corman's *Origin.* Eshleman notes that he kept up a few correspondences for his made-up poet, even fending off people who wanted to date her. An edited set of the poems appears in Eshleman's collection *Under World Arrest,* and it is apparent, from this selection, that Eshleman is exploring his own relation to the persona created in almost every poem, in many cases directly addressing his "homuncula." Here is the fourth poem in the series:

to be an udder dripping in the lie

To feel acutely the size of trees,
the cutaneous test of wind,
to return on the body
spoken, as if in rim.

And to be in touch, womanic,
to lean back into noun.
But to be suffix, mother, to have other
buried behind an m,
I lie

in

her lie,
a supporting beam in the Tomb of M. (78)

The personae of Eleanor Antin are illustrative of a radically different approach to personae. In playing the role of Eleanora Antinova, a black Russian dancer, possibly the last to dance with Diaghilev in Paris in the 1920s, Antin does nothing to disguise her complexion or change her accent. She appears live, as at the MLA some years ago, or on tape, as in apparently archival film footage, as Antinova, one in a series of roles Antin has assumed over her career. Yet, strikingly, Antin, whose personae have never involved deceit about her identity, tells a story of a curator dismissing the significance of her work with this telling remark—"Oh Eleanor Antin—she's a fraud!"

I have been called a fraud myself and more than once, perhaps in part for speaking in forked tongues . . . or maybe just because my tongue was not forked enough, not forked in the way designed to pass muster, or that is, was tongued in a way that called to mind forks and spoons and not the real world of emotional truths beyond, or perhaps under, the table. In this context, it's worth bringing to mind that the accusation of fraudulence is routinely used against those who question certain conventional wisdom, including conventional literary wisdom. The charge of fraud not only says that the poems are no good but also that those involved in editing or publishing them, or critics who praise them, or even readers who enjoy them are somehow on the aesthetic take, conspiring with the fake poets to pull a fast one on authentic literary values. Accusing someone of being a charlatan, rather than simply a bad artist or one who has ideas with which you disagree, is the fastest way to end discussion: it short-circuits the kind of ideal speech situation envisioned by Jürgen Habermas or Richard Rorty. It reinforces an us/them consciousness on both sides of the erected barrier. Ironically, outrage at the frauds of charlatans is one of the main sources of literary frauds, as if the only way you could exorcise the fraudulent is through fraud—to teach these snake oil salesmen a lesson. This is where I want to begin a brief discussion of *ressentiment* in James McAuley and Harold Stewart's Ern Malley, Timothy Barrus's Nasdijj, Kent Johnson's Araki Yasusada, and Alan Sokal's Alan Sokal, each of which uses a fraud as a way of ridiculing what the perpetrators see as the fraud of modernism, poststructualism, or multiculturalism.

Literary fraud is an ethically troubling activity not because it undermines the rhetoric of sincerity, which it may or may not do, but because it violates the good-faith relationship of parties making a cultural exchange, in particular undermining the trust between editor and authors necessary especially for literary presses where contracts are rare and legal suits impractical (which is what makes the Ern Malley affair so unusual). Note that literary fraud does not, in itself, destabilize truth claims or authorship, since in many cases, as in the three just mentioned, the fraud depends on a highly stable idea of authorship for the deception to work. Once unmasked, the authority of the author is all the more crucial; or to put this more accurately, what remains stable is an assumption that there is a true state of affairs that underlies the deceptive surface of the fraud—this is a prerequisite for the fraud to be a fraud. Indeed, the frauds of Sokal, McAuley and Stewart, and Johnson are not critiques of moral discourse—that is, attacks on the social codes of honesty and integrity. On the contrary, these frauds were used as a way of shoring up moral discourse against the perceived relativism of contemporary culture. These authors embraced fraud not in a joyous or comic dance with the improbabilities or insufficiencies of authenticity, but rather out of a sense of moral outrage—specifically of white male rage.

Let me begin with Sokal. The Spring/Summer 1996 "Science Wars" issue of *Social Text* included an article by New York University physicist Alan Sokal entitled "Transgressing the Boundaries: Towards a Transformative Hermeneutics of Quantum Gravity." But the boundary it was transgressing was not related to quantum theory but to authorial sincerity. Sokal's intent, as he noted in articles and interviews, was to mock the gravity of antifoundational literary theory; *Social Text* was viewed as a veritable witches' coven of this treacherous approach to reality. The story of Sokal's duplicity received front-page attention in *the New York Times*. Indeed, Sokal's fraud was widely hailed as exposing the fraud of both postmodernism and poststructualism.

The Sokal affair solicited the kind of moral indignation that draws lines in the sand at the beach of the Ideological State Apparatus. Consider a comment by Dr. Jonathan Katz, from the October 1999 issue of the journal *Physics Today*, cited in a *New York Times* article by James Glanz. Dr. Katz, the *Times* reports, assures us that "the only reasonable conclusion [to be drawn from the hoax] is that postmodernism is nothing more than a scheme to obtain cushy university jobs for its practitioners."[6]

Alan Sokal's deception was aimed at exposing what he viewed as an intellectual fraud. If Sokal had wanted to dispute the premises of *Social Text* editor Andrew Ross or others' views about science, he could, of course, have written an essay on this topic—as polemical or scathing as he chose to be—and submitted it to *Social Text*. Presumably, Sokal's choice to ventriloquize arguments that he would later expose as preposterous was motivated by his sense that the editors of the special issue of *Social Text* in which his essay appeared were pulling the wool over someone's eyes—not Sokal's, who knows which way is up (but alas not which way is upside-down and sideways), but those of more tender readers who may not have the intellectual acuity to fend off the seduction of this intellectual con. Sokal wished to expose *Social Text*'s assault on truth for what it was—irrational, gibberish, nonsensical—patent nonsense, let's say, in the sense of patent medicines, if not patent leather tap shoes. To expose this deception he chose to be deceptive, fighting fraud with fraud, and so entering into that genre of literary fraud I want to term "hostile or retributive frauds"—frauds without a sense of humor, which is not to say they may not be quite funny. (Brian McHale sees this type of fraud as

---

6. James Glanz, "Reconciling Nothingness in the Universe and the Soul," *New York Times*, December 7, 1999, sec. 5, p. 5, col. 2.

punitive—hoaxes with a trap.)[7] Sokal's fraud was necessitated by moral outrage, with all the self-righteousness such outrage typically entails. The Ern Malley affair is the now classic example (see especially the account by Michael Heyward in *The Ern Malley Affair*).[8] And while those of us on the sidelines may appreciate the Sokal affair as a literary event, a bit of mischievous fun, Sokal's own glosses of the hoax give no comic relief and indeed are filled with high moral tone in the defense of empirical truth.

It should be noted that by their nature, the social and aesthetic effects of fraud are hard to predict. This is a volatile social medium. McAuley and Stewart would not likely have been able to be anticipate that their prank would end up having such an acute and chronic impact, just as they could not have imagined that the poems they wrote in ridicule would be valued for their comic innovation by the very audience they intended to send up. In Kent Johnson's case, the author may well have been primarily concerned with the creation of the persona of Yasusada, and related literary documents, and less concerned about the hoax through which this work entered the world. However, if that is the case, it raises further questions not only about reestablishing credibility after a hoax but also about the specter not just of deception of others but self-deception (as to motive and outcome). I don't want to get trapped by an assertion of the author's intentions. More useful is to read these works as social texts.

While considering the perplexing problem of fighting fraud with fraud, I happened to have a conversation with Susan Howe in which she explained that during the seventeenth-century witch trials in New England, the courts were able to convict those accused of witchcraft on the basis of "specter evidence"—testimony about their phantom doubles. That is, testimony was accepted from the accusers not about what we might say were the actual actions of the accused but rather based on the action of the accused's ventriloquized "specter" (as reported by the accusers). In other words, those accused of projecting phantom devils onto innocent persons were convicted on the basis of ventriloquized projections of themselves. Specters fighting specters, through the medium of ventriloquism. As if fraud could vanquish fraud.

Ern Malley is an invented ghost. The Australian trial of Max Harris, the young editor of the modernist journal *Angry Penguins*, who in 1944 had published Ern Malley thinking it was a "real" person, used the testimony of this

7. Brian McHale, "Archaeologies of Knowledge: Hill's Middens, Heaney's Bogs, Schwerner's Tablets," in *New Literary History* 30.1 (Winter 1999): 236.

8. Michael Heyward, *The Ern Malley Affair* (London: Faber and Faber, 1993).

specter against him. Harris was convicted by the word of a ghost text of an invented dead poet. The text of Ern Malley was produced by the prosecutors as proof of the indecent thoughts of Max Harris; the specter text's sexual and aesthetic indiscretion, as fantasized by the court, convicted Harris.

Sokal projected his own "bad" specter to pull down the specter of post-structualism.

Kent Johnson's Yasusada is a phantom set out in the world to destroy a phantom. In saying this I am not denying the temptation and indeed value in reading *Doubled Flowering* strictly as a work of persona.[9] I am rather focusing on the way *Doubled Flowering* entered into the world as ventrilo-quism, through a series of concerted deceptions and choreographed du-plicities.

The Yasusada hoax took place over a period of a few years in a number of poetry magazines, including *Conjunctions, American Poetry Review,* and *Grand Street*. Translations of the work of a Japanese poet, Araki Yasusada, began to appear, with the explanation that Yasusada was a survivor of the atomic bombing of Hiroshima who had died a few years ago. The work was interesting, quite unexpected in its style from the little most of us knew about postwar Japanese poetry, oddly familiar. Only it turned out that the work was by an American, not a Japanese, and some of the editors who pub-lished it felt betrayed and duped. One said he would not have published it if he had known the actual authorship and, of course, this seems the reaction the forgery was set out to provoke. Is a work valuable as poetry because it is authentic in its witness? Is a poem worth publishing only because it is a poem by a survivor, otherwise not? Is the poet's identity or autobiography more important than the poem? Is the value of poetry now primarily its value in conveying cultural information rather than aesthetic exploration (including the exploration carried out by the forgery)?

In this respect, the most straightforward of all the responses to *Doubled Flowering*, and the one that is, in a sense, least open to dispute as to the first-order reality of this work, was written by Juliana Chang, Walter K. Lew, Tan Lin, Eileen Tabios, and John Yau—the only collective response amidst many quite intricate reactions to appear in the Summer 1997 is-sue of the *Boston Review*.[10] Their response is notable because it reflects the

9. Araki Yasusada [© Kent Johnson], *Doubled Flowering: From the Notebooks of Araki Yasusada* (New York: Roof Books, 1997).

10. Juliana Chang, Walter K. Lew, Tan Lin, Eileen Tabios, and John Yau, "Displacements," in *Boston Review* 22.3 (Summer 1997), http://bostonreview.net/BR22.3/Chang.html, accessed February 2006.

views of several of the most formally innovative poets of the present moment, a group that, while acknowledging the significance of their Asian American backgrounds, has worked to articulate identity in ways critical of the identity poetics of those who, presumably, might be disturbed most by the false witness of the Yasusada hoax. Ironically, *Doubled Flowering* has received commendation from those who lean toward a poetics of witness and authenticity. The response of Chang et al. is scathing, but not because of the issue of false witness, per se:

> It is disturbing that Kent Johnson, the alleged perpetrator of the hoax, found it necessary to reprise the stereotype of the deferential Asian in order to point out the relationship between a classical Japanese form, renga, and the postmodern practice associated with Ron Silliman's "new sentence." In so doing, as Perloff notes, Johnson displaces and diminishes the accomplishments of contemporary Japanese poets. This is not an isolated incident: *Beneath a Single Moon*, the anthology of contemporary American Buddhist poetry that Johnson co-edited with Craig Paulenich, similarly displaces Asian American poets from the practice of Buddhism. As Walter K. Lew has written of that volume:

>> The 45 American poets whose essays and poetry on Buddhist practice comprise the anthology are all Caucasian, and the book only mentions Asians as distal teachers (ranging from Zen patriarchs to D. T. Suzuki), not as fellow members or poets of the sangha. . . . When one considers the relative obscurity of some of the poets included in the book, one wonders how it was possible not to have known the Buddhistic poetry of such writers as [Lawson Fusao] Inada, Al Robles, Garrett Kaoru Hongo, Alan Chong Lau, Patricia Ikeda, and Russell Leong. . . . [Gary] Snyder's introduction deliberates the question—"Poetry is democratic, Zen is elite. No! Zen is democratic, poetry is elite. Which is it?" . . . Perhaps he should have also asked whether Zen and poetry, as reconfigured in American Orientalism, are racist.

The response by Chang and company ends this way:

> Like most hoaxes, Johnson's is fueled mainly by the potential for self-gain. And like all hoaxes it is complex—his act of yellowface at once plays into an existing and apparently vigorous orientalist fantasy, exposes American ignorance of both Japanese poetry and recent Japanese history, and levels a critique against an experimental writing community to which the author

also seeks to ingratiate himself. In this last respect, Johnson's act is doubly disturbing: he wants the taint of scandal without having to take responsibility for the stereotypes he celebrates.

While sales for *Doubled Flowering* have been modest (about seven hundred copies in ten years since publication, according to publisher James Sherry),[11] the book has received an enormous amount of attention—not as much as Alan Sokal, but for small-press standards, an extraordinary number of papers and essays as well as international media exposure, in Japan, Australia, and the U.S. I think it is safe to say that much more has been written on the imaginary Japanese poet Araki Yasusada than on any work of Japanese poetry published in English translation in the 1990s. A 1998 bibliography compiled by Johnson listed a couple of dozen reviews or articles regarding *Doubled Flowering*, and this number has doubled in the years since.[12] Compare this to approximately one review received by *May Sky*, edited by Violet Kazue de Cristoforo, both a history and a collection of haiku by Japanese Americans interred in U.S. concentration camps, published by Sun & Moon Press in 1997.[13] The idea that *Doubled Flowering* might increase interest in or understanding of the poetry of Japanese holocaust survivors or Japanese poetry in general appears unsupported. Nor should this be a criterion in judging this work. *Doubled Flowering* is a work of American poetry and its reception has taken place within this frame.

It is an important part of the story that the substantial interest in the *Doubled Flowering* hoax has not translated into a comparable interest in the poems themselves. Indeed, the hoax is what is primarily interesting about this work. In contrast, the Ern Malley poems continue to engage a great deal of interest and have emerged as among the great poetic works of the 1940s, despite their author's desire to write the worst possible poems (something like writing a "pits" or "Flarf" poem from the Experiments List).[14] Ironically, and unlike James McAuley and Harold Stewart, Kent Johnson appears to

11. James Sherry, publisher of Roof Books, personal correspondence, June 24, 2007.

12. Kent Johnson, "Araki Yasusada: A Partial Bibliography" (September 1998), http://www .lang.nagoya-u.ac.jp/~nagahata/yasusada-bib.html, accessed February 22, 2006.

13. Violet Kazue de Cristoforo, ed., *May Sky: There Is Always Tomorrow—An Anthology of Japanese American Concentration Camp Kaiko Haiku* (Los Angles: Sun & Moon Press, 1997). The epigraph quoted above (p. 206) is from p. 269.

14. Experiments List, http://writing.upenn.edu/bernstein/experiments.html, accessed February 22, 2006.

have wanted to write poems of great value. The "gotcha" of the Malley hoax was to show that nonsensical poems would be published in *Angry Penguins* because the editor was himself a fraud, making nonsensical literary judgments. It turns out that McAuley and Stewart were quite wrong about this; Max Harris had made a good choice. The "gotcha" of the Yasusada hoax was quite different, exposing the fact that good poems would be overlooked because of who their author was, that the "authenticity" of the author's identity was eclipsing aesthetic merit.

What I am suggesting is that the way *Doubled Flowering* entered into the world is an indelible part of its meaning. If it had been initially presented as the work of Kent Johnson, as a work of a literary persona, part of a venerable literary tradition, it would not only have received far less attention, but it would be far less interesting as a literary work. The social aggressiveness of the hoax is defining and not biodegradable. At the same time, the nature of this deception apparently means that the author cannot, or in any case has so far been unwilling to, fully confront the more dystopian politics of resentment at its core. In a 1998 interview, Johnson makes the implausible claim that "there was never any desire to taunt anyone through this work—only to present poems that imagined another life in the most compelling way possible to their author. . . . The Yasusada author did not try to hide the work's fictionality—it was there from the start, for everyone to see."[15] But isn't this what every confidence man says to himself: let the buyer beware; if only you had paid attention you would have seen; it's your own fault for believing what I said. That really, in the end, this fraud is no fraud at all, just another literary work. What's the fuss all about?

Let me spell this out. The idea of the hoax, though not necessarily the persona, was to trick unsuspecting editors into showing that they publish work not on the basis of its intrinsic aesthetic merit but rather on the basis of who is writing it, with presumed favor being shown to victims, whether of discrimination or tragedy. For the hoax to work—to show up the editors and the values of the larger literary world in which they operate—enough clues to the fraudulent signature of the poems must be given, so that the perpetrator can claim a kind of moral justice in entrapping the editors who commit the crime of sloppy reading, making politically and socially—rather than aesthetically—motivated literary judgments, and, not the least, lapsing into sentimentality toward the plight of the author as survivor. Indeed,

15. Kent Johnson, "An Interview with Kent Johnson, Conducted by Norbert Francis," *Jacket* 5 (1998), http://jacketmagazine.com/05/yasu-larsen.html, accessed February 22, 2006.

the perpetrator of the fraud actually gets to claim the moral high ground, gets to be not the criminal but the police on a sting operation. This moralism fatally compromises the aesthetic giddiness that is possible with more comic or destabilizing frauds or spoofs.

The memoir frauds of James Frey and Nasdijj (Timothy Barrus) are worth considering in this context. The epigraph from Nasdijj (quoted above, p. 206)[16] is from a website now removed by the author, Timothy Barrus, a white man, winner of the 2004 PEN/Beyond Margins Award,[17] who successfully posed as a troubled American Indian named Nasdijj. A bio of Nasdijj was posted on the website of the Native American Authors Project, Internet Public Library, of University Michigan School of Information (it has since been removed from the site):

> Nasdijj, 1950–
>
> Navajo
>
> Nasdijj, whose name means "to become again" in Athabaskan, was born in the southwestern U.S. to a mother of Navajo heritage and a cowboy father. His first published essay, "The Blood Runs Like a River Through My Dreams," appeared in *Esquire* in June, 1999. It has since been published in a collection of autobiographical essays that bears the same title. He currently lives in Chapel Hill, NC.[18]

According to Matthew Fleischer's *LA Weekly* story on the fraud, " 'The cover letter was this screed about how *Esquire* had never published the work of an American-Indian writer and never would because it's such a racist publication,' recalls editor in chief David Granger. 'And under it was . . . one of the most beautiful pieces of writing I'd ever read.' By the time the piece was published in the June issue, the writer (who lives on an Indian reservation) had a book contract."[19]

---

16. Nasdijj website, http://www.nasdijj.typepad.com, accessed February 22, 2006 [since removed].

17. PEN Beyond Margins Award website, http://www.pen.org/page.php/prmID/929, accessed September 19, 2010.

18. Internet Public Library, Native American Authors: http://www.ipl.org/div/natam/bin/browse.pl/A500, accessed February 22, 2006 [since removed].

19. Matthew Fleischer, "Navahoax," in *LA Weekly*, January 23, 2006, http://www.laweekly.com/index3.php?option=com_content&task=view&id=12468&Itemid=9&pop=1&page=0, accessed February 22, 2006.

If Nasdijj's "memoir" traffics in loss and tragedy, his blog revealed "a very angry man," according to the *LA Weekly* piece. "If in the books his passion and fierceness are modulated and concentrated, his blog posts are full of rants and denunciations. Targets include the American health care system, government treatment of Indians, middle-class values and, especially, the publishing industry." Fleischer offers this quote: "Jews [in publishing] would sell the gas chamber shower heads if they thought it might make a buck."

Commenting on the Nasdijj affair in *Time* magazine, Sherman Alexie wrote:

> As a Native American writer and multiculturalist, I worried that Nasdijj was a talented and angry white man who was writing as a Native American in order to mock multicultural literature. I imagined that he would eventually reveal himself as a hoaxer and shout, "You see, people, there is nothing real or authentic about multicultural literature. Anybody can write it." . . . So why should we be concerned about his lies? His lies matter because he has cynically co-opted as a literary style the very real suffering endured by generations of very real Indians because of very real injustices caused by very real American aggression that destroyed very real tribes.[20]

Unlike McHale, I view *Doubled Flowering* as a retributive/punitive hoax, what he calls a "trap hoax" (238). It seems to me this is not only an essential part of the work but also one of the things that is more aesthetically and historically interesting about it. The attempt to efface the hoax after the initial "gotcha" has been realized *is itself a hoax*, a double cross that comes with a double scold—first against those who fell for the trap and then against those who can't take a joke, who recoil from the first hoax. This double is the doubled flowering of the title, if we take the flowers to be Baudelaire's *fleurs du mal*. Under this interpretation, *Doubled Flowering* goes beyond its initial highly volatile deception to lead a second, fraudulent life as an authentic work of persona. For this reason, *Doubled Flowering* may actually be closest to McHale's category of "genuine hoax" (236). To deflower this doubly retributive hoax, to make *Doubled Flowering* more palatable, ends up undervaluing the work; making it more genial takes away not only its noxious odor but also its double edge.

20. Sherman Alexie, "When the Story Stolen Is Your Own," *Time*, January 29, 2006, http://www.time.com/time/magazine/article/0,9171,1154221,00.html, accessed February 22, 2006.

We see this deflowering of *Doubled Flowering* as a persistent note in several of the critical responses to it, whether positive in the case of Forrest Gander and Eliot Weinberger or negative in the case of Charles Simic. All insist it really doesn't matter who wrote it; what matters is the poems themselves. According to Simic,

> Our literary politics being what they are, we can expect more hoaxes. I have no objection to them whatsoever. If the poems are first-rate, I'll bow down to them in deepest reverence even if the claim is being made that they were composed by a left-behind space alien or a love-starved orangutan in the San Diego Zoo. No matter what anyone tells you, as in music, carpentry and all the other ancient arts and true crafts, it always comes down to the work itself. [*Boston Review* symposium.]

Gander, in his review in *The Nation*, takes a more positive tack: "Let's consider a Yasusada poem and ask ourselves whether the fiction of the poem's authorship makes it less emotionally authentic."[21] He goes on to suggest that *Doubled Flowering*'s use of persona is an "act of solidarity" that produces an "astonishing success" (31).

Finally, Weinberger writes that—

> those who dismiss the Yasusada poems as a cruel imperialist joke are assuming the author is a white American male, which in turn is based on the assumption that anyone who is not a white Euro-male wants to speak only in an "authentic" voice. The identity of the Yasusada Author has become so refracted that we are approaching the condition where We Are All Yasusada—though I prefer to think of the author as a young woman in Senegal.[22]

Weinberger suggests that the meaning of *Doubled Flowering* would be comparable whether its author were an African woman facing the ravages of AIDS in her country or an American college professor from the Midwest contemplating the rejection of his manuscript from poetry magazines because of perceived reverse discrimination. It seems to me this misses what is most profoundly interesting, and disturbing, about *Doubled Flowering*— that the effect of the hoax depends on the fact that it was written by a white,

21. Forrest Gander, "Poetic License & the Bomb," in *The Nation* 267.2 (July 13, 1998): 30.
22. Eliot Weinberger, "Can I Get a Witness?" and "Postscript: I Found a Witness," *Jacket* 5 (1998), http://jacketmagazine.com/05/yasu-wein.html, accessed February 22, 2006. Repr. in part from *Village Voice Literary Supplement* (July 1996).

male, heterosexual American. It is not insignificant that all of the hostile literary frauds I am discussing here were written by men. The gender of these frauds is as much a part of their social poetics as any other fact about them. "We" are not the world and the world is not "U.S."

The idea that it doesn't matter who actually wrote the poem is a tried but not so true shibboleth from New Criticism. Of course it matters; it always matters. Who speaks in a poem is never inconsequential, and the identical text written by someone else would not be the same poem. I take *that* to be the lesson of *Doubled Flowering*, not the opposite. A poem shorn of historical and social being in the world amounts to almost nothing, an empty husk. There is no poem "itself" but only a work that exists in a social space in which such a hoax plays itself out. To deny the meaning of the fraud is to negate the work almost entirely. This works exist, fundamentally and primarily as a social text—a social text whose meaning cannot be controlled by its author, much less its publishers. Taking away the issue of fraudulent authorship strips *Doubled Flowering*, as it would the Ern Malley poems, of what makes it significant *as a poem*. Indeed, the authorship of *Doubled Flowering* is even more, not less, crucial for this work than it is for most contemporary poems, and this is only highlighted by the author's dramatics concerning authorship. The claim that *Doubled Flowering* proves the insignificance of who wrote it brings up a basic problem with *Doubled Flowering*, for the idea that there is any such thing as the poem itself is a species of the jargon of authenticity. *Doubled Flowering* does not so much give lie to the idea that only "white Euro-males" question authenticity as demonstrate the desire for authenticity of at least some "white Euro-males." The problem with *Doubled Flowering* is not that it is a fake, but that it is not fake enough.

Johnson makes this problem explicit when he writes, in the 1998 interview, "Rather than being 'fakes,' I would offer that the Yasusada writings represent an original and courageous form of authenticity—one that is perhaps difficult to appreciate because of the extent to which individual authorial status and self-promotion dominate our thinking about, and practice of, poetry."

This could hardly be stated better: the point of the fraud is authenticity; but this authenticity can be claimed only at the price of falling prey to the very enshrining of authorial status and self-promotion that the author claims to want to critique.

As Marjorie Perloff points out, the *Doubled Flowering* hoax makes a valuable critique of the primacy of the authentic witness in a poem: the belief that actually *being there* is more important than the literary artifact that results.[23] But for all that, it still must be registered that this attack on authenticity comes from a member of the race and gender group most apparently undermined by the interest, for American literary circles in the past two decades, with the authenticity of the witness of "others." If the Western canon often took the work of white males as universal witness of human experiences, the new emphasis on witness and testimony can seem to have replaced the insistence on the white male point of view with everything but. White male backlash has been intense, ingenious, and unrelenting. And this backlash often comes with a lesson to us all about its own ultimate high-order authenticity; for, in case you didn't know, the most abusive behavior is the most authentic because it alone is not coached in liberal niceties. Macho über alles.

Like Ern Malley and Nasdijj, Yasusada is not a nice or happy literary affair: it is constituted by bitter social aggression. Frauds like those of Sokal, Nasdijj, McAuley and Stewart, and Johnson require that the perpetrators see their projects as in some ways more authentic than what they are debunking. The idea that the deception of the fraud falls away to reveal an ulterior truth is the anti-historical fantasy of this set of frauds of forged identities. The paradox goes back to Epimenides: *The author is a liar.* The liar's claim to authenticity, like the Cretan's, has no face value. But it is just this truth that these frauds wish to overcome. And yet the more they struggle to free themselves from the knot they have so carefully tied, the tighter is its hold.

Echoing Alexie's remarks on Nasdijj, *Doubled Flowering* can be seen to represent the apotheosis of the poetics of resentment in the 1990s— resentment against the apparent new entitlements to those often invisible or inaudible in previous representations of contemporary literature; resentment, that is, against feminism, gay rights, and multiculturalism as arbiters of literary taste. Ironically, the more this motivation is denied (or repressed or unintended), the more the hoax assumes its grim office. The common theme of the critique of literary reverse discrimination is the idea that literature is now more about victimization than aesthetics. The perverse genius of *Doubled Flowering* is that by putting on not only "yellowface" (in the words of Chang et al.) but also the mask of grief of the holocaust survivor, the ventriloquizing author of *Doubled Flowering* willfully subjects himself

23. Marjorie Perloff, "In Search of the Authentic Other: The Poetry of Araki Yasusada," originally published in *Boston Review* (April/May 1997), collected at Perloff's EPC page, http://epc .buffalo.edu/authors/perloff/boston.html, accessed February 22, 2006.

to denunciation and humiliation, thus achieving identification as the victim he could otherwise not be as an American white, male heterosexual.

If an epic is a poem including history, then a fraud is a failed epic, a poem dissolving into its historicity.

Let me now take an abrupt turn to a literary fraud entirely unknown in the United States.

In the early summer of 1986, two young Austrian poets, Franz Josef Czernin and Ferdinand Schmatz, had the idea to write poems that closely resembled the poems they found most typical and at the same time most deplorable in contemporary poetry volumes—for example, the work of Reiner Kunze, Günter Kunert, and Sarah Kirsch. At first they had the idea to call the poet Irene Schweighofer (silent court), a poet born in a little town in upper Austria, who, familiar through schooling with the tenets of modernism, would need no time to forge her own distinctive style and upon being published would proceed to win many prizes and much praise. However, Czernin and Schmatz felt this process would take too long, and in order to shorten the "difficult and boring" process, decided to give authorship of the poems to Czernin. They completed the work in a few weeks, and the book was immediately accepted for publication under the title *Die Reise* (the journey). The book received positive attention, some of which suggested that at last Czernin had given up his thrashing about in the waters of experimentation and found a more profound and authentic voice. When Czernin broke the news of his own duplicitous relation to the poems in *Der Spiegel* in March 1987, a furious hail of criticism descended upon him, not the least from the publisher of the book, who felt he had been betrayed. Later the same year, Czernin and Schmatz published a book-length account of the story together with exchanges between them and several interlocking essays.

Here is of one of the poems from *Die Reise: In achtzig Gedichten um die ganze Welt*:

fahr-plan

> ist mein blick
> nicht eine schere,
> deren beine
> schritte machen,
> die alle fernen
> auseinanderschneiden?

hat denn die schere
keine augen,
die zu ringen werden
jener finger,
die auf ihre ziele zeigen?

und gehen diese ziele
nicht auf zwei füssen,
deren zehen
auf nägel treten,
die meine ganze reise
zusammennageln?[24]

agenda

is my glance
not a scissor
whose leg
makes steps
that cut through
all distances?

had, then, this scissor
no eyes
which will strive
to finger
loins of desire?

and will not such loins
walk on two feet
whose toes
tread on pins
fastening together
my whole journey?

---

24. Franz Josef Czernin, *Die Reise: In achtzig Gedichten um die ganze Welt* (Salzburg und Wien: Residenz Verlag, 1987), 30.

Schmatz and Czernin created a literary scandal with this and the other poems in the collection, but they were able to focus the discussion of issues of quality and judgment and to avoid the more abusive aspects of the Ern Malley and Yasusada hoaxes. Indeed, *Die Reise* is motivated by a desire to critique the jargon of authenticity rather than to reinscribe it, as we find in the Yasusada case. There is no claim here that these are necessarily good poems or that we should look to the "poems themselves" for the meaning. The texts here have meaning in relation to the literary valuations into which they make an intervention; their meaning is social and diacritical. Indeed, late in 1987, Schmatz and Czernin published *Die Reise: In achtzig flachen Hunden in die ganze tiefe Grube*, a book about the affair in which they address explicitly the questions of authorship and motivation. In this book, Czernin describes *Die Reise* as a form of literary self-criticism. "Perhaps one must, to make a better poem, know how one makes a worse poem," he writes. "I think it was Novalis who said that good literature is made from worse literature. He was right that there must be, in any case, worse poetry from which better poetry can originate, whereas for me it is self-evident that the contrary can also be valuable."[25] *Die Reise*, then, can be understood as an investigation of aesthetic judgment. And yet, as the Ern Malley poems also show, what is written out of a desire to expose the limits of a particular style (or rhetoric) may ultimately become exemplary of unrealized potential in the style; ironizing of the style may create a thickening of the artifice and with it an intensification of the aesthetic experience. Over time, the poems of *Die Reise* take on charm that goes beyond parody. In any case, Czernin is not asserting the objectivity of any such judgments, but rather that "every objectivity is fictional." His purpose then, as befits a poet who has written a study of Karl Kraus, is satiric adjudicative: the fraud remains a fraud.

I want to end this brief on literary fraud by revealing one for the first time. I am thinking of the meteoric rise of Nick Gallansky, who has recently had poems in *APR* and an interview in *AWP* (so far his major publications have been restricted to magazines with titles abbreviated by three letters). Gallansky's *AWP* interview is particularly revealing:

25. Franz Josef Czernin, "Die Verdopplung des Igels," in Czernin and Ferdinand Schmatz, *Die Reise: In achtzig flachen Hunden in die ganze tiefe Grube* (Linz-Wien, Austria: Edition Neue Texte, 1987), 21.

As a member of Gen X, I reject the ideologized poetry wars of the seventies and eighties. I don't have to choose. I can like x and y, from the elegant elegiacs of Pinsky to the radical disjuncture of Graham to the exhilarating new formalism of Timothy Steele. I am particularly engaged with recuperating white male identity as both gentle and engaging.

Here is an excerpt of Gallansky's most critically acclaimed poem:

The sweet smell of nicotine on my fingers
A glimmering surrender to the charred forces
Below the surfaces of my coy graces
As if all that I know is in smoke that lingers
Swayed by the push and pull of my paces

It is my duty to tell you all this evening: Gallansky is a fraud.

FULCRUM INTERVIEW

What is and what isn't poetry? What is poetry's essential nature (if any)?

Poetry is not an essence but a practice. The term is not honorific but generic. A bad poem's still a poem. A newspaper article presented as a poem is a poem. By the same token, a song lyric printed in a CD insert is not a poem, though presented in another context that designation might change.

Poetry is the art of (verbal) language.

What is the most important poetry?

What is being written now.

Who are the greatest poets?

The ones who write the greatest poems.

What do they accomplish?

Nothing.

What is the relationship between poetry and truth?

Poetry is to truth like rubber to the rubber tree: it bounces.

Is there such a thing as poetic truth?

From time to time.

Fulcrum 4 (2005).

How does poetry relate to the human condition?

Poetry doesn't relate to the human condition, it articulates ways of encountering & acknowledging it; sometimes it changes it.

Poetry, by necessity, rejects the human condition.

Is there (or can there be) a meaningful philosophy of poetry?

Meaningful to whom? The poem, the poet, the reader, the human condition, or the kid on the street who is right now dancing on the head of a pine?

Can there be a poetry of philosophy?

Can there be a meaningful philosophy of philosophy?

Anyway, why call it a philosophy of poetry when the name is poetics?

Does the fundamental nature of poetry change over time?

There is no fundamental nature of poetry & it changes over time.

It just changed while you were reading this. It changed in a different way while I was writing this.

There.

It done did it again.

Is there one "poetry" or are there "poetries"?

All poetries are equal but some are more equal than others.

Now the new Pope, he's got a sure answer to this kind of question.

It is our duty as poets to repudiate the doctrines of the new Pope.

I will not endorse any poet who proclaims allegiance to the Pope.

Each of the pervious sentences is false.

The space between the sentences pertains to truth as long as you consider at least three such spaces.

What makes a genuinely great poem?

Chutzpah.

What is the relationship between tradition and innovation in poetry?

Tradition is the record of innovation. Innovation is a response to tradition. There are no first acts in poetry & no last acts either.

Is a particular poetic method (e.g., the "lyricist," "formalist," "free verse," "experi-
mental," or any other approach) preferable?

Yes, depending on time & motive.

    Free verse is not a method but an imperative, which we ignore at our
peril. But verse can only be as free as we are.

Are there deep associations between poetics and politics?

Yes, & superficial ones too. Commonly, the two levels are confused, with
the superficial associations (for example, a poem's theme) taking the role as
deep & vice versa. See immediately prior answer.

Please give some evidence.

I prefer not to.

What fundamental misconceptions about poetry annoy you most, and how would
you correct or refute them?

I get annoyed early & often. An occupational hazard.

    A change of fortune will never abolish irritation.

RADICAL JEWISH CULTURE /
SECULAR JEWISH PRACTICE

1. Some years ago, one of the editors of a forthcoming, prominent anthology of Jewish American literature mentioned to me that he thought Gertrude Stein (among other poets of particular importance for innovative American poetry) would not be included in the book. It struck me as deliciously odd that in a time of affirmation of the many distinct cultures that make up U.S. literature, these editors would consider leaving out of their anthology perhaps the most famous Jewish poet of the modernist period. Evidently, being Jewish was not enough to be a Jewish poet. By the same token, my children go to a Jewish camp for those who have no religious Jewish beliefs, a camp with a seventy-five-year history of secular Jewish commitment; but I wonder whether there are Muslim or Pentecostal or Catholic camps for nonbelievers? But that's because, at least in some sense, you can't really be a lapsed Jew.

Yes I know I am trading on the ambiguity of religion and ethnicity. I mean to continue to do so.

9. Here is the set of questions I posed to a 2004 panel on "Radical Jewish Poetry / Secular Jewish Practice": What are the innovations and inventions of American Jewish poets, over the past century? Can we say that there is a distinctly Jewish component to radical modernist and contemporary

Presented as part of a program I organized for the American Jewish Historical Society at the Center for Jewish History in New York on September 21, 2004. Paul Auster, Kathryn Hellerstein, Stephen Paul Miller, Marjorie Perloff, and Jerome Rothenberg joined me on the panel. A video of the panel and a related 2010 dialog with Norman Fischer on the topic is at PennSound, http://writing.upenn.edu/pennsound/x/AJHS.html (accessed May 30, 2010). The panel was a spark for what became *Radical Poetics and Secular Jewish Practice*, edited by Stephen Paul Miller and Daniel Morris (Tuscaloosa: University of Alabama Press, 2010), where this essay was first published.

poetry? What is the relation of Jewish modernist and contemporary poets to the historical avant-garde and to contemporary innovative poetry? How do Jewish cultural life and ethnic and religious forms and traditions manifest themselves in the forms, styles, and approaches to radical American poetry? What role does a distinctly secular approach to Jewishness by poets and other Jewish artists mean for "radical Jewish culture"?

4. Over the past weeks leading up to the panel, several of the participants, but most notably me, expressed confusion about the topic—are we being asked to put forward some positive correlation between Jewish poets, or we might say poets of Jewishness, and innovative poetic practice, or to affirm the value of Jewishness in reading or valuing such work? I feel a deep ambivalence on all these issues, and I want to insist that this ambivalence itself, the questioning of Jewishness, is just as Jewish as the designer yarmulkes and Glatt kosher Peruvian restaurants of my neighborhood, the deep Upper West Side.

Remember Kafka's question: "What have I in common with Jews? I don't know what I have in common with myself."[1] Or, in a recent translation, I wouldn't want to have an ethnicity that would automatically count me in its number . . . when the saints go marching in . . .

Am I Jewish? Is this Jewish? I am no more Jewish then when I set my Jewishness adrift from fundamentalist religious practice. I am no more Jewish than when I refuse imposed definitions of what Jewishness means. I am no more Jewish than when I attend to how such Jewishness lives itself out, plays tunes not yet played. Jewishness can, even must, in one of its multiple manifestations, be an aversion of identification—as a practice of dialogue and as an openness to the unfolding performance of the everyday. Call it the civic practice of Jewishness.

10. Amos Oz, in an essay published in 1993 writes:

> Now suppose a new Kafka is growing up right now, here in San Francisco,
> California: Suppose he is fourteen years old right now. Let's call him Chuck
> Bernstein. Let's assume that he is every bit of a genius as Kafka was in his
> time. His future must, as I see it, depend on an uncle in Jerusalem or an expe-

1. See Kafka's *Diaries 1914–1923*, edited by Max Brod (New York: Schocken, 1976), entry for January 8, 1914, 252. Joseph Kresh translates the second sentence, in full, as "I don't have anything in common with myself and would be content to stand quietly alone in a corner, satisfied that I can breathe."

rience by the Dead Sea, or a cousin in a kibbutz or something inspired by the Israeli live drama: Otherwise, with the exception of the possibility that he is growing up among the ultra-Orthodox, he will be an American writer of Jewish origin—not a Jewish American writer. He may become a new Faulkner, but not a new Kafka.[2]

If would be as if I wrote:

> Now suppose a new Kafka is growing up right now, in Tel Aviv. Suppose he is fourteen years old right now. Let's call him Amachi Oz. Let's assume that he is every bit of a genius as Kafka was in his time. His future must, as I see it, depend on an uncle in Miami or an experience learning Yiddish in the Catskills or the complete DVD set of *Curb Your Enthusiasm* and all Mel Brooks's movies, or something inspired by Bob Dylan or Jerry Lewis. Otherwise, with the exception of the possibility that he is growing up among transplanted Upper West Siders who have memorized Gershwin, Berlin, and Sondheim, he will be an Middle Eastern writer of Jewish origin—not a Jewish writer. He may become a new Darwish, but not a new Kafka.

No one would accept this except as a spoof, but is the Oz quote any less problematic? In the absence of a proliferating European secular Jewish culture in the wake of the Systematic Extermination Process, the United States has developed its own Jewish culture, and more to my point its own secular Jewish culture, that doesn't play second fiddle to Israel, which has over this time cultivated its own distinct brands of Jewishness, no more or less authentic than ours (and certainly no less treacherous). Israeli writers don't get to dictate who's Jewish or what's Jewish (and neither do Israeli rabbis). Israel does not provide a litmus test for Jewish identity, and indeed American Jewish culture has as much claim to the continuation of the culture of the European Jews as does any other Jewish culture. Judaism is a religion whose practices are marked by an infinite series of historical disputes/commentaries/reconstructions. Jewishness, in contrast, is cultural: a social practice and set of affinities, subject to change. The Jews who thought they were excommunicating Spinoza really just cut themselves off from a mainline Jewish culture that persists to this day; they became less Jewish. This

---

2. "Imagining the Other: 1" in *The Writer in the Jewish Community: An Israeli–North American Dialogue*, edited by Richard Siegel and Tamar Sofer (London: Associated University Presses, 1993), 122. I quote the same passage in the autobiographical interview in *My Way: Speeches and Poems* (Chicago: University of Chicago Press, 1999).

is what it means to practice Midrashic Antinomianism. Want your "birth right" as a Jew? Come to Brooklyn and have a blintz.[3]

Fortunately, we have America so as not to need a Mr. Oz to police who is Jewish or, indeed, what is Jewish. But this America, unfortunately, is still somewhere over the rainbow.

333. My friend Kenny Goldsmith, after a Jewish poetics panel at the Sixth Street Synagogue in New York, wrote me that I had a lot invested in the discussion. I agreed: it's an investment made for me that I am trying to make the best of, or maybe just acknowledge, or just not sink under the weight of, or free myself from without selling at a loss, or then again selling to you, wholesale.

A blogger, responding to a talk by Norman Fischer and me at the Jewish Meditation Center in Brooklyn, wrote that, as much as he liked our talk he didn't want to be "boxed in" by Jewish identification. If he meditated just a little longer he'd realize we are always boxed in. *Get used to it:* it's already used to you. "The chosen people" doesn't mean you get to choose: you've been chosen and you can fight it, deny it, explain it away, or accept it, but none of that changes if not the historic, than the psychiatric insistence (not to say intrusiveness) of Jewishness.

When the Messiah comes . . . then you will be freed from this burden or opportunity or challenge or irrelevance or calling or curse.

I come to this discussion out of annoyance, not conviction or belief. I don't want other people speaking for *the* Jews rather than *some* Jews. As for me, I'm just *a* Jew and not a particularly good (or bad) one at that.

I am a Jewish man trapped in the body of a Jewish man.

Jewishness is not a condition, an essence, a religion, a stigma, an aspiration, an albatross. *Not only.* It's a frame. And not just a frame that queues the way people interpret (interpolate) me, but a frame that taints (or illumines, as you prefer) the way I interpret the world. I can no more cast off the chains or frames of my Jewishness than I can escape history or dematerialize my body.

2. The obsessive focus in literary journalism on the American Jewish novel has had the effect of cutting off consideration of the formal and processural

3. The two preceding paragraphs are from a 2010 response to Robin Tremblay-McGraw linked at http://abigjewishblog.blogspot.com/2010/05/norman-fischer-charles-bernstein-on.html, accessed May 30, 2010.

features of secular Jewish art. We have ended up with a set of representative figures for an approach in and to a culture that highly values the rejection of such graven representations.

In other words, the often frame-locked focus on Jewish content as the sine qua non of Jewish literature has distracted from recognition—not so much of Jewish forms, whatever they might be, as of formal, rhythmic, dialectical and dialogical and colloquial dimensions of literary, musical, and visual works that do not have explicit Jewish thematic focus. In happy contrast, we do have such recent anthologies as *The Norton Anthology of Jewish American Literature* and *Jewish American Poetry: Poems, Commentary, and Reflections*, edited by Eric Selinger and Jonathan Barron, along with Jerome Rothenberg's groundbreaking *A Big Jewish Book* (and its shorter version, *Exiled in the World*).

5. & yet, increasingly, official American Jewish discourse has been dominated by concerns for Jewish demographic sustainability viewed through the frame of Jewish family life and defined by affiliation to organized religious institutions, when it is not strafed by concern over the catastrophe of Israel. This duel focus—the Scylla of ethnic preservation (as if Jewish life were already a museum show, a kind of Lower East Side Sturbridge Village) and the Charybdis of Palestine—is explicitly (and legitimately) paranoid in orientation; but the effect is counterproductive insofar as it disenfranchises sectors of current and future, and indeed historical, Jewish life, just that part of Jewish culture that can be called secular—and which had its greatest flourishing in the United States in the left Yiddishkeit culture of the 1920s and '30s, that world of nonreligious, indeed often antireligious, Jewish artists, intellectuals, socialists, comedians, musicians and songwriters, and assorted freethinkers that thrives in New York even to this day.

7. While Jewish secular culture has sometimes, maybe often—well sometimes or often, I really can't be sure—wanted to erase (or shall we say put under erasure?) its explicit Jewishness, especially insofar as such identity-politics might remove or ghettoize us from the larger culture of which we are an integral part—nonetheless there is no particular reason, in other words, no necessity, to take such bracketing of Jewishness as anything other than Jewish. *Read the text of this aversion. Interpret it. Talk back to it.* Within historical Jewish time there are certain icons of radical secular Jewish thought, icons that don't define a poetic practice for Americans but suggest a constellation of possibility. This is a constellation most explicitly noted

by Isaac Deutscher in his *Non-Jewish Jew* and that includes Spinoza, the three Marxes (Chico, Karl, and Groucho), & the three Steins—Ein, Wittgen, & Gertrude; our own Yiddishe Trinity—Freud, Kafka, and Celan; Irving Berlin's "White Christmas" and the Gershwins' "It Ain't Necessarily So"; Emmanuel Levinas's faces, Emma Goldman's dancing at the revolution, & Fanny Brice's Baby Snooks; Alfred Stieglitz & Chaim Gross; Allen Ginsberg's "Kaddish," Edmond Jabes's imaginary rabbis, and Jacques Derrida's midrashic commentary; Hannah Weiner's dialogic voices and Larry Eigner's linguistic fields; Ad Reinhardt's shades of black & Lenny Bruce's "Religion, Inc."; the space between Morton Feldman's notes and Arnold Schoenberg's scales; and, lest we forget, Mickey Katz's foundational "Borscht Riders in the Sky."

In this respect, I want to acknowledge the important work of John Zorn's Radical Jewish Culture series & beyond that the work of Sander Gilman and Daniel and Jonathan Boyarin and Maria Damon.

6. The weekend before the panel, several of us participated in a centennial celebration at Columbia and Barnard for Louis Zukofsky, who along with Charles Reznikoff, George Oppen, Muriel Rukeyser, and Laura Riding constitute an important constellation of Jewish Second Wave Modernist poets. The interest in this work should not be understated: the capacious philosophy hall lounge was filled to capacity. But of course the interest was not primarily because of Zukofsky's Jewishness.

The first conference to celebrate the Objectivist poets, and, in effect, Jewish American modernist poetry, was not in America at all but in France, in 1989 at Royaumont. I remember after a talk I gave on Reznikoff,[4] Carl Rakosi sternly reprimanded me for the Jewish motifs in my piece: "We were secular," he said, and Jewishness was not a legitimate lens through which to read the work. While Rakosi's remarks seemed particularly ill-suited to Reznikoff, for whom Jewishness is an explicit and central concern, it is, nonetheless, an important statement of poetic license that I do not wish—entirely—to ignore. (An even more striking rejection of Jewish identification is to be found in Laura [Riding] Jackson.) But you can't separate Jewishness, and in particular the Jewish cultural context from which, for example, Zukofsky emerges as a poet, from his work, even if this aspect of his poetry was rarely mentioned at the conference (Rothenberg's concluding address being a significant exception). Consider only that Zukofsky's

4. "Reznikoff's Nearness," in *My Way: Speeches and Poems.*

first major work, "A Poem Beginning 'The,'" is not only a Jewish response to Eliot's "The Waste Land" but also an extraordinary poem about the tensions of assimilation for the young poet with Yiddish in his ears into an Anglophilic literary culture. In this respect, I want to commend Stephen Fredman's recent book on Reznikoff, *A Menorah for Athena*, the title itself playing out the tensions that would underlie some of the most important formal innovations in Second Wave Modernist American poetry, for example the way Reznikoff, Oppen, and Zukofsky insist on resistant particulars against airy generalization.

8. Several years ago I wrote the libretto for *Shadowtime*, an opera about Walter Benjamin.[5] A collaboration with composer Brian Ferneyhough, *Shadowtime* was commissioned by the Munich Biennale. The opera opens with the death of Benjamin; not the suicide, by the way, because whatever else, to think Benjamin committed suicide is too easy an out for all of us. Perhaps "suicided." After this scene, the opera envisions a journey for "our" imagined Benjamin, as told, largely, through a chorus of angels, a chorus of the angels of history. Much of the secular Jewish culture in Europe was wiped out between 1937 and 1945, along with the rest of European Jewish culture. What would have become of all these intellectuals and artists? We have to imagine our character "Benjamin" living in New York. It is interesting that two people living in America created an opera in English, commissioned and premiered in Munich, on this character. Our "Benjamin" is born in the space of contemporary American thought. The historical person leaves the face of the earth, but not our imagination. How do we "hear" him? How do we hear the flapping of the wings of history? That's also a translation: how is "Beniamin" translated into "Benjamin"?

In other words, at a certain point it became apparent to me, and not just me of course, that the secular Jewish culture that was wiped out in the Second War—I realize this was not the only Jewish culture destroyed— stranded the correlative developments in America. Imagine Klezmer music played by Jews in Poland, not as museum pieces but as a living culture? Imagine European poetry and philosophy by the descendents of Benjamin and Heine? But, to a large extent, this is not to be, or anyway, insofar as it is to be, it too must be the task of secular Jewish culture on this side of the

5. The libretto was published by Green Integer in 2005; for the synopsis and extensive commentary on the opera see, http://epc.buffalo.edu/authors/bernstein/shadowtime, accessed May 30, 2010.

Atlantic and of our radical poetry and ambiguating poetics. I think it is difficult to acknowledge this unwanted and perhaps even insufferable task; certainly it has been difficult for me. But perhaps this is what we have been chosen for.

11. Not long ago I had an extended discussion with the secular Jewish Zen poet and priest Norman Fischer. Our questions wove in and out of the midrashic practice of textual dialog and interpretation: the insistence that the fixed text was nonetheless open to multiple, possibly infinite (but then again, *maybe not*) interpretations; the revelation that any text, like any word, poem, event, person, or people, requires complex interpretation in terms of its multiple levels. Call it the PRDS of interpretation—the truthfulness of the refusal of the literal in the pursuit of meaning: **Peshat**—literal meaning; **Ramez** (remez)–suggested meaning; **Drash** (derush)—allegorical meaning; **Sod**—hidden or mystical or esoteric meaning. You can call it Paradise but maybe it's just People Really Digging the Secular. We wondered whether such a practice of deliberately delicious ambiguation and intoxicating complexifaction could lead to a greater ethical and aesthetic responsiveness in and resonance with the social world, such as we associate with secular Jewish politics and art. *Some dare call it reason.* Norman and I ended with more questions than we started with; this is how we knew that the conversation had value for us. But how Jewish was it? As Bartleby might put it, I'd prefer not to say.

POETRY SCENE INVESTIGATION: A CONVERSATION WITH MARJORIE PERLOFF

Marjorie Perloff: Charles, almost twenty years have gone by since that fateful MLA when you delivered the lecture "The Academy in Peril: William Carlos Williams Meets the MLA" (1983). I still remember what a tempest you caused and how furious the old timers like M. L. Rosenthal were at your demolition job. You were, in those days, a great fighter against "official verse culture." How does the "situation in poetry" today relate to that earlier moment? Do you feel the fight against official verse culture has been won? Can it ever be won? How would you describe the current scene vis-à-vis that of 1983?

Charles Bernstein: I remember after that speech—and it was more a speech than a "paper"—Allen Ginsberg told me that while he liked what I said, I should talk more slowly and breathe between phrases. I think I must have been going at twice the words per minute of other people at the MLA, but they seemed to get the drift. I don't think I've slowed down in the meantime, but then I'm more a tortoise type than quick like a bunny.

MP: You a tortoise?? You'll have a hard time convincing your friends of that because you are in fact super-quick on the uptake, though I agree you're not a bunny!

CB: Well, slow and steady and all that, if not unrelenting.

This e-mail conversation took place between October 15 and November 22, 2002. I moved from Buffalo to Penn the next year. *Fulcrum* 2, 2003.

I take it as a given that the situation has changed; but I believe the necessity to respond to our current predicament is as acute now as ever. In 1983, I didn't anticipate that my remarks would provoke repeated waves of applause, though I did expect the ire. The response to that talk, and lots of other interventions many of us were making at the time, suggested that certain long-entrenched views about American modernist poetry were collapsing under the weight of their own dogmatism, if dogmatism can be said to have weight and not just bark. It was a commonplace, in those distant days of yore, to accuse those of us questioning such dogmatism of being dogmatic; but I have long found that some of the more narrow-minded people are the quickest to cry "Ideologue!" at those who question their prerogatives. Of course—

> Today we live in far different times:
> We have no poetry wars, no aesthetic crimes;
> At last, we are all one big family
> Under the tent of art and harmony.

(I sometimes ask Felix, my ten-year-old son, if my silliness is going to cause him some future harm—I mean things like breaking out into doggerel in the middle of lunch, or telling jokes that are all schtick and no punch line.)

What I think has changed is that the radical modernism I was putting forward in that address—poets and poetics—has received much greater acknowledgment since that time, both inside and outside the academy, as the result of the advocacy of many poets, scholars, and editors. At the same time, modern and contemporary poetry is, if anything, becoming more peripheral to literary studies, in the universities but also in elementary and high schools. Nor has the problem with "official verse culture" disappeared, despite far greater prominence for several of my contemporaries and the continued resilience of many of the approaches to poetry that met with so much resistance in the '70s and '80s. I do think that creative writing programs, taken in aggregate, are more open now to alternative approaches to poetic composition; but when I read the *Writer's Chronicle* of the Associated Writing Programs, I mostly see the same problems many of us criticized two decades ago, though now expressed with the kind of embattled, nostalgic tinge of those who know their ground is more like thin ice: better to skate on than to pound. I find the publication rather charming, in a perverse way.

Almost any poet will tell you not enough poetry gets reviewed in publications-with-wide-circulation (PWC): big city newspapers, the newsweeklies, and the national journals of culture and opinion. Part of the problem would simply be solved if poetry were treated by these publications as a national cultural "beat": if poetry were covered the way art or TV is. But the reality is that poetry is economically too small-potatoes (even if the potatoes are sweet) to be able to count this way. The larger problem is that contemporary poetry books suffer the same neglect as contemporary philosophy books (as Peter Hare pointed out to me recently) or really any number of "scholarly" books, books not intended for a "general" audience partly because the general audience is kept ignorant of their existence and the chronic significance for their lives, if we consider the life of the mind essential for the body politic. And while you might make an argument for the fact that poetry ought to be of greater "general" interest than these other "difficult" books, I wouldn't, since I see the fate of all of us as related to a lack of judgment, a lack of cultural and intellectual commitment, on the part of the PWC. In contrast, I am impressed and grateful that such small publications as the *Boston Review* and *Rain Taxi* can offer more thorough and thoughtful book reviewing than the combined efforts of the PWC.

When it comes to poetry, the PWC do a great disservice to their readers: their coverage is, to use the terms of opprobrium so popular in their reviews, inadequate and of poor quality. Almost no coverage is given of the field, something that is otherwise the prerequisite of journalism, and the choices of what is reviewed seem at best arbitrary, though obviously skewed to the trade presses, even though these presses, by almost anyone's measure, are responsible for only a small proportion of the significant poetry of our time. (Sometimes this point gets misunderstood: It's not that I think that any given book that is reviewed is no good or that no book I care about is ever reviewed nor that I think only the books I prefer should be reviewed or that if a few of them were that would solve the problem.)

In any case, and to put it baldly, I think only a very few of the poetry books published over the past twenty years that you or I would value most highly have received any attention in the PWC; no matter how important these works may be for many of us involved with the art, they remain invisible to the literate reader who relies on these publications for news of what is going on in poetry. There is a connection here to literary prizes, too: not so much who wins them—since there are a great number with many different perspectives—but which ones get reported in the PWC. The Pulitzer, one among many prizes at least its equal (and one with a track record as bad as, but similar to, the PWC)—gets the most attention because it comes packaged with so many journalism awards. Given by a group that cares little or nothing for poetry, the Pulitzer is covered as a significant poetry award because it serves the PWC's self-promotion. I recall when Jackson Mac Low won the lifetime achievement award (then called the Dorothea Tanning and now the Wallace Stevens prize) from the Academy of American Poets in 1999, there wasn't even a mention of that in the *New York Times*, which nonetheless has often reported on the award, calling it poetry's best-paying prize; but then Mac Low, even when honored by nothing less than Official Verse Culture at its best, is presumably one of the unmentionables in the land of the PWC.

Does it matter? It's not that the books don't circulate or are not taught in universities or discussed in small press and web journals or on listserv discussion groups. What difference does it make? I know a lot of people are indifferent, criticizing universities more than they criticize the PWC. Yet I think what Andrew Ross called "the oxygen of publicity" matters quite a bit. Poetry survives and thrives nurtured by its committed readers and practitioners; I think the value of poetry is not just for us but indeed for this wider public, and that the culture suffers when it isolates itself from its poets.

MP: What you describe seems to me entirely accurate, but it's more symptom than cause, isn't it? If the PWCs felt that the public "out there" had even the slightest interest in the material in question, of course they would review it and write articles about it. And the university presses would want to do more to promote the work. So where did this vacuum come from? Is it that English Departments themselves have abdicated their "literary" role, wanting desperately to teach and study anything but "literature"? Is it just a general dumbing down of the culture? But if the latter is the case, why do certain very difficult works get quite a bit of attention? For instance Oulipo. Perec's *Life: A User's Manual* had, I recall, a front-page review in the *TLS*, and even *La Disparition*, translated by Gilbert Adair, did relatively well. And then in the architecture world, people will pour into shows of very arcane and avant-garde material—I'm thinking of a recent Coop Himmelblau exhibit at the Schindler House in LA—and my hairdresser, to give just one example, went all the way to Bilbao to see the Frank Gehry Guggenheim Museum and he'll go see Surrealist art shows at this or that museum.

So what is it about "poetry" today that makes it seem so "specialized" to people? Or, to put the question another way, why do people accept the "new" and unexpected in architecture and often in the visual arts in general, but want their poetry to be "clear" à la Billy Collins?

CB: You tell me. There are so many directions to go in answer to your question I feel like the guy at the end of Bergman's *The Passion of Anna* who is pacing from the left to the right of the screen with that drop-dead chilling voiceover, "This time his name is Andreas Winkelman." *This time its name is American poetry.* On the one hand, yes of course the PWCs are responding to a profound lack of interest in poetry as an art form; but, on the other hand, do they aid or even foment this disinterest, or are they just the messengers reporting the news? Why do they cover the poetry they do cover rather than something else? Why is the aesthetic right given such free reign to trash "radical poetry" while the views of the other sides (all 44 and a half of them) go largely unheard? By the standards of the "massed" media, none of this poetry—not any of it—amounts to a hill of beans in Iowa or a barrel of orangutans in the new Times Square. On the one hand (if you can keep all these hands away from the threshing machines), some poets and poetry do-gooders think the answer is to go with the flow, to try to make poems that, while still unpopular at the Prom of American Culture are a little more popular (and don't assume I am not one of them). The classic '50s response is to become Raincoat Adolescents, the hip-without-being-cool dropouts or rebel saints that figure, as social gesture, into the Romantic Ideology of a Rock 'n' Roll culture that replaces poetic work with poetic attitude and whose heroes are not poets at all but pop stars like Jim Morrison or Bob Dylan or Patti Smith. I don't really need easy listening poetry if I can listen to the Sex Pistols, or New Formalism if I have Randy Newman. For "My Generation" (formally the journal of the American Association of Retired Persons), it's not the antimodernist poetry championed by the Mediocracy that is clawing at poetry's share of the consciousness of the American muddled class, but the Golden '60s Boxed Set rerereleases of *The Who's Greatest Hits* (What's on second, Leonard Cohen shortstop, Joni Mitchell on bass). They paved Poetry Paradise and put up a Pop Music Lot.

Popularity or immediate accessibility is not a criterion of value for poetry in our time. Poetry can provide not an extension of the dominant values in American culture—as the poetry favored by the PWC does—but multiple, discrepant alternatives to them: often messy, inchoate, disturbing, unhappy—indeed sometimes *worse*—alternatives to boot. How the culture and how the PWC respond to this is a judgment on them. A culture's refusal of its poetry is not without consequence or redress. So when you ask if "the public [has] even the slightest interest in the material in question," I would say that the PWC's spurning of this, indeed, *material in question*, is a direct violation of the public interest, that we won't have a public worthy of the name until we engage with such material, in poetry, philosophy, history, sociology, theology, and, indeed, politics.

MP: Touché. I think there's also a "skill" or "expertise" problem. To be an architect, you do have to learn very specific things. And a composer obviously has to know something about music. But anyone, it seems, can be a poet. The *New York Times* praised Dana Gioia precisely because he had worked for ten years for General Foods and made his mint before turning to poetry—evidently something one can do by a sheer act of will. One declares oneself a poet, period. So then anyone of course can also be a poetry critic and comment on the quality of the poetry. This past week the *Wall Street Journal* announced that Gioia was one of "our finest poets" without ever saying how or why. It seems their columnists simply *know*. And in response to the staggering multimillion-dollar Gertrude Lilly bequest to *Poetry* magazine, Joseph Parisi, the venerable journal's current editor, produced some sobering statistics. For instance, the circulation of *Poetry* today is 10,000. But every year the journal gets 90,000 submissions. Poetry, it would seem, is much more fun to write than to read!

Clearly, PhD programs like the Poetics Program at Buffalo have gone a long way in rectifying this situation and demanding some knowledge on the part of their would-be poets. Could you comment on how this has worked at Buffalo? Since the program is largely your brainchild, how did you go about inventing it? What are its best features? Are there things you would now do differently?

CB: In terms of reviewing and awards, there is sometimes a presumption that a person who never reads poems and has no apparent interest in poetry should be able to judge what's good or bad in poetry, because we are all "human beings" after all, as the coordinator of a recent very-minor-award panel informed me a few days ago. Sometimes that goes for the "general reader" qualifications of the reviewer/judge and sometimes it's a criterion used to evaluate poetry. The "we're all humans" proposition is not just a harmless shibboleth: it is a chief means of riding roughshod over aesthetic and ideological differences and enforcing—now here's a ten-buck word—*uniformitarianism.* The poets I most care about are, maybe, trying to *become* human—or nonhuman; anyway, they are not so quick to assume what the human is or how it manifests itself.

The problem with lots of poetry that bills itself as easy reading is that there's not a lot of there there, or what there there is doesn't hold up to more than a quick and casual glance. The irony is that "difficult" poetry may actually provide a good deal more immediacy and affect than much of the more "I am my subject matter and don't you forget it" variety. That's why I would cast the issue in terms not just of aesthetics but aestheticism—*linguistic sensation*. There is much still made of the alleged problem that lots of the poems you and I like to read are not point, click, and play; but the alternative provided is not like asking the readers to write their own poems (though that's a fine activity too, for another time) or stare into the abyss (though that may be something that comes up along the way). The difference is more like the one between riding a motorbike and taking a taxi (substitute your own engine-free metaphor if you like). Personally, I prefer teleportation, since that gives me more time for reading hard-core poetry.

As to the Poetics Program: university English departments typically separate poetry writing courses from poetry reading courses and we all know that the former are on the rise while the latter are on the wane. The Poetics Program, as we formed it in the early 1990s in Buffalo, rejected this dichotomy, not just in an informal, or class-by-class, basis, but as a matter of policy; and not just at an undergraduate or master's level, but also, and even primarily, in the PhD program. The poets teaching in our graduate Poetics Program—Susan Howe, Robert Creeley, Myung Mi Kim, Loss Pequeño Glazier, Dennis Tedlock—teach not creative writing but rather doctoral seminars; the students don't submit poems or manuscripts, but essays and dissertations. The Poetics Program students are often poets, and we support the activity of writing poetry as a positive contribution to teaching literature classes, writing criticism, and doing scholarship. This is not to say that all the Poetics students are poets, but lots of them are, and they have formed their own immediate local context of exchanging work, publishing magazines and books, and organizing reading series.

No poetry community is without troubles, and ours has its share, but it is vital and sizable and even formidable, since our program, having surprising little competition among PhD programs, has attracted (in early and not-so-early stages) some great poets, scholars, critics, and editors over the years. Because we have some funds available, we are able to provide a small amount of money to any of the students who want to have a series or press—and that little bit of money goes a long way. This approach to funding—giving to a highly decentered not to say idiosyncratic set of projects can lead, as Joel Kuszai put it a while back, to a place with "all leaders and no followers"; but at least it avoids the committee-driven decision making of many official university magazines and reading series, where money is centralized and consensus is emphasized. Anyway, this has been my philosophy. We also have lots and lots of visitors, who meet with students in seminars as well as give readings or lectures. So it's all very poetry-intense, with lots of fellow poetry devotees and lots of activities. And also a strong web presence, with the Electronic Poetry Center and also the Poetics List.

Looking back, I think the Poetics Program was an intervention particularly relevant for the 1990s and so one that now needs to undergo some serious and necessary transformations, as I think all institutions do, less they become stagnant, victims of their own successes or preoccupied with their own failures.

There is always a lot of concern expressed among poets about the relation of poetry to the academy. (I wish I could say there was comparable concern in the literary academy for this topic.) Without jumping into the quicksand of this topic, I would say that my own commitment has been to find ways to use the university and its resources to support poets and poetry, especially poets outside the academy. As I said in an interview with Andrew Epstein for *Lingua Franca* on this topic, the issue isn't that, as a poet, you have a university job, but what you do with it.

MP: I've always felt that the "issue" of the poet in the academy was a red herring. Poets have to make a living somehow, and some choose teaching even as others (Kit Robinson, Ron Silliman) work in the computer industry, and others as lawyers or psychiatrists. But enough sociology; I want to turn now to your poetry, which, it seems to me, has gotten somewhat short shrift vis-à-vis your essays, manifestos, lectures, etc. Especially in the UK, critics and reviewers talk of you as the *chef d'école* of the Language school rather than as the very particular poet that you are.

Suppose we look at what I take to be a particularly brilliant recent poem, "The Manufacture of Negative Experience," in *With Strings* (Chicago, 2001). What was the actual process of composing this long poem? Where did you begin? Do you start with a particular conception and then "fill in," or does one perception immediately lead to a further perception, as Olson put it? Do you assemble the found texts ahead of time? Do you move passages around a lot? In short (ha!), can you describe for our readers how the composition took place.

CB: I wrote the poem, using some notes I had assembled over the previous year, in Provincetown in August 1992. I was there with Susan of course, but also with Emma, who was seven (echoes of her presence in §41—"When I say 'no' I mean / maybe, probably not, what's / the matter with you?, do I / make myself clear? . . ."), and Felix, who, at a few months old, may well be the "beeper" of §333. Like most of my poems, I wrote this one in a bound "sketch"-type notebook, then typed it up and revised.

"The Manufacture of Negative Experience" is one of a number of longish serial poems: loosely linked stanzas, all bouncing off, or getting sucked into, the black hole of the title. It's a constellation or array, or then again maybe something like a charm bracelet. One of the charms is §482: the set of jokes in the form of one-line questions, all with same answer, "No." One of my obsessions has been to include—fully and faithfully (or is it faithlessly, I always get those confused)—a set of Henny Youngman-style jokes within a poem. So here it's eleven questions spread over fifteen lines. And those questions also rhyme with similar jokes or quasi jokes in other parts of the poem. (Was that a real joke or did you just mess it up?)

There are thirteen parts to the poem. Another way I think of this is as something like conical sections arcing around a numinous center (negative experience). That's one way to understand the erratic numbering (3, 17, 37, 38, 41, 46a, 57, 71, 333, 334, 482, 501, 788), which is both one of those stock jokes I like so much, while at the same time giving a sense of the space between the sections. The form is probably more like Wittgenstein's *Philosophical Investigations* than Olson's *Projective Verse*, but it's true I want the parts to concatenate.

Lots of contrasting materials by way of language, style, prosody, subject matter: fractured aphorisms and slogans (§38), semi-nursery rimes (§17, §57), speech acts (§41), riddles with no answer if not no for an answer, and some parts that combine these (§3). A lot of the poem sounds like you've heard it before but can't place it or just when you think you remember, it's on the slip of your tongue until it gets bounced out of mind by a quick dissolve to the next illusionless allusion or allusive elision, or a pop fly to third when you still don't know who's on first.

And that, again, brings up the title as organizing principle: less negative experience as in "I had a very negative experience at polka night at the supper club" and more as in Adorno's "Negative Dialectics": "Truth is the antithesis of existing society" (which is the epigraph to a related poem, "Emotions of Normal People" in *Dark City*). Or like that great "Not this" in Ron Silliman's *Tjanting*.

Section 37 is taken from a school report on my twin nephews, who were in elementary school at the time. I jotted those sentences down when I was over to my sister- and brother-in-law's house for Thanksgiving. I am one of these mildly unsocial people at family gatherings who do things like that: scribble things in my notebook from school reports, scan the popular magazines on the table, record overheard conversation, all in the endless quest for material. School reports are classic fodder for my hypnopompic mill: such school-blotter characterizing may not kill you, but the wounds . . . they don't so much heal as morph. I identify with everything that's said about David and Ian, and so those statements form the poetics of the piece.

I guess, to get back to your question, a lot of the poem is pulled from the air, from signs in my mind and on the street, from what I am reading in the newspaper or hearing on the radio; everything gets considered as possible material to be transmuted, sputtered, turned topsy turvy or tipsy flopsy. As if "negative experience" could be the portal into a world next to the one we usually pretend to inhabit, less through the looking glass than the blank side of the mirror that doesn't reflect but allows for reflection.

For example, in writing this I was casting around for an adjective to go with "mill" to describe the fuzzy logic of interconnections in the poem; for some reason hypnogogic came to mind, but I wanted something that meant the opposite, which is when I lit on hypnopompic: a state of dawning consciousness, just after sleep. Meanwhile, while I was working on this explanation, and it was getting late, Emma wanted to use the computer to play a biology CD-ROM, so all of a sudden, out of the blue, I heard this disembodied, hypercalm voice, talking about the plasma membrane of a cell as a "fluid mosaic," and I realized this was another way of talking about poetic structure; in this case, the internal elements that make up each section as well as the relations among the sections.

Which leads me to §3: "Madder / than a scratched eel at a / Crossing Guard kettle-shoot." The kettle shoot is always the highlight of the Crossing Guard annual convention in Whipsalantamariaozoola, even though the scratched eel underwater diving meet is my personal favorite. Well you'd have to have been there to take it in fully; this was the best way to evoke the experience, a painful one that I will remember for the rest of my life.

What else to say? As you see, I guess I am more tempted to write another stanza than offer up an explanation. Not that I mind explaining anything, which anyway is always more a supplement than a substitute, or so I would hope.

MP: Your account shows how absurd it is to talk of yours as a poetry where "anything goes," indeed, how carefully you plan the poem's overall architecture. But I still have some questions. First and foremost—and this would apply to most of your poems, whether in *With Strings* or in earlier volumes— how does the reader deal with the hermeticism of the allusions? In §37, for example, once you explain that Ian and David are your sister-in-law's twins, the section is perfectly clear. But if I didn't know that, I would assume that Ian is a character, perhaps in Cowper's *Task*, perhaps in another Cowper poem or related text, and that you're modernizing the situation for parodic effect. Now, you can say it doesn't matter, that the thematic import would be the same. But it does help (I've found) if the reader knows the New York world you're so often referring to—a world of those Henny Youngman jokes and phrases like "a wolf in schlep's clothing." So I wonder whether you think some day your poems will or should be annotated by editors? And of course if this were the case, the annotations would be longer than the original poem or perhaps themselves a new poem, which might be fun.

I'm of two minds about the question of reference. Part of me feels that anyone living in today's media world, whether in Helsinki or Hackensack, will read "The Manufacture of Negative Experience" with a big smile and a great shock of recognition. But then I'm always surprised how many people even in (or perhaps especially in) our own social circles have never heard of NoDoz, pastrami, the Aswan Dam, or the self-help movement. For example, at the recent Modernist Studies Association meeting in Madison, I was astonished to learn that none of the people I was dining with—the poet Cole Swensen, the philosopher Jean-Pierre Cometti (French visitor, very sophisticated, who writes on Wittgenstein and Musil), or the young poet-critic-academic Craig Dworkin—had ever seen *The Godfather* or knew anything about it. I assumed EVERYONE had seen that film, or part of it, at one time or another.

So—to pose what is probably an impossible question: how do we deal with difficulty in the Age of Billy Collins and Dana Gioia? Yours is, to quote William James on Gertrude Stein, "a fine new kind of realism." I see you as one of the central chroniclers of our culture. But can we ask readers to know what Charles Bernstein knows?

CB: We have to make the reader an offer she can't refuse, can't even imagine refusing, whether or not all the references are known, and all this within the limits of poetry alone (that is, the threat is not of diminished physical capacity but of diminished aesthetic capacity, which remains a looming threat for many Americans). By *refuse*, I mean that turning away in the face of the daunting challenge of decoding the references, conceits, forms, before even starting to read the poem. My idea, and certainly not mine alone, was to make poems that allowed for ambient access, that you start by getting the hang of, more than figuring out. It doesn't mean that at some other point in your experience with the poem you won't ponder those obscure references, but that the poem encourages you to go on what you experience, not just what you already know. Pragmatism, pragmatism, joggity jag.

You'll remember the Chinese translator, in the giddy conclusion to *A Test of Poetry* (in *My Way*), who asked just the question you raise about the title of my poem "No Pastrami" ("Does the pastrami refer to a highly seasoned shoulder cut of beef?"). But, then, what is the meaning of *pastrami*? Would it be enough to define it ethnically, or would you really have to have a slice and not just a slice but a pastrami on rye at the Carnegie, but wouldn't the Stage be better?, or maybe only the Second Avenue Deli would do.

Yes we have no pastrami, yes we have no pastrami today.

The interesting thing about the translator's questions in *A Test of Poetry* is that the difficulties posed by the poems were not syntactic or grammatic or even structural but rather questions of cultural reference, especially from American popular, local, and mass culture. That's partly because this particular translator was a scholar of American poetry and was able to navigate through those formal aspects of the poems more readily; though another reader, someone who shared my mass and pop cultural experience but not my poetic interests, might have just the opposite difficulty. Still, the Chinese translator's predicament is hardly unique to non-Americans, but, rather, is a defining condition for everyone in American culture.

Anyone who teaches contemporary literature will have the experience that the most common cultural references of their own younger days are as obscure as Greek myths to those waves of ever younger people who were not "in" the culture at that time. The bigger they are, the harder they fall. ("All right, Mr. DeMille, I'm ready for my close-up," as some of us will recall Norma Desmond saying in *Sunset Boulevard*.) You sometimes hear people lament the decline of the big three TV networks as creating a crisis of decentralization, as if Lloyd Bridges on *Sea Hunt* provided a shared national experience that we now suffer from the lack of, as we contend with the dispersed sons of Lloyd: Beau and Jeff. I use this example—knowing full well that you may never have heard of *Sea Hunt*, which had its TV first run from 1957 to 1961 and which had a kind of ominous, not quite existential, feel—because it was turned down by the networks and was an early example of syndication that ultimately robbed "us in the U.S." of the common culture . . . like they had over there in Russia, with the one TV station?! The web, which makes '50s TV syndication seem like the tiniest hairline fracture of network hegemony, provides quick information on an amazing range of once-famous references, *Sea Hunt* and the Aswan Dam included. (I guess for my work you can't go too far wrong thinking of the '50s and the Cold War as a possible backdrop, once you start to see the pattern.) Google is both a veritable Guide to the Perplexed and a fomenter of perplexity, both a handle on, and a downward slope into, the Babel (or is it Bible?) of information on the Internet and the concomitant eclipse of central authority. (Lately I've been fascinated by the difference between the websites developed for poets, say on the EPC, and the fan sites you get for every manner of thing, like the one for *Sea Hunt*.)

You touch on some of these issues in fundamental and illuminating ways in your recent essay, "The Search for Prime Words: Ezra Pound as Nominalist," on the use of proper names in Pound; and Yunte Huang also addresses this issue in a recent piece, "Was Ezra Pound a New Historicist?" The question in both your essays is—How are we supposed to know the significance of certain anecdotal references in *The Cantos*? In both Eliot's and Pound's modernist practice, there is a professed commitment to a canon of Historical Events and Cultural Works that are presented with the (implied) injunction that readers have an obligation to know what they are or, if not, learn about them. Stein and Williams might stand for the opposite if those Proper Names weren't ones that you and I, after all is done and said, would expect those reading this exchange to know about (or if they didn't, possibly prompt them to find out). The problem you and Yunte raise in regard to Pound's work is whether we are to take his anecdotal references as such luminous details, especially if they refer to his own particular experiences, such as restaurants he visited in New York or Paris. (Do readers of this exchange really need to know the difference between the Stage and the Carnegie?) Yunte argues that you always need paratextual information and that there is not necessarily a value in imagining a poem as self-evident: I stare at the page and all the significance of the Proper Names immediately manifests itself to me, to ponyback (or is it pigtail?) on Pound's famous and equally problematic remark about the status of the Chinese written character.

Poems can't go it alone and never could, relying, as they so often do, not only on the kindness of strangers but the testimony of friends.

Poetry is too important to be left to its own devices.

Interpretation is act, editing a form of writing, translation a condition of reading.

There is no end to what you might need to know to read a poem and maybe no beginning either. In my textual economy, each poem is an initiation into a world of particulars both inside and outside the reader's information databank. The question is: Does that which is unrecognized in the poem make the work more forbidding or more beckoning. In the kind of poems I want, you don't need secret "abracadabra" words or some special knowledge or even explanatory annotations to open the door of the poem. Rather, all that's needed is a willingness to jump into the middle of a flow of experience, just as you do every time you open up the door to your house onto that other world we sometimes call everyday life. The fact is that as a culture we don't share a fixed set of given, all-purpose, cultural and historical references or, insofar as we do, there are relatively few of them and, taken as topological points, they make an inadequate map of our history, our contemporaneity, our aspirations and destinies. I don't want my poems to impose a sense of what's most important on the world or on those readers who care to take the journey the poems offer. But the ecology of reference does concern me: creating a mix so that everyone gets some things but no one can get everything—and counting on both.

You mention the wolf in schlep's clothing, but I remain more concerned about the schleps in wolf's clothing, the paper tigers of poetry. Or there is the one about the difference between the schlemiel and schlemazel: the schlemiel is the one who spills the soup; the schlemazel is the one it gets spilled on. You could say that this is just the difference between the poet and the reader, in my semiotic economy.

So maybe, going back again to §37, the dedication to William Cowper's *The Task* is the more significant frame, and I was leading you down the garden path of anecdote in my comments on David and Ian. Negative experience necessarily engages what you don't know: The manufacture of negative experience—going on in the midst of uncertainty of reference, bearing, morality, truth—is the task of poetry. In *The Task* (1782–1785), Cowper writes:

When Winter soaks the fields, and . . . feet
Too weak to struggle with tenacious clay,
Or ford the rivulets, are best at home,
The task of new discoveries falls on me.

At such a season and with such a charge
Once went I forth, and found, till then unknown . . .

If the task of poetry is "new discoveries," what is the task of criticism?

MP: I love the aphorism "*Poetry is too important to be left to its own devices.*" Vintage Bernstein in that it sounds at once wholly familiar (we're always talking about something being too important to be left to its—or his or her—own devices) and yet it is completely absurd. Or is it? Poetry does have "devices"—rhyme, repetition, anaphora, assonance, onomatopoeia, metaphor, metonymy, pun, simile—but device alone can't make something poetry, as too few "poets" realize. So your little proverb is only too true, it turns out. The particular feat of your poetry, I'd say, is this doubleness or tripleness or quintupleness. . . . Every statement looks in more than one direction, which is, of course, what poetry is all about and always has been.

The reader needn't know all the allusions. When I first read "Gertrude and Ludwig's Bogus Adventure" (*My Way*) I had no idea what those Pete Hewitt "Excellent Adventure" films were. Boy films, kid films, science fiction—not at all my thing. But even without knowing the actual films referred to, the meanings come through well enough. On the other hand, once told about the films, I became quite intrigued with looking them up, rather the way I now love reading about "the cake shops on the Nevsky" Pound writes of and which he never saw any more than I've seen them! That's what makes poetry so infinitely re-readable. And poetry that has none of this thickness quickly gets boring.

But there's another point. Yes, one can do without knowing all the references, but there's also the unavoidable fact that sooner or later, readers WILL look them up. In twenty years' time, someone will write an essay or thesis on your poetry and they'll go to the Stage and the Carnegie and have a look at the pastrami!! After all, in their day, Eliot and Pound, not to mention Stein or Duchamp, were felt to be hopelessly hermetic, and now students talk about the Oculist Witnesses in the *Large Glass*, as if it were all part of normal discourse. And in the case of Frank O'Hara, where I used to think most of the person and place names were intentionally fortuitous, now scholars are writing solemn treatises about the significance of lunching at Larré's on 56th Street, or on the meaning of *Gauloises*. And since younger people have no idea who Billie Holiday was, there's much writing about her voice, cultural role, and so on.

So time catches up with the poetry! And that's OK because, in the end, nothing substitutes for "close reading," which needn't be arid New Critical exercise at all, but just the habit of paying attention to the words and sentences on the page or on a CD—whatever. I will sound like an Old Wolf in kvetch clothing when I say it's a practice that has been largely lost. So afraid are teachers and their students of actually looking at a text, so fearful that they will be endowing that text with "autonomy," that crucial things get missed. I was dismayed the other day in my graduate class when, in reading Stein's "Miss Furr and Miss Skeene," three of the eighteen seminar members thought Helen Furr was the same person as Mrs. Furr and that she had left her husband to be with Georgine Skeene because she was stifled by bourgeois capitalism, or some such thing. The seven-page story does refer to Helen not liking to live "where she had always been living," which—common sense tells us—could hardly have always been with her husband, could it? And on the next page we read explicitly that Helen Furr went home to visit "her mother and father." Accordingly, when you get this kind of reading, you know the student hasn't actually read through the text.

Teaching poetry thus remains a challenge. And I can't think of a more perfect comment on all this than your words in "What's Art Got to Do with It?":

> The shortest distance between two points is a digression. I hold for a wandering thought just that I may stumble upon something worthy of report.

Who knows, ahead of time, what those items worthy of report, might be?

CB: And that goes as much for criticism as poetry, where the value, in part, comes from the searching for something not yet defined. Maybe close reading would get a better rap if we called it *PSI: Poetry Scene Investigation*. Of course, that would mean treating the poem as a crime, but maybe it is: a crime against mass culture.

"Poetry is too important to be left to its own devices" also means that poems can't do all the work of poetry by themselves. For poems to come into being, we need editors, publishers, designers, proofreaders, booksellers, websites, teachers, critics, detractors, supporters, and of course, not to leave them out of the picture entirely, poets and readers. I think the phobia about explication comes from the fact that some of what calls itself that is obtuse, dishearteningly literal or thematic, in short, deadening. But bad teaching about poetry is a problem comparable to bad writing of poetry; poetry as an art may seem to suffocate under the blankets applied in a well-meaning effort to keep it warm (as if the body of the text were growing as cold as a corpse), but poems go their merry way irrespective and irregardless. Cut-'em up, mangle their meanings, weigh them down with unsupportable symbolism, reduce them to a sentiment, strip them to their empty cores . . . and they still keep coming back for more. Poems are remarkably resilient, and far less likely to be injured by incursions into their autonomy or excursions into their associations, than we have any reason to expect.

Yet if poems are uncannily resilient, poets, alas, are not.

But, there I go again, off on a tangent. (How many tangents can play the harp on the edge of a pin? Or is it pine?)

That is, I don't mean to suggest that criticism is always, or even mostly, agonistic. Your own approach to close reading is not as a contest between poem and reading, but like dance, the two in tango. Moreover, without such external interventions, poetry would, indeed, be a dead art.

The poem is not finished even when it is completed. Completion or publication marks not the end of the poem but rather its entry into the world through the responses to it. And that's another dimension of the sort of close reading you encourage; for the poems we reread over time become cultural time capsules, linguistic dioramas in which each phrase is an imaginary hyperlink for our further exploration of—or reentry into—a particular time and place. In other words, crucial to any sense of the cultural details in a poem is the world they constitute; not only what the particulars are but also the economy of the particulars—how they are distributed and arranged. That's the way poems lend themselves, are made for, reinhabitation; why chasing down the references or the milieu the references evoke doesn't detract from the poem but rather opens it up.

Inspiration is not what comes before the poet writes the poem but what happens when the poem is read (or heard).

A criticism is responsible to the degree it is able to respond.

Criticism engages and extends the work of the poem, but criticism is not the end of poetry. Nor is the poem the final destination of a process of analysis and research.

The poem is an initial point of embarkation on journeys yet to come, on earth as they are in the imaginary space between here and there, now and then, is and as.

So, hey, if you have time now, let's go together on a trip to those cake shops on the Nevsky.

IS ART CRITICISM FIFTY YEARS BEHIND POETRY?

In *Frank O'Hara: The Poetics of Coterie*,[1] Lytle Shaw's ostensive subject is how "coterie" works in the poetry and poetics of Frank O'Hara. The opening chapters provide a cogent discussion of the role of proper names in O'Hara's poetry within the context of a linguistics-inflected examination of naming and reference. Shaw notes the different levels of proper naming in O'Hara's work—figures of popular culture, political and social figures—as well as different levels of his personal circle (from identifiable artists and poets to obscure names).

For Shaw, coterie is not a closed world of intimates but an interlocking, open-ended set of associations and affiliations. He links coterie to the socio-historically self-conscious poetics of the local, community, and other collective formations. The poetics of coterie is presented by Shaw as an alternative to universalizing conceptions of poetry. O'Hara's location of himself not in a homogenous elite but rather in intersecting constellations of persons (real and imagined affiliations), together with his famous time-stamping of his poems (it's 12:18 in New York as I rewrite this sentence) both work against the Romantic Ideology of timeless poems by great individuals.

Still, no discussion of coterie can completely free itself from the negative connotations of *clique* and *scene*. For best effect, the first chapters of Shaw's book should be read beside Andrew Epstein's *Beautiful Enemies: Friendship and Postwar American Poetry*.[2] Epstein offers exemplary Emersonian readings of the intricate web connecting individual talent and collective investment in the poetry and poetics of John Ashbery, Amiri Baraka, and O'Hara. Averting the Cold War myth of the individual voice in the wilderness of conformity, Epstein gives us voices in conversation and conflict, suggesting

Parkett 84 (2009).
1. *Frank O'Hara* (Iowa City: University of Iowa Press, 2006).
2. *Beautiful Enemies* (New York: Oxford University Press, 2006).

that resistance to agreement is at the heart of a pragmatist understanding of literary community.

The role of proper names and the nature of O'Hara's personal circle are not the only concerns of *Frank O'Hara: The Poetics of Coterie*. In the book's final chapters, another theme emerges with equal force: O'Hara's approach to the visual arts in his poems and criticism. Shaw sees O'Hara's art writing as a powerful and necessary counter to the monological and hyperprofessional rigidity that descends from Clement Greenberg (who dismissed O'Hara's art writing) to Michael Fried and, I'd add, extends to the *October* brand, the epitome of, let's just say, High Orthodoxical art criticism. For if the luminous rigor and prodigious insights of Greenberg and Fried end in the tragedy of misrecognition, the self-serious vanguardism of the High Orthodoxical ends in the farce of academic gatekeeping and market validation. In other words, Greenberg's and Fried's insistence on *conviction* and *agonism* morphed into a practice of regulation by exclusion.

For Shaw, the aversion of poetry in both formalist and High Orthodoxical art criticism is a sign of its own aesthetic failure. In contrast to Greenberg's and Fried's rebuke of "poetic" art criticism, he suggests that O'Hara was doing an "art-critical" poetry that, for example, has resonances with Robert Smithson's writing.[3] "O'Hara moves toward modes of hybridization and proliferation that are diametrically opposed to the narrowing lexical range Greenberg and Fried imagined as the cure to a threatened art criticism of the 1950s and the 1960s" (171). Shaw illustrates his point with a section of O'Hara's poem "Second Avenue" that explicitly addresses DeKooning:

> The silence that lasted for a quarter century. All
> the babies were born blue. They called him "Al" and "Horseballs"
> in kindergarten, he had an autocratic straw face like a dark
> in a DeKooning where the torrent has subsided at the very center
> classism, it can be many whirlpools in a gun battle

3. See Robert Smithson, *The Collected Writings*, edited by Jack Flam (Berkeley: University of California Press, 1996). One of Smithson's signature works for poetics, and by extension criticism, is his 1967 "Language to Be Looked at and/or Things to Read": "Simple statements are often based on language fears, and sometimes result in dogma and non-sense. . . . The mania for literalness relates to the breakdown in the rational belief in reality. Books entomb words in a synthetic rigor mortis, perhaps that is why 'print' is thought to have entered obsolescence. The mind of this death, however, is unrelentingly awake. . . . My sense of language is that it is matter and not ideas—i.e., printed matter" (61).

or each individual pang in the "last mile" of electrodes, so
totally unlike xmas tree ornaments that you wonder, uhmmm?
what the bourgeoisie is thinking of. Trench coat. Broken strap.[4]

O'Hara practiced a complicit[5] and promiscuous criticism that stands in stark contrast to the ideologies of formalist criticism of his time and the *October*-tinged orthodoxicalities of the 1970s and 1980s. As Shaw puts it, "O'Hara's painting poems present . . . a special kind of interdisciplinarity, or what Michael Fried would call 'theatricality.' . . . They . . . initiate almost infinite substitutions among discourses in their rapid, line-to-line attempt to imagine contexts for painting. *It is for that reason that they seem, and are, antiprofessional*" (179; italics added).

Both formalist and the later *October*-branded criticism and its many knockoffs preached views of meaning that, while at odds with one another, were sufficiently proscriptive as to void the full range of aesthetic approaches in the art championed and to simply dismiss (as "pernicious," as Fried called "Dada")[6] work that contested the limits of received ideas of meaning-making. This criticism operated not by "negating" or deconstructing meaning (the empty encomium of the High Orthodoxical Art) but by articulating newly emerging constructions of meaning-as-constellations (a poetics of affiliation, association, combine, conglomeration, collage, and coterie). In effect, both formalist and High Orthodoxical criticism see theatrical or allegorical methods, respectively, as emptying meaning. But while the former decries the putative demise of opticality and the latter valorizes it, neither has a sufficiently pliable approach to engage with the new semantic embodiments of the "frail / instant," as O'Hara puts it in his poem "For Bob Rauschenberg."[7] O'Hara's "frail / instant" could be called the weak absorption of coterie, which, like the "unevenness" of everyday life is both discontinuous and fluid, self-aware and constructive, "semantically

4. Donald Allen, ed., *The Collected Poems of Frank O'Hara* (Berkeley: University of California Press, 1995), 148–49.
5. See Johanna Drucker, *Sweet Dreams: Contemporary Art and Complicity* (Chicago: University of Chicago Press, 2005).
6. Shaw, 204, quoting Fried's 1965 "Three American Painters," from *Art and Objecthood* (Chicago: University of Chicago Press, 1998), 259. Fried's object of scorn is the neo-Dada of Rauschenberg and Cage.
7. Quoted by Shaw on 200, from O'Hara's *Collected Poems*, 322.

various and unstable," atomized and chaining.[8] O'Hara—in his reviled poeticizing—was able to articulate a poetics of adjacency, of queer juxtapositions, to which his critical others remained blind.

Thomas McEvilley makes the point very succinctly in his 1982 essay "Heads It's Form, Tales It's Not Content," prefacing his remarks with a quote from O'Hara's "Having a Coke with You"—

and the portrait show seems to have no faces in it at all, just paint
you suddenly wonder why in the world anyone ever did them . . .

Here's McEvilley:

In the attempt to free art from the plane of content, the formalist tradition denied that elements of the artwork may refer outside the work toward the embracing world. Rather, the elements are to be understood as referring to one another inside the work, in an interior and self-subsistent esthetic code. The claim is imprecisely and incompletely made, however, because the formalists take much too narrow a view of what can constitute "content." Greenberg, for example, often uses the term "non-representational" to describe "pure" artworks—those purified of the world. But as he uses it, the term seems to rule out only clear representations of physical objects such as chairs, bowls of fruit, or naked figures lying on couches. Similarly, Fried assumed that only "recognizable objects, persons and places" can provide the content of a painting. But art that is nonrepresentational in this sense may still be representational in others. It may be bound to the surrounding world by its reflection of structures of thought, political tensions, psychological attitudes, and so forth.[9]

As Shaw acidly notes, to cast "the poetic" as the last bastion of private insights, or indeed "as a kind of metaphysics of content, of pure meaning,"

8. "Unevenness" is Shaw's word to describe the mixed textures (both surfaces and fields of reference) in O'Hara's poem (202). "Semantically various and unstable" is Shaw's term for a work by Robert Rauschenberg (207).

9. McEvilley's essay was originally published in *Artforum*, November 1982. It was collected in his *Art & Discontent: Theory at the Millennium* (Kingston, NY: Documentext/McPherson, 1991); the passage is from p. 29, and the Fried citation is from "Three American Painters" (see note 2).

requires a concerted effort to ignore the formally radical poetries outside the domain of Official Verse Culture and especially those poetries that explore collage, collision, disjunction, overlay, and contradiction. Mispresented "as such it is no wonder that the poetic has had a long list of detractors—stretching from Greenberg and Fried to Benjamin Buchloh and James Meyer" (220). Indeed, "they"—both the prophets of a sublime late modernism and the apostates who argued for dystopian postmodernism—"were all cheated of some marvelous experience / which is not going to go wasted on me which is why I am telling you about it," as O'Hara wryly puts it in the final lines of "Having a Coke with You."[10] O'Hara is not, *not nearly*, a better critic than Greenberg and Fried, and Shaw shows O'Hara's allegiances as being more to the *in between* than to any one of his shifting positions—curator, poet, critic, lover, social magnet, arts administrator. But more than "they" he recognized that "form is never more than an extension of content."[11]

This is certainly not to say that the normative, descriptive, fashion- and market-driven modes of art criticism are to be preferred, whether written by poets or not. The problem is not that art criticism is too conceptually complex but, on the contrary, that—even at its putatively most theoretical—its poetics and aesthetics are too often willfully stunted, marked by a valorized incapacity to respond to how meaning is realized through multiple, incommensurable, or overlaid discourses—*kinship*, in Shaw's terms—within a single work. Meaning is not an end but a between.[12]

The significance of O'Hara (or McEvilley or Shaw) is not that they are poets who do criticism, which is also true of Fried, but the polymorphous dexterity of their writing; their aversion of simple description (of visual appearance or of ideas) in pursuit of phenomenological unevenness (in Shaw's terms) or complexity found in the visual artwork they address. This is the legacy of Baudelaire, Mallarmé, Apollinaire, and Stein, not the "belle lettristic" approach that is often, and banally, contrasted with orthodoxical criticism.

---

10. "Having a Coke with You," in *The Collected Poems of Frank O'Hara* (Berkeley: University of California Press, 1995), 360.

11. Robert Creeley quoted by Charles Olson in his 1950 essay "Projective Verse," in his *Collected Prose*, edited by Benjamin Friedlander (Berkeley: University of California Press, 1997), 240.

12. "The poem is at last between two persons instead of two pages," as O'Hara puts it in his 1959 essay "Personism: A Manifesto," in *Collected Poems*, 498.

Shaw's approach provides a useful historical context for such projects as M/E/A/N/I/N/G.[13] In doing so, it helps to explain not only the aversion of radical poetics and poetry in formalist and October-flavored criticism of the 1960s to 1980s, but also the fear of the taint of poetry by even such apparently poetry-related artists as Lawrence Weiner (who declines to have his work exhibited in poetry-related contexts). Consider, for example, that Meyer, in his introduction to a recent collection of the poetry (and other writings) of Carl Andre, barely mentions contemporary poetry or poetics as an active context in which to consider this work.[14] The lesson is that linguistic works of Weiner or Andre (Vito Acconci or Jenny Holzer) can be deemed significant *as art* only if they are purged of any connection to (radically impure, content-concatenating) poetry and poetics.

As Dominique Fourcade noted at the (Poetry Plastique) symposium, poetry literarily devalues visual art (we were talking about how Philip Guston's collaborations with Clark Coolidge had a lower economic value than comparable works without words).[15] But perhaps this devaluation provides a necessary route for removing visual art from any Aesthetic System that mocks both aesthesis and social aspiration.[16]

Reading Shaw's study of the 1950s and '60s underscores, once again, how, indeed, *pernicious* is the cliché that poetry is fifty years behind visual art. On the contrary, art criticism, insofar as it succumbs to a paranoiac

13. M/E/A/N/I/N/G focused on artists' writing about the visual arts, with an emphasis on considerations of both feminism and painting, and included many essays by poets. Edited by Susan Bee and Mira Schor, it published twenty issues from 1986 to 1996 and continues to publish, intermittently, online. See http://writing.upenn.edu/pepc/meaning, accessed July 6, 2009. This essay continues my reflections in "For M/E/A/N/I/N/G," which was published in the first issue of the magazine, December 1986, and collected in M/E/A/N/I/N/G: An Anthology of Artists' Writings, Theory, and Criticism, edited by Susan Bee and Mira Schor (Durham, NC: Duke University Press, 2000).

14. Carl Andre, Cuts: Texts 1959–2004, edited by James Meyer (Cambridge: MIT Press, 2005). Since Andre himself refers to his work as poetry, some history of Andre's childhood relation to poetry, and to the contemporary poetry of his youth most *unlike* his own, is provided. But Meyer does little to situate Andre's poetry into the context of related poetic work, either radical modernist or contemporary, and prefers not to address the formal and aesthetic issues foregrounded by Andre's poetry with reference to the considerable body of critical writing on poetry (including visual poetry) that explores similar issues.

15. Several collaborations by Coolidge and Guston were shown at the "Poetry Plastique" show, which I cocurated with Jay Sanders, at the Marianne Boesky Gallery in 2001. See http://epc .buffalo.edu/features/poetryplastique. See also catalog essay above, p. 187.

16. Johanna Drucker addresses some of these issues in "Art Theory Now: from Aesthetics to Aesthesis," a lecture given at the School of Visual Arts, New York, on December 11, 2007.

fear of theatricality that induces frame-lock, lags behind poetry at its peril. Meanwhile, the visual and verbal arts remain complicit with one another fifty years ago and today.

POST SCRIPT: IS POETRY FIFTY YEARS BEHIND POETRY? IS ART FIFTY YEARS AHEAD OF ART? THE SHOCKING AND UNEXPURGATED TRUTH . . . TOLD HERE FOR THE FIRST TIME

In a response to this essay on the San Francisco Museum of Modern Art blog (July 5, 2009), Kevin Killian gently chides me for not giving the original source of my ironic title, which I guess I took for granted. But the sentiment has become a kind of received wisdom, removed from the specifics of Brion Gysin's original remark:

> Writing is fifty years behind painting. I propose to apply the painters' techniques to writing; things as simple and immediate as collage or montage. Cut right through the pages of any book or newsprint . . . lengthwise, for example, and shuffle the columns of text. Put them together at hazard and read the newly constituted message. Do it for yourself. Use any system which suggests itself to you. Take your own words or the words said to be "the very own words" of anyone else living or dead. You'll soon see that words don't belong to anyone. Words have a vitality of their own and you or anybody else can make them gush into action.[17]

Killian and I would both be sympathetic to Gysin's point—and indeed my "experiments list" (based in part on Bernadette Mayer's) is indebted to Gysin (http://writing.upenn.edu/bernstein/experiments.html). Gysin was arguing for a poetry that challenged the conventional norms of Official Verse Culture—that would use cut-ups, visual display, parataxis, and appropriated language to create a new kind of poetry. But it was never true that the actual practice of poetry was ahead or behind the visual arts. Gertrude Stein may get less respect in the mainstream than Pablo Picasso, but the

---

17. Brion Gysin, *Cut-Ups Self-Explained*, in William S. Burroughs and Brion Gysin, *The Third Mind* (New York: Seaver Books, 1978), 34.

one is neither ahead or behind the other. Frank O'Hara is as significant in his poetry as Robert Rauschenberg in his art, to take an example from my review. And poetry has one advantage in the postwar period: its publication and criticism is not dominated by market values. (Of course, for the poète chétif this is hardly an advantage at all.) Certainly, naïve conceptions of representations, narrative continuity, and expression (what I once called "ideational mimesis") have great credibility in Official Verse Culture, but no more so than in the stylistically straitjacketed critical writing (and enforced copyediting) of the major art magazines. (As I've said before: I don't blame the writers, but the market-driven focus of the editors/publishers.)

No one owns art. You can own the objects, but no one—not museums, not artists, and not art critics, not art historians or poets—can contain how they come to mean in the world, what they mean to us, what we make them mean. What I value most in art criticism and art history (the two are as if one intertwined figure) is thinking that defies the established norms, that refuses to bow to received values, that reinvents the aesthetic *at every turn.*

A critical writing that is dialogic rather than proscriptive. (But is that itself a prescription?)

Art criticism and art history, just as literary criticism and literary history, are made up of words and can't avoid poetics, can't avoid the problems of representation or the implications of tone. When art criticism represses its own writerly investments, then it falls prey to the same naïve positivism as the most conventional representational portrait, no matter how sophisticated it claims to be. The modes of representation in art criticism are just as much at issue as they are in a work of visual art or a poem. That's, of course, where O'Hara comes in.

I hadn't given that much thought to the significance of O'Hara's art criticism until I read Shaw's book. O'Hara's art criticism had always seem slight, compared to his poetry and also to the art criticism of many of his contemporaries. But Shaw makes a compelling and complex case for O'Hara's art writing and its interconnection to his poetics. Shaw's book is primarily, or at least at first, about "coterie"—a term he turns from dark to light, a feat of transvaluation that is at the center of this exemplary historical study. Killian makes the crucial point that *coterie* has been used homophobically, belittling those stigmatized with it, from O'Hara's circle to Jack Spicer's; and there is a lesson to be drawn from that, well known, but relevant: that it is often those who claim to be free of "special" interests that have the greatest vested interests. It occurs to me that you could look at art criticism in terms of coterie too, but by reversing the stigma, pointing how much the tone of interest-free imperious authority, self-assured knowledge, and doctrinaire aesthetics functions because it is . . . *coterie criticism.*

We are all coteries now (only some are in more denial about it than others, and they are the ones that trouble my sleep).

My idea is not that we should all get along, and certainly not that the same things should be on our radar, but rather that we'd be better off not to cast our disagreements in terms of the ignorance of those with whom we disagree. This is harder than it may seem. Stigmatizing aesthetic or ideological disagreement as if it were the results of ignorance, fraudulence, or insignificance is too often the way both art (and poetry) business is conducted by those who fiercely police what they too often regard as their own turf.

No Trespassing!

Don't get me wrong: I *am* ignorant, I make mistakes *at every turn*; it's my awareness of that, to the degree I can be, that is my guide.

I am as partial and partisan as anyone. Preference and selection are a necessary part of aesthetic judgment. Yet, my radar might be the exact map of another person's exclusions, just as another's exclusions might begin to map my paradise. The relation of these two ideas (conviction in one's aesthetic judgment and its inevitable limitations) is not irreconcilable but dialectical.

The axiomatic wounds art. And yet art seeks this wound and deepens in relation to it. The fashion of the day is almost never fashionable enough unless you make it so yourself. This is as much a problem for poetry as for visual art, for poetics as much as art criticism.

It is the same problem.

POETRY BAILOUT WILL RESTORE CONFIDENCE OF READERS

Chairman Lehman, Secretary Polito, distinguished poets and readers—I regret having to interrupt the celebrations tonight with an important announcement.

As you know, the glut of illiquid, insolvent, and troubled poems is clogging the literary arteries of the West. These debt-ridden poems threaten to infect other areas of the literary sector and ultimately to topple our culture industry.

Cultural leaders have come together to announce a massive poetry buyout: leveraged and unsecured poems, poetry derivatives, delinquent poems, and subprime poems will be removed from circulation in the biggest poetry bailout since the Victorian era. We believe the plan is a comprehensive approach to relieving the stresses on our literary institutions and markets.

Let there be no mistake: the fundamentals of our poetry are sound. *The problem is not poetry but poems.* The crisis has been precipitated by the escalation of poetry debt—poems that circulate in the market at an economic loss due to their difficulty, incompetence, or irrelevance.

Illiquid poetry assets are choking off the flow of imagination that is so vital to our literature. When the literary system works as it should, poetry and poetry assets flow to and from readers and writers to create a productive part of the cultural field. As toxic poetry assets block the system, the poisoning of literary markets has the potential to damage our cultural institutions irreparably.

As we know, lax composition practices since the advent of modernism led to irresponsible poets and irresponsible readers. Simply put, too many poets composed works they could not justify. We are seeing the impact on

A statement read at an event marking the release of *Best American Poetry* 2008, at the New School, New York on September 25, 2008. David Lehman is the series editor of *Best American Poetry*, and Robert Polito is the director of the writing program at the New School. Published the following day on *Harper's* website.

poetry, with a massive loss of confidence on the part of readers. What began as a subprime poetry problem on essentially unregulated poetry websites, has spread to other, more stable, literary magazines and presses, and contributed to excess poetry inventories that have pushed down the value of responsible poems.

The risks poets have taken have been too great; the aesthetic negligence has been profound. The age of decadence must come to an end with the imposition of oversight and regulation on poetry composition and publishing practices.

We are convinced that once we have removed these troubled and distressed poems from circulation, our cultural sector will stabilize and readers will regain confidence in American literature. We estimate that for the buyout to be successful, we will need to remove from circulation all poems written after 1904.

This will be a fresh start, a new dawn of a new day. Without these illiquid poems threatening to overwhelm readers, we will be able to create a literary culture with a solid aesthetic foundation.

I'm Charles Bernstein and I approved this message.

IV

Recantorium

RECANTORIUM
(A BACHELOR MACHINE, AFTER
DUCHAMP AFTER KAFKA)

I, Charles, son of the late Joseph Herman, later known as Herman Joseph, and Shirley K., later known as Sherry, New Yorker, aged fifty-eight years, arraigned personally before this Esteemed Body, and kneeling before you, Most Eminent and Reverend Readers, Inquisitors-General against heretical depravity throughout the entire Poetry Commonwealth, having before my eyes and touching with my hands, the Books of Accessible Poets, swear that I have always believed, do believe, and by your help will in the future believe, all that is held, preached, taught, and expressed by the Books of Accessible Poets.

I was wrong, I apologize, I recant. I altogether abandon the false opinion that National Poetry Month is not good for poetry and for poets. I abjure, curse, and detest the aforesaid error and apostasy. And I now freely and openly attest to the virtues of National Poetry Month in throwing a national spotlight on poetry, so crucial to keeping verse alive in the twenty-first century.

I was wrong, I apologize and recant. I altogether abandon the false opinion that only elitist and obscure poetry should be praised. I abjure, curse, detest, and renounce the aforesaid error and aversion. And I now freely and openly

First publicly attested at "Conceptual Poetry & Its Others," Poetry Center, University of Arizona, Tucson, May 29, 2008; subsequently attested with codicil at Ecole normale supérieure in Lyon at "Modernisme et illisibilité" on October 23, 2008; later translated into French by Abigail Lang and published in *Nioque* 5 (2009); reattested and confirmed, with additional codicil, at the Museum of Chinese in America in New York, as part of Performa 2009, on November 14, 2009. Published in *Critical Inquiry* 35.2 (Winter 2009) and (excerpts) in *Harper's* (January 2009).

attest that the best way to get general readers to start to read poetry is to present them with broadly appealing work, with strong emotional content and a clear narrative line.

I was wrong, I apologize, I recant. I altogether abandon the false opinion that, to raise the profile for poetry, events involving celebrities reading poems, such as the one each year that is the centerpiece of National Poetry Month, are not as valuable as events presenting poets reading their own work. I acknowledge and regret my error. Poets would turn off the large and wealthy audience of arts patrons. Like the retarded or crippled stepchildren in fairy tales, it is for the best to have the poets stay in the back room during the party, lest they frighten the guests.

I was wrong, I apologize, I recant. I altogether reject, abjure, and denounce the sarcasm that just now has undercut the sincerity of my confession. My comments about poets as retarded or crippled stepchildren are offensive. I abase and prostrate myself in humbly and sincerely asking your forgiveness and the forgiveness of all those who seek, above all, sincerity and authenticity in poetry.

I was wrong, I apologize, I recant. Midway in my journey as a poet, I have given my name in encomium and book cover endorsement, both for ads and announcements, catalogs and brochures, print and digital, to works that are not of the highest order as established by Time, Authority, and Fashion, lapsing into stubborn selection based on personal preference or appreciation or liking, on intuitions and hunches, rather than rational principle and promulgated theory.

I was wrong, I apologize, I recant. I altogether abandon and renounce the false opinion that poetry is a social and ideological construction and not the expression of the Pure Feeling of the Poet (PFP) and declare the Sovereign Human Self (SHS) to be the sole origin of authentic expression and meaning. In full recognition and acknowledgment of my error, I hereby declare and swear, to all present company, that I must not hold, defend, or teach in any way whatsoever, verbally or in writing, the said false doctrine.

I was wrong, I apologize and I recant. I altogether abandon the false opinion that the head of a major writing organization was out of line when he called me "morally repugnant" for not sharing his views about poetry. As one of the Blessed of the doctrine of Authentic Poetry pointed out in rebuking me, he is entitled to his views, and my criticism of him was divisive and partisan and morally repugnant.

I was wrong, I apologize, I recant. I altogether abandon the false opinion that Official Verse Culture, through prestigious prizes awarded for merit and reviews in nationally circulated publications selected for major importance, and including the appointments of the poets laureate, does not represent the best and the finest, the most profound and significant, the richest and most rewarding, poetry of our nation. And now that I myself, in my person and through my work, have ascended into this Exalted Company, and joined the rarefied and incorrigible company of Official Verse Culture, do here cast stones and sticks and call an abomination and curse and scorn and repudiate any who would not cherish and adore both the process and product of that Official Verse Culture that has embraced, with trepidation and embarrassment, and with noses tightly pinched and ear muffs in place, my unworthy ascent.

I was wrong, I apologize and recant. I altogether abandon the false opinion that there was a value in working together collaboratively with other poets along the lines of shared aesthetic engagements. I abjure, curse, and detest the aforesaid error and aversion. I now see clearly and openly, and without coercion acknowledge to all virtually or actually present, now and in the future, in this life and in all subsequent lives, on earth as well as on other planets populated by intelligent beings, that only poets working in solitude and individually can produce poems of enduring value.

I did wrong, I'm sorry, I recant. Having advocated, in youth, a set of radical approaches to poetry, I later abandoned or altered or undermined these very approaches of my own and my comrades, devising, shifting my views with the tides, putting my personal aesthetics above these principles, my preferences and interests above the ideals and interests of the group.

I did wrong and was wrong, I recant and renounce. The time for my ways erroneous and peripatetic, errant and wandering, has expired; the time for a poetry of the doggedly particular and the quotidian detail, of the unsymbolical, of the minor and the off-key, has expired; just as the time has expired for obscurantist theories propping up obscurantist poems, poems that turn their backs on meaning, story, emotion, and pleasure, as these values have been promulgated in the Books of the Accessible Poets, which is the only sure guide away from empty rhetoric and toward the pure achievement of meaning, story, emotion, and pleasure. I now, and I aver this before you assembled here, virtually and actually, before you I aver and embrace, a poetry without limits of time or place, a poetry of universal address and true to the timeless human spirit.

I was wrong, I apologize, I recant. I altogether abandon the false doctrine of social poetics in which poems are read in their cultural and bibliographic contexts. I abjure, curse, and detest the aforesaid error and apostasy. I now declare, openly and without fear of punishment, ridicule, neglect, disparagement, or coercion, to all virtually or actually present, now and in the future, in this life and in all subsequent lives, on earth as well as on other planets populated by intelligent beings, that social poetics demeans poetry, which should be read, in its purest form, as a Timeless Expression of Universal Human Feeling (UHF).

Wrong was I and wrong still am I, yet and still, 'til now as I renounce my unseemly and self-mocking infatuation with performance and here declare for all of you to hear clearly and without equivocation: the performance of a poem undermines its essential and heart-felt meaning, for poetry is the Supreme Art of the written word and the written word only. To contaminate poetry with performance, as I have done and advanced with arguments both sophistical and deplorable, is an abomination to be scorned with stigmas.

I was wrong, I apologize, I recant. I totally and absolutely, with shame and guilt, abandon the false doctrine that social and cultural history might include poetry in its field of study or use poetry as models for thinking about society and culture. I abjure, curse, detest, and renounce the aforesaid error and aversion. I now admit and acknowledge, proclaim and announce, openly and without coercion or fear or punishment or ridicule or disparagement, to all virtually or actually present, now and in the future, in this life and in all subsequent lives, on earth as well as on other planets populated by intelligent beings, that prose narratives are the only suitable works for cultural and historical study and that expository prose can provide the only suitable models for such study.

I was wrong, I apologize, I recant. I altogether and totally, completely and thoroughly, without reservation, quibble, or question, and with newly faithful heart, abandon the false doctrine that meandering, digressive, or paratactic prose, prose that fails to state clearly its meaning, sentences that get caught up in their own rhythms and sounds and cadences, nuances and nooks, rather than in getting to the point or meat or heart of the matter or meaning or substance, as I say, I abandon and renounce the false doctrine that crooked and bent prose can have any value for truthful discourse or accurate representation. I abjure, curse, and detest the aforesaid error and aversion and the many related errors and aversions that flow inevitably as a consequence of the aforesaid error and aversion, as a baby inevitably flows from its mother or an ocean from its rivers or a false conclusion from a flawed premise or a disease from a virus or death from repeated blows with a blunt instrument or gorging from a starving child given food. Clearly written expository prose, with a delineated argument including a beginning, middle, and end, is the only guarantor of Rational Mind.

I done and went wrong, disregarding the views of Joe Sixpack in my desire to ingratiate myself with Nunnely Ninepack. I here before you assembled renounce the idea that American poetry has anything to learn from French poetry, whether from its Baudelairean decadence, its Rimbaudian dark mysticisms, its Lautréamontian obfuscation, or from its Mallerméan dandifying and aestheticism, a dandyism and aestheticism that takes us away from the thinking of the common man and toward a fetishizing of language and its sounds and its placement on the page, on unhealthy and irrational thought processes, on chimerical values that lead away from manly truth and toward a girly preciousness and pretentiousness. I furthermore denounce and renounce the value of difficulty—of *illisibilité*—in poetry, which is no more than a cynical ploy to garner attention from work that is empty. And so I today renounce the white space of the page as empty, meaningless, signifying nothing to no one, no way no how, a void, a black hole of erased life, from vitality and vibrancy and natural meaning, which is, which must always be, red, white, and blue.

I was wrong, I apologize and recant. I altogether abandon the false doctrine that ambiguity and irony are anything more than sophistry. I abjure, curse, and detest the aforesaid error and apostasy, which I have lapsed into again

and again, like a habitual drinker seeking his five o'clock martini, or an ero-
tomaniac seeking nonprocreative sexual experiences, or a worker idling on
the job, or a habitual truant passing notes in class.

I was wrong, I apologize, I recant. I altogether abandon the false opinion
that abnormal poetry techniques such as fragmentation, dissociation, discontinuity, collage, disjunction, seriality, constellation, and unnatural constraints of whatever kind have any contribution to make to poetic craft.
After it had been notified to me that the said doctrine was contrary to the
Books of the Accessible Poets, I wrote and published works in which I discuss this new doctrine already condemned, and adduced arguments of
great cogency in its favor, without presenting any negation of these, and
for this reason I have been vehemently rebuked. I abjure, curse, detest, and
renounce the aforesaid errors and aversions, which are symptoms of a queer
and degenerate avoidance of meaning, coherence, truth, morality, and the
literary tradition (if rightly understood). I must not hold, defend, or teach
in any way whatsoever, verbally or in writing, the said false doctrine.

I was wrong, I apologize, I recant. I altogether abandon the false opinion
that form in poetry is political and social. I abjure, curse, and detest the
aforesaid error and aversion, which is a symptom of a queer and degenerate
avoidance of meaning, coherence, truth, morality, and the literary tradition
(if rightly understood). Form in poetry is a transparent means of conveying
the emotional truth of the poem and should never interfere with, or contra-
dict, the emotional truth of the poem.

I was wrong, I apologize, and I recant. I altogether abandon, disavow, and
retract the false doctrine that the Imagination is anything more than can be
grasped by Rational Mind. I abjure, curse, and detest the aforesaid error and
aversion, which I have lapsed into again and again, like a milkman singing
on his route or a pony that refuses to be ridden.

I was wrong, I most humbly apologize, I recant. I altogether abandon, disavow, and retract the false doctrine that poets should write poetics and criticism. I recant my cant. I abjure, curse, detest, and renounce the aforesaid
error and apostasy and the many related errors and apostasies that flow
inevitably as a consequence of the aforesaid error and apostasy, as a baby
inevitably flows from its mother or an ocean from its rivers or a false conclusion from a flawed premise or a disease from a virus or death from repeated

blows with a blunt instrument or gorging from a starving child given food. Poetics and critical thinking inhibit the creativity of the poet and should be left to academics.

I am filled with regret and overcome with the errors of my ways, for I have preferred the crooked path over the straight, the bent over the upright, the hunched over the erect. I recant my cant. I recant and cant my recantation. While supporting the work of small and independent and noncommercial publishers, presses, magazines, zines, mags, rags, periodicals, blogs, organizations, groups, galleries, websites, series, centers, and noncenters, I nonetheless, with callous disregard for these loyalties and affiliations, have betrayed, abandoned, and disappointed these publishers, presses, magazines, zines, mags, rags, periodicals, blogs, organizations, groups, websites, series, centers, and noncenters by arranging and agreeing to have my work published, presented, and co-opted by established and mainstream and commercial publishers, presses, magazines, journals, periodicals, blogs, organizations, groups, galleries, websites, series, and centers.

I am with regret fillèd and by errors o'erwhelmed, having chosen the broken path over the righteous, the warped over the erect. I cant and recant. I altogether abandon the false doctrine that poets can remain radical while working as academics. After it had been notified to me that the said doctrine was contrary to the Books of the Accessible Poets, I wrote and published works in which I discuss this new doctrine already condemned, and adduce arguments of great cogency in its favor, without presenting any negation of these, and for this reason I have been vehemently and justly rebuked. I abjure, curse, and detest the aforesaid error and aversion. Academic employment is the mark of a compromised poet who has sold out. Radical poets prove their authenticity through poverty.

I am with regret fillèd and by errors o'erwhelmed, having chosen the broken path over the righteous, the warped over the erect. I cant and recant. I altogether abandon the false opinion that advocacy or partisan positioning has any place in poetry and poetics. Poetry and poetics should be reserved for those who look beyond the contentions of the present into the eternal verities, the truths beyond this world that never change, as represented in the Books of the Accessible Poets. I further stipulate that I recant, categorically, that poetry is an activity of the intellect and herewith and hereby declare and proclaim that true poetry is an affair of the heart and only the heart.

I was wrong, I apologize most humbly before you, and with great contrition I recant. I altogether abandon, renounce and revile the use of found or appropriated texts in poems, whether attributed or unattributed, or the use of any external constraints, operations, procedures, algorithms, engines, or devices, whether machinic or manual, automated or calculated, digital or analogic, real or imaginary, virtual or actual. Such approaches to poetry soil, defame, and besmirch all traces of human expression, which is the necessary foundation for all poetry, and in pernicious and insidious ways foster depersonalization and inauthenticity by means of the substitution of the plagiarized and manufactured for the original and creative.

I was wrong, I apologize, I recant. I altogether abandon, renounce, and revile syntactic and grammatical turpitude, improper coupling of subjects and verbs and objects, run-on sentences and sentence fragments, suppression of natural connectives, erosion of necessary subordination of clauses, intentional and unconscious solecisms, or any relaxation, deviation, perversion, or inversion of the highest and strictest standards for English.

I am with regret fillèd and by errors o'erwhelmed, having chosen the broken path over the righteous, the warped over the erect. I cant and recant. I altogether abandon and renounce the false opinion that American poetry is founded on a mixed and miscegenated overlay of languages from the native tongues of immigrants to the echoes of Africa to the lost language of natives, indigenous to our social space. I abandon and altogether renounce the false opinion that slangs, patois, pidgins, accents, dialects, and ideolects are any more than bad grammar deserving an F and a slap on the face by those who uphold grammatical correctness and decry the deterioration of proper English usage and pronunciation. I altogether abandon and renounce the false opinion that bilingualism, trilingualism, and n-lingualisms have any place in our literature and I endorse those efforts, real and imaginary, to build a wall, from shore to shore, that separates us from any foreign contamination of our linguistic norms.

I am filled with regret and overcome with the errors of my ways, for I have preferred the crooked path over the straight, the bent over the upright, the hunched over the erect. I recant and cant my recantation. I altogether abandon the fetishizing of the sounds and forms and appearances and rhetoric of a poem. The innermost meaning of poems reveals itself when sound, form, appearance, rhetoric, and oratory fall away.

I was wrong, I apologize, I recant. I altogether abandon the false opinion that beauty can be found in the tattered, torn, ripped, battered, crippled, crumpled, odd, discounted, inconsequential, or in the asymmetric, particular, approximate, conceptual, cacophonous or cacophanous, in the clotted or off-key, in stray marks on the page, or in the transient or ephemeral. Beauty is always and only the manifestation of the ideal or perfect; beauty is only and always the image of the eternally true. After it had been notified to me that the said doctrine was contrary to the Books of the Accessible Poets, and the beliefs and doctrines of all poets and readers who believe in authenticity of expression, whether true or not, memoir or fake memoir, lyric or epic, nonetheless and still, even though I had been warned and cursed, I persisted, wrote, and published works in which I discuss this new doctrine already condemned, and adduced arguments of great cogency in its favor, without presenting any nullification of these arguments, in accord with decency and right thinking and the moral approach to poetry and poetics, and for this reason I have been vehemently rebuked. And I say and declare, vow and proclaim, to all assembled here or who may read this document, in printed or digital form, or who may hear it through audio recordings: I must not hold, defend, or teach in any way whatsoever, verbally or in writing, the said false doctrine.

I was wrong, I apologize, I recant. Like the black sheep who strays too far from the adoring flock, or like the drunk with a pale green beret who, deep into the night, and desperate for one more absinthe before closing time, babbles uncontrollably to the deaf and crippled barkeep, I embraced an elitism that put me out of touch with the sentiments, feelings, convictions, beliefs, preferences, perspectives, and dyspepsia of everyday, ordinary, run-of-the-mill people, the Johns and Joans and Janes and Jills, the Billys and Bobs, the Shirleys and Toms, the Frans and Fritzes, Millys and Moes, not only thinking I was better than John and Joe, Mary and Harry, but that their sentiments, feelings, convictions, beliefs, preferences, perspectives, and dyspepsia did not matter. I spent my time hunting for thoughts rather than hunting quail. My solipsism overcame me, so that I wrote, and professed for others to write, words that communicated to no one, that meant nothing, that defied the laws of meaning and the fundamentals of grammar; praising—over and above clear sense and good syntax—the incoherent, the nonsensical, the aberrant, the foolish, the deformed, the contradictory, the awkward, the frivolous, the ungainly, the self-indulgent, the infantile, the stubborn, the phony and fake, the prevaricating, the disorderly.

In my promiscuous dalliance with affect rather than emotion, I cast my lot with the excessively cerebral and the cerebrally excessive. I recant this cant. Now I stand before you to repudiate and abjure, to cast away and revile, this stiff-necked arrogance in order to dedicate myself to the freedom in right thinking.

I was wrong, I apologize, I recant. Like a rat seeking a dark cavity to eat its hapless prey, I succumbed to the dictatorship of relativism, a state of profound confusion in which I could not recognize anything as definitive and based my judgments solely on my own ego and desires. In this graceless state, I falsely believed that the real tyranny was intolerance to those who do not adhere to the aesthetic values of honesty, coherence, clarity, and truth as revealed to all with a moral conviction and a commitment to the time-less human story. I repudiate this gutless indulgence toward benighted and fallen ideas and commit myself to the dictatorship of obedience.

I was in error, I apologize, I recant. I altogether abandon the false doctrine of Midrashic Antinomianism and Bent Studies, which I have promulgated in writings, lectures, and teaching, with its base and cowardly insistence on ethical, dialogic, and situational values rather than fixed and immutable moral laws. I loved language more than truth, discourse more than reality, and so allowed to spread, in myself and in others, an intellectual virus that uproots the plain sense of the word.

I was wrong, I apologize, I recant. I altogether abandon the false opinion that the sun is the center of the world and immovable, and that the earth is not the center of the world, and moves. I must not hold, defend, or teach in any way whatsoever, verbally or in writing, the said false doctrine.

Quivering with tiny, rapid oscillations, these recantations are inscribed upon the bed of my thought, as a harrow incises the ground before the seeds are planted. My sentence is written onto me as I merge with it, yet I cannot comprehend it, even as it apprehends me. For yet, you have already seen, my errors abound around me and I, I am engulfèd by them, as a harpooned whale is overcome by the very waters that had buoyed him. I am in anxi-ety and in sorrow, for my wrongs known and unknown. For I have, here, now, in this very moment, done badly and wrongly with the hypocrisy, the bad faith, of this recantation, which reflects pride and arrogance, flippancy, sarcasm, resentment, hyperbole, and a fundamentally false analogy, and I

regret, already as my mouth speaks the words, my unsupportable and offensive identifications, in placing myself, even if only imaginatively or rhe-
torically or didactically, even if only parodically or satirically or ironically,
in the position of poets and writers and artists and scientists in the past
who confronted most cruel, most terrible, and most violent sanctions for
their work, for their thinking, and for their discoveries, but also poets and
writers and artists and scientists in the present, now, in this moment, as we
speak and as we listen, here and in other places, at home and abroad, who
daily and even hourly confront most violent, most terrible, and most cruel
sanctions for their work, for their thinking, and for their discoveries, while
I am at leisure, relatively free of fierce and wounding reprisals and may
cant and recant, recant and cant, for the most part, at my own discretion.
So, verily, I have fallen into error deep, an error I cannot ironize or satirize
or joke my way out of, and I have a queasy feeling of unease in my regret,
for I realize I am making a mistake, that these words are all out of proportion and grotesquely exaggerated in suggesting an equivalence of violent
political repression with often minor and petty, silly and stupid, ignorant
and harmless, doctrines, beliefs, and sentiments, or, indeed, sometimes
perfectly reasonable views and perspectives, with which I have had cause to
quarrel, and whose only crime is my disagreement, fomented by an increasingly inexcusable and unjustified crankiness, ungratefulness, belligerence,
and abetted by a morbid fascination with the structure of such disciplining
machines, perfected by a series of reigns of terror, from all of which I have
been spared (or else such exercises as this would be impossible, since it is
my freedom, however relative and circumscribed, that both lets me compose this and is the measure of its failure). For after all is done and said,
after the fury and the sound, after the pomp and bombast and self-regard,
after the myopia and insufferably inappropriate and unjustified delusions
of persecution, this recantation enacts a false and offensive analogy to woe-
fully pernicious, life-destroying belief systems, states, or religions. And for
this I recant my cant, cant and recant. I am wrong, I have strayed from the
path of decency, restraint, and honor.

Therefore, desiring to remove from the minds of your Eminences, and of
all faithful Poets and Poetry Readers, this vehement suspicion, justly conceived against me, with sincere heart and unfeigned faith I abjure, curse,
and detest the aforesaid errors and aversions, and generally every other error, apostasy, and sect whatsoever contrary to the said Books of Accessible
Poets and I swear that in the future I will never again say or assert, verbally

or in writing, anything that might furnish occasion for a similar suspicion regarding me; but that should I know any dissenter, or person suspected of dissent, I will denounce him to the Inquisitor of the place where I may be and also to the Inquisitor that is in me, that I have become. Further, I swear and promise to fulfill and observe in their integrity all penances that have been, or that shall be, imposed upon me. And, in the event of my contravening any of these promises and oaths, I submit myself to all the pains and penalties imposed and promulgated in the canons and other constitutions, general and particular, against such delinquents as myself.

I, the said Charles Bernstein, have abjured, sworn, promised, and bound myself as above; and in witness of the truth thereof I have with my own hand subscribed the present document of my abjuration and abjection, and recited it word for word at Tucson, formally S-cuk Son, at the base of the Black Mountain, in the long shadow of Baboquivari, in the County of Pima, State of Arizona, on the border of Estados Unidos Mexicanos, on the Last Day of May, in the year Two Thousand and Eight of the current era.